7 0 NOV 2019

D0588180

NOW

THAT'S WHAT I CALL MUSIC

THE
QUIZ!

WITHDRAWN
FROM
STOCK

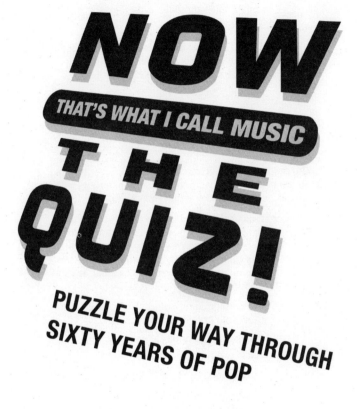

NOW

THAT'S WHAT I CALL MUSIC

THE
QUIZ!

PUZZLE YOUR WAY THROUGH
SIXTY YEARS OF POP

TRAPEZE

First published in Great Britain in 2019 by Trapeze,
an imprint of The Orion Publishing Group Ltd
Carmelite House, 50 Victoria Embankment,
London EC4Y 0DZ

An Hachette UK company

1 3 5 7 9 10 8 6 4 2

Copyright © Michael Mulligan 2019

The moral right of Michael Mulligan to be identified as
the author of this work has been asserted in accordance with
the Copyright, Designs and Patents Act of 1988.

All rights reserved. No part of this publication may be
reproduced, stored in a retrieval system, or transmitted
in any form or by any means, electronic, mechanical,
photocopying, recording, or otherwise, without the
prior permission of both the copyright owner and the
above publisher of this book.

A CIP catalogue record for this book is
available from the British Library.

ISBN (Paperback): 978 1 409 17992 4
ISBN (eBook): 978 1 409 17993 1

Designed by Goldust Design

Printed and bound in Great Britain by
Clays Ltd, Elcograf, S.p.A

MIX
Paper from
responsible sources
FSC
www.fsc.org
FSC® C104740

www.orionbooks.co.uk

Contents

Introduction

For more than thirty-five years, the team at NOW That's What I Call Music have been selecting the most popular songs to appear on their phenomenal, billion-selling series of albums. In 1985, two years after they captured all the latest hits on their very first compilation, they branched out into genre specific and themed collections, beginning that May with *NOW Dance: The 12" Mixes*, followed in November by *NOW... The Christmas Album*.

Two hundred or so of these albums (and now playlists) later, they have cast their net over all sorts of genres, events, themes, years, decades, happenings and countries, along the way capturing the songs of countless multi-hit megastars and one-hit wonders who have graced the UK Singles Chart since the early 1950s.

Inspired by those same NOW albums, this book contains one thousand brand new pop quiz questions, covering the same broad and diverse range of musicians and songs they have featured.

Whether you were a teenager in the fifties or you are looking forward to being one in the next decade, there are questions here for you. The book also includes lots of additional 'I never knew that' facts, perfect for testing friends and family members who think they know it all.

So, whatever your age, whatever your musical taste and wherever you are, it's time to puzzle your way through more than sixty years of pop.

NOW

THAT'S WHAT I CALL A

DECADE

Answers from page 218

NOW

THAT'S WHAT I CALL

Sixties

It's been said that if you can remember the sixties, you weren't really there. It's time to test your knowledge of songs from the decade known as 'Swinging'.

1. Which song originally recorded by The Beatles gave British group The Overlanders a number 1 hit and their only Top 40 single in 1966?

2. **Reggae singer Eddy Grant had his first solo number 1 in 1982 with 'I Don't Wanna Dance', but he previously topped the chart in 1968 as the frontman of which British pop group?**

3. Which singer had fifteen Top 40 hits in the sixties and made her first NOW appearance in 1990 with a Top 20 hit written for her by Pet Shop Boys?

4. **In 1967, Gene Pitney had a number 5 hit with 'Something's Gotten Hold of My Heart', and had his only number 1 in 1989 when he rerecorded the same song as a duet with which singer?**

5. American band Tommy James and the Shondells had their only number 1 in 1968 with 'Mony Mony', but which former punk had a seventh Top 40 solo hit with his 1987 cover version?

6. **Two of Wet Wet Wet's three number 1 singles were covers of sixties' Top 10 hits. Which songs were they?**

7. Name the British rock group who followed up their only number 1 single in 1967 with the number 6 hit 'Homburg'.

8. **Right Said Fred had their only number 1 in 1992 with 'Deeply Dippy', but who had a 1962 Top 10 single with the song 'Right Said Fred'?**

9. Noel Gallagher shares a writing credit for Oasis' 1994 number 3 'Whatever' with Neil Innes. What was the name of the band with which Neil had a number 5 hit in 1968 with 'I'm the Urban Spaceman'?

10. **Which hugely successful chart-topping artist used the pseudonym Apollo C. Vermouth when he produced that Bonzo Dog Doo-Dah Band single?**

DID YOU KNOW?
When 66 year-old Louis Armstrong reached number 1 in August 1968, it made him the oldest artist to top the singles chart, a record that stood until 2009 when 68 year-old Sir Tom Jones appeared on the Comic Relief single 'Islands in The Stream'.

Sixties Dance

Do you know your Mashed Potato from your Monkey? Can you spot the difference between the Jerk and the Twist? Put your dancing feet up and try our dance-themed sixties' posers.

1. What amazing animal did Simon Smith have according to the 1967 number 4 single by the Alan Price Set?

2. **In 1985, David Bowie and Mick Jagger had a number 1 hit with 'Dancing in the Street'. Who originally recorded and had a hit with the song in 1964?**

3. Which American vocal group with eighteen Top 40 hits first charted in 1960 with the singles 'Dance with Me' and 'Save the Last Dance for Me'?

4. **Chris Montez made his chart debut in 1962 with which song that shares its title with number 1 hits by David Bowie and Five?**

5. Name the American guitarist who had twenty instrumental hits between 1958 and 1986, including the 1962 number 4 'Dance with the Guitar Man'.

6. **After two number 1s as a backing group, which instrumental quartet had six number 1s of their own, including the 1962 chart-topper 'Dance On!'?**

7. The song 'Land of a Thousand Dances' was written and originally recorded by Chris Kenner in 1962, but who had a Top 40 hit with the same song in 1966?

8. **What demand did Sly and the Family Stone make in their 1968 single, resulting in their first and biggest Top 40 hit?**

9. Who was in the Top 40 to 'Dance, Dance, Dance' in 1965 and returned to have 'Fun, Fun, Fun' in 1996?

10. **In 1968, Love Sculpture reached number 5 with a version of 'Sabre Dance' from Khachaturian's ballet *Gayane*. Which chart-topping Welsh guitarist fronted Love Sculpture?**

NOW

THAT'S WHAT I CALL

Seventies

Folk, rock, glam, disco, pop and punk –
the seventies had it all. Were you paying
attention to the charts or were you out on
your Chopper bike or Space Hopper?

1. Which British band had a run of ten Top 40 singles
   that began with 'The Seeker' in 1970 and ended with
   'Who Are You' in 1978?

2. **Which Scottish singer-songwriter who had three
   Top 40 hits of his own in the seventies also
   produced The Proclaimers' 1987 debut single
   'Letter from America'?**

3. Mott the Hoople's 1972 hit single 'All the Young
   Dudes' was written by David Bowie, but can
   you name the three other great British pop acts
   mentioned in the lyrics?

4. **Name the British act who racked up seventeen
   Top 40 singles in the seventies, including the Top
   10 hits 'Love Is Life', 'A Child's Prayer' and 'Put
   Your Love in Me'.**

5. What four-word instruction concludes the lyrics of ELO's 1978 number 6 single 'Mr. Blue Sky'?

6. **Name the 1979 number 1 disco anthem that was also a Top 40 hit for Diana Ross and Chantay Savage in 1996, Cake in 1997 and Leah McFall in 2013.**

7. When rock group Free split in 1973, singer Paul Rodgers and drummer Simon Kirke formed which other successful rock act?

8. **Wild Cherry scored their only Top 40 hit with the 1976 number 7 'Play That Funky Music'. Who had a number 10 hit in 1991 with their own version of the song as the follow-up to a 1990 number 1?**

9. Bill Withers made his chart debut in 1972 with 'Lean on Me'. Which glam-rock outfit had their fifteenth and most recent Top 40 hit when they released their version of the song in 1976?

10. **Which New York quartet had their only hit single with the 1977 number 7 'Black Betty'?**

NOW

Seventies Dance

Do you know your 'D.I.S.C.O.' from your 'Y.M.C.A.'? Can you tell a 'Bump' from a 'Bus Stop'? Slip off your platform boots and try our dance-themed seventies' questions for size.

1. DJ Sir Terry Wogan had two Top 40 hits: 'Silver Bells' in 2009 and which number 21 hit in 1978?

2. **Who reached number 12 in 1974 with the song 'You Can Make Me Dance, Sing or Anything (Even Take the Dog for a Walk, Mend a Fuse, Fold Away the Ironing Board or Any Other Domestic Shortcomings)'?**

3. By what name did singer Barry Green have Top 10 hits in 1973 with 'Dancin' (on a Saturday Night)' and 'Do You Wanna Dance?'?

4. **Which American band had seven consecutive Top 40 hits in the seventies, including 'Dance, Dance, Dance', 'Everybody Dance' and 'My Feet Keep Dancing'?**

5. Name the British pop duo that had the first of their two Top 40 hits with the 1978 number 3 'Dancing in the City'.

6. **What was the family name of sisters Linda, Anne, Maureen, Bernadette and Coleen who had their biggest hit in 1979 with 'I'm in the Mood for Dancing'?**

7. Which chart-topping British icon added the word 'Again' to the title of his 1972 number 12 hit and took it to number 12 again in 1979?

8. **In 1979, Violinski had their only Top 40 hit with 'Clog Dance'. Which chart-topping British rock group was violinist Mik Kaminski previously a member of?**

9. Name the American dance group whose only chart entries were the Top 10 hits 'Get Dancin'' in 1974 and 'I Wanna Dance wit' Choo (Do Dat Dance)' in 1975.

10. **Prior to his spells with rock giants Rainbow, the Michael Schenker Group and Whitesnake, which drummer had a solo chart hit in 1974 with 'Dance with the Devil'?**

NOW

THAT'S WHAT I CALL

Eighties

Did you listen to heavy metal or hip hop on your Walkman? Was your mobile phone bigger than your shoulder pads? Put down your Rubik's Cube and test your knowledge of eighties' hits.

1. Which two-word song title provided different eighties' Top 10 hits for both David Bowie and The Jam?

2. **Name the English duo who had the first of two Top 40 hits with the 1985 number 3 'Lean On Me (Ah-Li-Ayo)'.**

3. Which Australian group had their only Top 40 hit with the 1983 number 7 single 'Waiting for a Train'?

4. **The Communards' two biggest hits were both cover versions of seventies' disco favourites. Harold Melvin & The Blue Notes 1986 number 1 'Don't Leave Me This Way' was one, but what was the other?**

5. What 1985 number 3 hit for Dee C. Lee provided Girls Aloud with their eleventh consecutive Top 10 hit in 2005?

6. **The theme to the 1985 James Bond film *A View to a Kill* gave Duran Duran their second US number 1. Which other eighties' pop star played the villainous May Day in the film?**

7. Name the group that backed Yazz on her 1988 number 1 'The Only Way Is Up'?

8. **Chart-topping British pop group T'Pau took their name from which famous science-fiction series?**

9. Which member of the original 1984 Band Aid line-up had his biggest hit the previous year with 'Calling Your Name'?

10. **Which American singer's 1987 debut hit starts with the spoken introduction 'Sweetheart, listen, I know the last few pages haven't been good for the both of us ...'?**

NOW

THAT'S WHAT I CALL

Eighties Party

Which number 1 hit best sums up the eighties for you? 'Red Red Wine' by UB40 or 'I Should Have Known Better' by Jim Diamond? Time to test your knowledge of some eighties' party favourites.

1. In 1982, Madness had their only number 1 with 'House of Fun' and made number 5 with which other 'House' song?

2. **In 1983, which two-word song title provided different Top 20 hits for both Marillion and Mezzoforte?**

3. Which 1983 UK and US number 1 single begins with the Emerald Express playing the traditional Irish tune 'Believe Me, If All Those Endearing Young Charms'?

4. **In 1984, which Liverpool band gave the Mike Stock, Matt Aitken and Pete Waterman production team their first number 1 single?**

5. Which American female duo started out as Two Tons o' Fun, before changing their name and having a number 2 single in 1984?

6. **Who had their only number 1 single in 1984 with a song written by Prince, featuring harmonica from Stevie Wonder and a rap from Melle Mel?**

7. Which American band's run of thirteen consecutive Top 20 singles – including five number 1s – ended in 1982 when 'War Child' peaked at number 39?

8. **In 1990, Don Pablo's Animals had their only Top 40 hit with a cover of Shocking Blue's only Top 40 hit, from 1970. But who had their ninth Top 40 hit with the same song in 1986?**

9. In 1988, Phil Collins teamed up with legendary Motown songwriter Lamont Dozier to write 'Loco in Acapulco', the thirty-first and most recent Top 40 hit for which American vocal group?

10. **Which British singer made her chart debut in 1981 and had the first of twenty Top 40 hits with a number 2 single written by her father and her brother?**

DID YOU KNOW?
In 2011, readers of *Rolling Stone* magazine voted Starship's 1985 number 12 hit 'We Built This City' as the worst song of the '80s. In 2012, Starship singer Grace Slick went even further, telling *Vanity Fair* magazine it was "the worst song ever".

NOW
THAT'S WHAT I CALL

1983

The very first volume of *NOW* was released on 28 November 1983, featuring thirty songs and including eleven number 1 hits. Here are ten questions to test your knowledge of that first album.

1. Phil Collins opened the first *NOW* album with his number 1 version of 'You Can't Hurry Love', but who first took the song to number 3 in 1966?

2. **Which American singer and songwriter wrote UB40's first number 1, 'Red Red Wine', as well as 'I'm a Believer' by EMF and Reeves and Mortimer on *NOW 31*?**

3. Duran Duran made the first of ten *NOW* appearances with 'Is There Something I Should Know?', but who was the band's original singer, who made his only solo appearance on *NOW 5* with 'Icing on the Cake'?

4. **What playground pastime was the subject of Malcolm McLaren's 1983 number 3 single 'Double Dutch'?**

DID YOU KNOW?

Will Powers, aka photographer Lynn Goldsmith, is the only artist who appeared on the very first *NOW* in 1983, but has yet to feature on any other *NOW* collection.

5.   Under what name did Christopher Hamill make the first of his two *NOW* solo appearances?

6.   **Men Without Hats were the first band from which Commonwealth country to appear on *NOW*?**

7.   Who was the guest female singer on Heaven 17's biggest hit, the 1983 number 2 'Temptation'?

8.   **Ian Craig Marsh and Martyn Ware of Heaven 17 were previously members of which other band appearing on *NOW 1*?**

9.   Tracey Ullman made her first appearance with 'They Don't Know', a song written by Kirsty MacColl. Two of Kirsty's solo *NOW* appearances were with a cover of which 1968 single by The Kinks?

10. **Who was the Scottish female singer who provided vocals for Mike Oldfield's only *NOW* appearance, 'Moonlight Shadow'?**

1984

It was the year that Frankie Goes to Hollywood spent fifteen weeks at number 1, Band Aid released 'Do They Know It's Christmas?' and Culture Club won Best British Group at the BRIT Awards.

1. In 1984, which chart-topping duo had a number 4 single subtitled 'Nineteen Eighty-Four'?

2. **In October 1984, which British singer and songwriter had his only Top 40 hit with the number 9 single 'Missing You'?**

3. Stevie Wonder had the second-bestselling single of 1984 with 'I Just Called to Say I Love You'. Which film soundtrack was the song taken from?

4. **Which chart-topping artist married German recording engineer Renate Blauel on Valentine's Day 1984?**

5. Herreys won the 1984 *Eurovision Song Contest* with their song 'Diggi-Loo Diggi-Ley'. Which country were they representing?

6. **In the US, Mary 'Tipper' Gore, wife of former Vice President Al Gore, formed the pressure group Parents Music Resource Center (PMRC) after she heard her daughter listening to which Top 10 album?**

7. Singer and actor Murray Head had his only Top 40 hit with 'One Night in Bangkok'. Which hit stage musical was the song written for?

8. **In December 1984, who made his solo chart debut with the number 1 single 'I Should Have Known Better'?**

9. Two songs from the film *Footloose* made the Top 10 – Kenny Loggins's number 6 theme song and which number 2 hit for Deniece Williams?

10. **Who made his chart debut in October 1984 with 'Too Late for Goodbyes', nine months after his father had his twelfth solo Top 40 hit?**

DID YOU KNOW?
The first number 1 of 1984 is one of just two acapella chart toppers – The Flying Pickets 'Only You' spent five weeks at the summit, while The Housemartins 'Caravan of Love' managed one week in 1987. Bobby McFerrin almost had a third in 1988 but Whitney Houston with 'One Moment In Time' kept his 'Don't Worry, Be Happy' from the top spot.

NOW

THAT'S WHAT I CALL

1985

Ten questions about the year that Live Aid was watched by almost 2 billion people and 'Into the Groove' gave Madonna the first of her number 1 singles.

1. Which chart-topping artist had four Top 40 hits in 1985 but only reached number 42 with his memories of 69?

2. **Phil Collins and Philip Bailey spent four weeks at number 1 with 'Easy Lover', but which American soul group does Philip Bailey sing with?**

3. The bestselling single of 1985 spent five weeks at number 1, and was by an American singer who was born Heidi Stern. What was the artist's stage name?

4. **Who swapped a planned performance with his band for a solo rendition of an 'old northern English folk song' when the Live Aid concert at Wembley stadium overran?**

5. Dire Straits released their bestselling album *Brothers In Arms* in this year, which resulted in five Top 40 singles – all with three-word titles. What was the first single from the album, peaking at number 20 in May?

6. **After twenty consecutive Top 20 hits, a run that started in 1979, which chart-topping British act stalled at number 21 at the twenty-first attempt?**

7. In February 1985, a BRIT Award was given to the Best British Comedy Record for the first and only time. Who won it for his number 2 debut solo single?

8. **Which British singer made his Top 40 debut with the theme to the 1985 film *St. Elmo's Fire*?**

9. Name the boy soprano who appeared with Sarah Brightman on the number 3 single 'Pie Jesu'.

10. **In December 1985, which duo followed up their 1982 number 4 debut with a version of 'White Christmas'?**

DID YOU KNOW?
Before Nick Ashford and Valerie Simpson had their only Top 40 hit with the 1985 number 3 'Solid', they were staff writers at Motown Records, where they wrote the hits 'Ain't No Mountain High Enough', 'Ain't Nothing Like The Real Thing' and 'You're All I Need To Get By'.

NOW

THAT'S WHAT I CALL

1986

Ten questions about the year that Wham! split, The Communards had the bestselling single and *Spitting Image* told us to 'stick a deckchair up your nose'.

1. Which comedy actress had her only Top 40 hit with the number 2 single 'Starting Together'?

2. **Which American band had their biggest hit with a number 3 single that would later provide a Top 20 hit for Gun, Melanie G and Little Mix?**

3. Mike and the Mechanics made their chart debut with 'Silent Running (On Dangerous Ground)'. The band's two lead singers included Paul Young, who was previously singer for which other chart act?

4. **In March 1986, the Rolling Stones reached number 13 with their cover of the sixties' soul classic 'Harlem Shuffle'. Who had the original Top 10 hit in 1969?**

5. Who spent three weeks at number 1 in June with a song that had previously been a number 1 for Norman Greenbaum in 1970?

6. **Madonna made number 4 with which three-word song title that also provided different Top 10 singles for The Human League and M People?**

7. In October, what four-word command gave the former The Teardrop Explodes singer Julian Cope his first and biggest solo hit?

8. **Name the former singer with Chicago who had his only solo Top 40 hit with the theme from *The Karate Kid Part II*.**

9. What was the Christmas number 1 that first made number 6 in 1957 but was reissued in 1986 following its use in a TV commercial for Levi's jeans?

10. **Who wrote The Bangles' first Top 40 hit 'Manic Monday' using the pseudonym 'Christopher'?**

NOW

THAT'S WHAT I CALL

1987

It was the year Rick Astley had the bestselling single, and sales of CD singles counted in the chart for the first time. How much do you know about the hits of 1987?

1. Name the soul-music legend who had her only number 1 single in February 1987 when she teamed up with George Michael.

2. **Jody Watley had the first of four solo Top 40 hits when 'Looking For a New Love' made number 13 in June, but can you name the R&B trio with whom she'd previously had eleven Top 40 hits?**

3. Which 1971 Bill Withers' single did Club Nouveau reach number 3 with in April, giving them their only Top 40 hit?

4. **In May, which Irish singer and songwriter became the first artist to win the Eurovision Song Contest twice?**

5. Which band, whose line-up included three brothers, made their Top 40 debut with 'Need You Tonight'?

6. **In June, U2 had their seventh Top 40 hit when 'I Still Haven't Found What I'm Looking For' reached number 6, but can you name the Scottish act who had their biggest hit in 1990 when their cover version also reached number 6?**

7. Which Hollywood A-lister made number 2 in July 1987 with his version of a song that had originally been a 1964 single for The Drifters?

8. **Abigail Mead and Nigel Goulding had their only hit when they made number 2 with which film-influenced 'military melody'?**

9. Which Australian artist made number 6 with his only Top 40 single, twenty years after he topped the Australian chart with 'Sadie (The Cleaning Lady)'?

10. **Who had the Christmas 1987 number 1 with their cover of the 1972 Elvis Presley hit 'Always on My Mind'?**

DID YOU KNOW?
In 1987, sales of Compact Disc (CD) singles counted towards the Top 40 chart for the first time. In June 1987, Whitney Houston had the first number 1 available on CD single (as well as 7-inch and 12-inch single), when 'I Wanna Dance With Somebody (Who Loves Me)' spent two weeks at the summit.

NOW

1988

Ten questions about the year teenagers Kylie Minogue, Debbie Gibson and Tiffany had twelve Top 10 hits between them, and Bros' first five singles all made the Top 5.

1. Kylie Minogue had her first five hit singles – two number 1s and three number 2s – including her version of 'The Loco-Motion'. Who had the original 1962 number 2 hit with this song?

2. **Which American singer made number 1 for the first (and only) time with 'First Time' in November?**

3. Wet Wet Wet had their first number 1 with a cover of The Beatles' 'With a Little Help from My Friends'. The single was a double A-side, featuring a version of 'She's Leaving Home' by which solo artist?

4. **Which singer, born Leslie Wunderman, had her biggest hit in February 1988 when 'Tell It to My Heart' reached number 3?**

5. Pet Shop Boys wrote and produced 'I'm Not
    Scared', the biggest single for which band fronted by
    actress Patsy Kensit?

6. **Which Irish artist had their first number 1 with a
    song about a South American river?**

7. In December, Australian singer Angry Anderson
    reached number 3 with the ballad 'Suddenly'. Which
    rock band is he also the singer for?

8. **Which Italian singer had her biggest hit when
    she reached number 3 in June 1988 with a song
    subtitled '(Summertime Love)'?**

9. Which male-female duo reached number 7 with a
    cover of a song by a chart-topping male duo that
    only made number 85 in 1985?

10. **Which supergroup made their Top 40 debut
    in November of 1988 with a line-up featuring
    'Nelson', 'Otis', 'Lefty', 'Lucky' and 'Charlie T. Jr.'?**

NOW

THAT'S WHAT I CALL

1989

After twelve volumes of NOW had spent a total of sixty-one weeks at number 1, a new Compilation Album Chart was introduced on 8 January 1989 to give other titles a chance at the top spot!

1. Who saw their first three singles top the chart but just missed out on the Christmas number 1 when Band Aid II knocked 'Let's Party' off the summit?

2. **Which American dance act reached number 6 in January with a song that combined Peter Frampton's 'Baby I Love Your Way' with Lynyrd Skynyrd's 'Freebird'?**

3. In June, who made the first of thirty-one Top 40 appearances when they reached number 28 with 'Orange Crush'?

4. **Felly, Ya Kid K and MC Eric were all featured vocalists on the first three singles by which Belgian act, who made their chart debut in September 1989?**

5. In April, Simply Red spent three weeks at number 2 with which song that had originally made number 9 for Harold Melvin & the Blue Notes in 1973?

6. **Which Italian act sampled Loleatta Holloway's 1980 disco hit 'Love Sensation' and finished 1989 with the year's bestselling single?**

7. In March, who made her chart debut as featured singer on Coldcut's number 11 hit 'People Hold On'?

8. **Which sister act made number 8 in April 1989 with a song that mentioned Rolling Stones, Fleetwood Mac, Pink Floyd and Dire Straits?**

9. Jason Donovan had his third number 1 single in June 1989 with a cover version of 'Sealed with a Kiss'. Who originally took the song to number 3 in 1962?

10. **Which British group had the biggest of their seven Top 40 hits when 'Baby I Don't Care' spent two weeks at number 3?**

DID YOU KNOW?
Forty years after he released his debut single 'Miss Martha King', 64 year-old Blues guitar legend B.B. King made his UK chart debut with the number 6 hit 'When Love Comes to Town', a collaboration with U2. His only other chart appearance came in 1992 when he teamed up with Gary Moore for the number 59 single, 'Since I Met You Baby'.

NOW

THAT'S WHAT I CALL

1990

Ten questions about the year Cliff Richard scored his hundredth Top 40 hit and the bestselling single was a twenty-five-year-old song by the Righteous Brothers.

1. Who had their only number 1 with a 'dub' version of a song that had originally made number 13 for the S.O.S. Band in 1984?

2. **Who is credited alongside Paula Abdul on her number 2 single 'Opposites Attract'?**

3. In June, Elton John had his third number 1 single with 'Sacrifice'. What was the other song on this double A-side release?

4. **Deacon Blue had their biggest hit with their *Four Bacharach & David Songs* EP, but which American country singer took the lead song, 'I'll Never Fall in Love Again', to number 1 in October 1969?**

5. Which British-American quartet had their biggest hit in October when 'I've Been Thinking About You' peaked at number 2?

6. **Which American singer made number 7 with a version of the theme tune from the TV series *Twin Peaks*?**

7. Despite twenty-four Top 40 hits with Eurythmics, David A. Stewart only had one solo hit with 'Lily Was Here'. Who was the Dutch saxophone player also credited on this single?

8. **Which American group made their chart debut with a number 6 single that mentioned Swiss luxury watchmakers Longines and Greek myth Jason and the Argonauts?**

9. Madonna's first greatest hits album, *Immaculate Collection,* featured two new songs, including the single 'Justify My Love', which was written, produced and featured backing vocals by which American rock singer and guitarist?

10. **Following the success of Kylie Minogue and Jason Donovan, which other *Neighbours* actor tried his luck, with the number 16 single 'Don't It Make You Feel Good'?**

DID YOU KNOW?

In September 1990, 'Groove Is In The Heart' by Dee-Lite and 'The Joker' by Steve Miller Band tied for the number 1 slot, having sold exactly the same quantity. Eventually, 'The Joker' was awarded the top spot as it climbed five chart places in the previous week compared to three for the Dee-Lite tune.

NOW

THAT'S WHAT I CALL

1991

Ten questions about the year Iron Maiden's twentieth Top 40 hit gave them their only number 1, while The Clash managed it after fifteen previous attempts.

1. In January, what song with lyrics in Latin and French by a German and Romanian group reached number 1?

2. **Which famous cartoon family became the first characters to top the chart since the Archies' 'Sugar, Sugar' in 1969?**

3. In June, R.E.M. had their first Top 10 hit with 'Shiny Happy People'. Who was the female guest vocalist on this song?

4. **Which American country-music singer had her first Top 40 hit for fifteen years after she agreed to 'Stand by the JAMs'?**

5. In August, which American hip-hop act reached number 3 with a song that sampled Spandau Ballet's biggest hit?

6. **Shara Nelson had five Top 40 hits in the nineties, but in June 1991 she was the singer with which Bristol band making their Top 40 debut?**

7. Which Manchester band reached number 2 with a rerecording of their own song that had made number 7 only two years earlier?

8. **Which Italian singer scored his first UK hit in May when a duet he recorded with Paul Young reached number 4?**

9. Who followed 'the Moskva down to Gorky Park' and found themselves at number 2 in October?

10. **In December, what became the only song to be Christmas number 1 twice for the same artist?**

DID YOU KNOW?
Heavy D & The Boyz had a number 2 hit in July 1991 with 'Now That We've Found Love', originally a 1978 number 10 for Third World. Singer Dwight 'Heavy D' Myers also had a successful acting career, including appearances alongside Tobey Maguire and Charlize Theron in 'The Cider House Rules', and Ben Stiller and Eddie Murphy in 'Tower Heist'.

NOW

THAT'S WHAT I CALL

1992

Ten questions about the year Simply Red's *Stars* was the bestselling album (again), David Bowie married model Iman and Bill Wyman announced he was leaving the Rolling Stones.

1. Who had their only number 1 single in June, with an EP featuring cover versions of four songs by ABBA?

2. **In April, which British male trio topped the charts with their third attempt after their previous hits stalled at number 2 and 3?**

3. Who had their biggest hit in August with a number 4 single that featured vocals from actress Kim Basinger and Black Sabbath singer Ozzy Osbourne?

4. **In June, Utah Saints reached number 4 with 'Something Good', sampling which 1985 single by Kate Bush?**

5. What Brian May song reached number 5 in September and number 15 in 1996 when it was

released as a Queen single, complete with a vocal from Freddie Mercury?

6. **Which Leeds indie outfit equalled Elvis Presley's thirty-five-year-old chart record when they had twelve Top 30 hits in one year, including their biggest hit 'Come Play with Me'?**

7. In July, which actor turned singer had his only number 1 with a song that includes the lyrics 'she says it's like in the song, remember, if you love somebody, set them free'?

8. **Which teenage duo wore their trousers back to front and reached number 2 in June by telling everyone to 'Jump'?**

9. Who followed up his 1986 number 1 with a cover of a thirty-three-year-old song that was used as the theme to a British TV police drama?

10. **Who went one better than Gerry Rafferty when they took 'Baker Street' to number 2?**

NOW

THAT'S WHAT I CALL

1993

Ten questions about the year Queen topped the chart without Freddie Mercury, and Freddie topped the chart without Queen.

1. Which big pink fellow had the Christmas number 1 and the first ever eponymous number 1 single?

2. **In October, Take That had the second of their three number 1s of the year with a cover of a 1979 song by Dan Hartman. Who was the featured vocalist on the Take That version?**

3. 'Ain't No Love (Ain't No Use)' was the only Top 40 hit for dance act Sub Sub, featuring Melanie Williams. Sub Sub later became which Manchester indie band who had nine Top 40 hits between 2000 and 2009?

4. **In May, the *Five Live* EP spent three weeks at number 1. Recorded at the 1992 Freddie Mercury Tribute Concert, it was credited to George Michael and Queen, with which female vocalist?**

5. In February, Duran Duran had their biggest hit for eight years with the number 6 single 'Ordinary

World'. In 2000 who went one better and took a dance version of 'Ordinary World' to number 5?

6. **What type of weather helped Canadian reggae singer Darrin O'Brien get a number 2 hit in March?**

7. In September, DJ Jeffrey Townes had a number 1 as half of a duo. His partner would go on to have another thirteen solo hits, including a second number 1. By what name were Jeffrey and his partner better known?

8. **The year's bestselling single had Lorraine Crosby asking, 'Can you build an Emerald City with these grains of sand?' and, 'Will you hose me down with holy water if I get too hot?' What was that single?**

9. Which song that had originally been a 1956 hit for Bing Crosby and Grace Kelly gave Elton John and Kiki Dee their second Top 10 hit together?

10. **The song's title 'What's Up?' doesn't appear in the lyrics of this 1993 single, but it made number 2 and gave which Californian female group their only Top 40 hit?**

DID YOU KNOW?

In February 1993, Elton John was forced to cut short a concert at the National Tennis Centre in Melbourne, Australia after an infestation of grasshoppers invaded the venue and forced him off stage.

NOW

THAT'S WHAT I CALL

1994

Ten questions about the year Prince had his only number 1 single, and Blur had the first of their six number 1 albums while Oasis had the first of their eight.

1. In February, Mariah Carey had her first number 1 with a cover of which song that had previously been a 1972 number 1 for Nilsson?

2. **Jack Radics and Taxi Gang were the featured artists on the first number 1 single of the year, but which reggae duo were the 'headline' act?**

3. Following its use on a TV advert for Levi's jeans, 'Inside' became a number 1 single in May for which Scottish rock group?

4. **In September, Danish singer Sannie Carlson ended Wet Wet Wet's fifteen-week stay at number 1 with the first of her five Top 40 hits. By what name is Sannie better known?**

5. Following their 1993 number 11 cover of Pet Shop Boys' 'West End Girls', East 17 reached number 3 in January 1994 with a song that shared its title with which other Pet Shop Boys hit from 1989?

6. **In April, who did Salt-N-Pepa team up with for the number 7 hit 'Whatta Man'?**

7. In August, which Canadian rock group reached number 2 with their chart debut, a song with a four-word title that contained only one letter?

8. **Who made their chart debut and had the first of twenty Top 40 hits with a cover of The Osmonds' 1974 number 1 'Love Me for a Reason'?**

9. In November, Jimmy Nail had his third Top 40 hit with the theme tune to a BBC TV series in which he played a factory worker who becomes a country-and-western singer. What was the song?

10. **Who had 'The Perfect Year' in 1994 thanks to Andrew Lloyd Webber?**

NOW

THAT'S WHAT I CALL

1995

Ten questions about the year Brit Pop dominated the charts, with number 1 singles and albums for both Blur and Oasis, and chart-topping albums for Elastica, Supergrass and Pulp.

1. In January, 'Protection' by Massive Attack featuring Tracey Thorn peaked at number 14. Tracey is better known as a member of what English duo?

2. **In March, 'Love Can Build a Bridge', the official *Comic Relief* single, reached number 1. Cher, Chrissie Hynde, Neneh Cherry and which British guitarist performed on the song?**

3. The fourth series of ITV drama *Soldier Soldier* spawned a number 1 hit following a performance by Fusilier Dave Tucker and Sergeant Paddy Garvey. By what name are the duo better known?

4. **The Outhere Brothers spent a total of five weeks at number 1, with 'Boom Boom Boom' in July and what other song that topped the chart in April?**

DID YOU KNOW?
Simply Red had their biggest hit when 'Fairground' spent
four weeks at number 1. It included a sample of 'Give It
Up', a 1993 number 5 for The Goodmen, which in turn
sampled 'Fanfarra (Cabua-le-le)', a 1992 recording by
Brazilian Jazz musician Sérgio Mendes.

5. In May, which single gave Oasis the first of their eight
    number 1s?

6. **Which Merseyside band took their name from
    a character in Harper Lee's 1960 novel *To Kill a
    Mockingbird*, and had the first – and biggest – of
    their seven Top 40 hits in March 1995?**

7. In August, Blur won the 'Battle of Brit Pop' when
    'Country House' beat Oasis' 'Roll with It' to number
    1. Which Young British Artist directed the video for
    'Country House'?

8. **Which American duo had their only Top 40 hit in
    September when 'I'll Be There for You', the theme
    to the TV series *Friends*, reached number 3?**

9. How did Royston Vasey help a 1976 number 5 single
    get back into the Top 10 in October?

10. **Thirty-nine years after his chart debut, which
    Cuban bandleader reached number 2 in May after
    his mambo tune 'Guaglione' was featured in an
    advertising campaign for Guinness?**

1996

Ten questions about the year the Spice Girls arrived, Take That departed (temporarily, it turned out) and 'Three Lions' topped the chart twice.

1. Which British artist launched his solo career in July with the number 1 single 'Forever Love'?

2. **East 17 reached number 2 with their sixteenth Top 40 single, 'If You Ever', featuring which female singer?**

3. Following a total of thirty-nine Top 40 hits with his two previous bands, who had his biggest solo hit in August 1996 with the number 5 single 'Peacock Suit'?

4. **What nationality were OMC, who spent fourteen weeks in the Top 40 with 'How Bizarre'?**

5. In March, American composer Mark Snow had his only Top 40 hit when he reached number 2 with the theme to which hit TV series?

6. **In the second half of 1996, which British act's first three singles went to number 1 and featured the B-sides 'Bumper to Bumper', 'Take Me Home' and 'One of These Girls'?**

7. In August, R.E.M. had their eighteenth Top 40 hit with the number 4 single 'E-Bow the Letter'. Who was the 'Godmother of Punk' who provided additional vocals?

8. **In October, The Chemical Brothers had their first number 1 with 'Setting Sun', with vocals from which artist making his 'solo' debut?**

9. What name did cast members of the TV series *Emmerdale* go by when they reached number 5 in November with 'Hillbilly Rock Hillbilly Roll'?

10. **Who followed up their number 1 debut with the singles 'Animal Army' and 'The Boy with the X-Ray Eyes', which charted at number 17 and number 32 respectively?**

NOW

THAT'S WHAT I CALL

1997

Ten questions about the year Paul McCartney received his knighthood, the Spice Girls launched Channel 5, and Katrina and the Waves won the forty-second Eurovision Song Contest.

1. The chart debut from Oklahoma-born brothers Isaac, Taylor and Zac was number 1 for three weeks in June. By what family name were the brothers better known?

2. **Who had a number 1 hit in January after her single was remixed by DJ Armand van Helden and given the subtitle 'It's Got to Be Big'?**

3. Which South American country gave German dance group Sash! their second Top 40 single?

4. **Film composer David Arnold made his second Top 40 appearance when he collaborated with Propellerheads on a reworking of which 1969 James Bond theme?**

5. Which Italian classical singer collaborated with Sarah Brightman on the number 2 hit 'Time to Say Goodbye (*Con te Partirò*)'?

6. **In June, The Verve reached number 2 with 'Bitter Sweet Symphony' but were later forced to change the songwriting credits after a legal challenge from which other band's record label?**

7. American R&B quartet 112 spent six weeks at number 1 when they were featured artists on which song recorded as a tribute to rapper the Notorious B.I.G.?

8. **In August, who celebrated their biggest hit with a whiskey drink, a vodka drink, a lager drink and a cider drink?**

9. In September, 'Candle in the Wind 1997' spent five weeks at number 1 and became the biggest-selling single of all time. But what other song was also on this double A-side single?

10. **All three singles Boyzone released in 1997 peaked at number 2. They were 'Isn't It a Wonder', 'Picture of You' and a cover of which 1988 Tracy Chapman single?**

DID YOU KNOW?
Boyband Five made their chart debut with the number 10 hit 'Slam Dunk (Da Funk)'. The band were put together after an advert in The Stage newspaper sought singers and dancers with "attitude and edge". The 3,000 hopeful auditionees included future comedian and actor Russell Brand.

NOW

THAT'S WHAT I CALL

1998

1998 was a good year for Irish acts, with B*Witched having three number 1 singles, Boyzone another two, and The Corrs' *Talk on Corners* being the year's bestselling album.

1. In January, which indie star made his solo debut with the number 5 single 'My Star'?

2. **Which American singer's fourth number 1 single spent seven weeks at the top while George Michael, E-17, Steps, Five, Boyzone and Jay-Z all took turns at number 2?**

3. After six consecutive number 1s, which band saw their seventh single stop at number 2 in March?

4. **Whose three number 1 singles in 1998 included a double A-side release that coupled cover versions of songs made famous by Red Hot Chili Peppers and Labelle?**

5. Name the American ten-year-old whose three Top 40 hits in 1998 included a cover of a Beach Boys' song that was originally a hit twenty-four years before he was born.

6. **Which indie band topped the chart for the first time with a song that begins 'The future teaches you to be alone, the present to be afraid and cold'?**

7. Who had their fourth number 1 in January with a song that shares its title with a 1989 number 1 by Lisa Stansfield, and a 1977 number 13 by The Jam?

8. **In May, Massive Attack had their first Top 10 hit with 'Teardrop', with lyrics and vocals by Elizabeth Fraser. Which Scottish indie band was she previously singer with?**

9. Which rapper's four Top 40 hits in 1998 included her collaborations with Melanie B and Nicole?

10. **In October, Fugees singer Lauryn Hill had her biggest solo hit with a number 3 single subtitled '(That Thing)'. What was the full title of this song?**

NOW

THAT'S WHAT I CALL

1999

Ten questions about the year Britney Spears had the bestselling single, Shania Twain had the bestselling album and Blondie had their sixth number 1 single after a nineteen-year gap.

1. Who left Albert Square and had a 'Perfect Moment' when she topped the chart in April?

2. **Name the Californian rock band who followed up their January chart-topper with the number 2 hit 'Why Don't You Get a Job?'.**

3. In February 1999, which Canadian band spent one week in the Top 10 with their song 'One Week'?

4. **Which Swedish act had their nineteenth and most recent Top 40 hit with the number 11 single 'Wish I Could Fly'?**

5. The number 3 hit 'Boy You Knock Me Out' saw Will Smith collaborate with another cast member from *The Fresh Prince of Bel-Air*. Who was she?

6. **The Vengaboys had four Top 10 hits in 1999, including the number 1 'We're Going to Ibiza!', which was based on the 1975 number 1 'Barbados' by which British band?**

7. At the end of September, Eiffel 65 started a three-week spell at number 1 with 'Blue'. But what was the three-'word' subtitle of this song?

8. **What name did French DJ Quentin Dupieux adopt for the hit 'Flat Beat', which spent two weeks at number 1 in April?**

9. After three consecutive number 2 singles, Five finally had their first number 1 with which song that shares its title with a 1989 number 5 hit for Soul II Soul?

10. **Westlife had the Christmas number 1 with a double A-side release combining a cover of ABBA's 'I Have a Dream' with a cover of which song that was a number 1 single for Terry Jacks in 1974?**

DID YOU KNOW?
Before he started in One Republic, guitarist Zach Filkins studied classical guitar in Spain and worked as a model; his image appeared on packaging for a popular brand of men's underpants.

Twenty-first Century

Inspired by the 2014 NOW compilation of the same name, here's one question for each of the first ten years of the twenty-first century.

2001. Who had the first of three Top 40 hits when 'Who Let The Dogs Out?' peaked at number 2 in November 2000?

2002. Who entered *The Guinness World Records* book as the Most Successful Virtual Band after their self-titled debut album sold more than half a million copies in the UK in its first twelve months?

2003. Which female trio had the first of six number 1 singles with a bit of help from Tubeway Army's 1979 chart-topper 'Are "Friends" Electric?'?

2004. At the BRIT Awards, Niomi McLean-Daley won Best Female British Solo Artist and Best British Urban Act. By what name is she better known?

2005. Although it was never a hit single for The Beatles, 'With a Little Help from My Friends' topped the chart for a third time when it became the debut hit for which duo?

2006. Name the Canadian singer who had a 'Bad Day' in 2005, even though his debut hit spent three weeks at number 2.

2007. Name the Finnish rock band that won the 2006 Eurovision Song Contest in Athens, and had their only Top 40 hit with 'Hard Rock Hallelujah'.

2008. Katie Melua had her first number 1 single when she recorded a version of 'What a Wonderful World' with which singer, who had passed away in 1996?

2009. Mint Royale knocked Rihanna off the top spot with their version of which song, usually associated with a 1952 Gene Kelly musical?

2010. What name did English duo Elly Jackson and Ben Langmaid go by when they made their chart debut with the number 2 hit 'In For The Kill'?

DID YOU KNOW?
American Rock group The Offspring had their biggest hit in January 1999 when 'Pretty Fly (For A White Guy)' spent one week at number 1. The band's songwriter and singer Bryan 'Dexter' Holland has a Ph.D in Molecular Biology from the University of Southern California.

NOW

THAT'S WHAT I CALL

A COMPILATION

Answers from page 235

NOW

THAT'S WHAT I CALL

Movies

Ten questions on actors who sing, singers who act and big hits from the big screen.

1. The biggest film of 1978 resulted in two number 1 singles for Danny Zuko and Sandy Olsson. Who are they better known as?

2. **Maria McKee spent four weeks at number 1 in 1990 with 'Show Me Heaven'. Which Tom Cruise film did it feature in?**

3. Survivor's only two Top 40 singles were the 1982 number 1 'Eye of the Tiger' from *Rocky III*, and which 1985 number 5 taken from *Rocky IV*?

4. **Starship had their biggest hit in 1987 with 'Nothing's Gonna Stop Us Now'. Which romantic comedy did the song originally feature in?**

5. Which Oscar-winning actress had a number 22 single in 2013 with her version of 'I Dreamed a Dream'?

6. **Jennifer Warnes twice made the Top 40 with duets from films. One was '(I've Had) The Time of My Life' with Bill Medley, from *Dirty Dancing*. What was the other hit, taken from *An Officer and a Gentleman*?**

7. In 1997, Ewan McGregor was the featured vocalist on 'Choose Life', a number 6 single that included dialogue from *Trainspotting*. Name the act responsible for the music.

8. **The theme from the Disney animation *Beauty and the Beast* gave Celine Dion her first Top 40 hit in 1992, but who was her duet partner on this song?**

9. In 1990, Cher had her first number 1 single for twenty-five years with a cover of 'The Shoop Shoop Song (It's in His Kiss)'. What film soundtrack was the song taken from?

10. **In 1988, American actor Patrick Swayze had his only Top 40 hit with 'She's Like the Wind'. Which female singer is also credited on this number 17 single?**

DID YOU KNOW?
Despite his nineteen Top 40 singles and his thirty-one Top 40 albums (ten of them number 1s) Bruce Springsteen has made just one *NOW* appearance, with his 1994 number 2 hit 'Streets Of Philadelphia' featuring on *NOW... Movies*.

NOW

THAT'S WHAT I CALL

Feel Good

Ten questions on the themes of bliss, delight, elation, euphoria, happiness, joy and pleasure. A ten out of ten score is guaranteed to make you feel good.

1. Which American trio had four Top 20 singles in 1982, including the number 7 hit 'I Can Make You Feel Good'?

2. **What 1967 number 12 hit for The Turtles also gave Jason Donovan the thirteenth of his sixteen Top 40 hits in 1991?**

3. Which southern African country was singer Rozalla born in? She had her biggest hit in 1991 with the number 6 single 'Everybody's Free (To Feel Good)'.

4. **In 1973, which band had the first of three Top 10 hits with 'Joybringer', based on 'Jupiter' from Gustav Holst's *The Planets* suite?**

5. Which British singer was just fifteen years old when she had her second number 1 single with 'Walkin' Back to Happiness' in 1961?

DID YOU KNOW?
Eastbourne indie group, Toploader, had their biggest hit in 2000 when 'Dancing In The Moonlight' reached number 7. Originally a 1972 number 13 US hit for King Harvest, their version failed to chart in the UK. Other covers of the song include recordings by Liza Minnelli in 1973 and Baha Men in 1994.

6. **What 1979 'list' by Ian Dury and the Blockheads included Buddy Holly, Woody Allen and John Coltrane?**

7. Which four-word song title provided different Top 10 hits for Stereophonics in 2001 and Bon Jovi in 2005?

8. **In 2003, which American singer had a number 3 hit with 'Feel Good Time', featuring English DJ William Orbit?**

9. What combination of drinks gave Dr Feelgood their only Top 10 hit in 1979?

10. **In 2013, which American singer-songwriter's four-week spell at number 1 was interrupted first by Pitbull featuring Kesha, then by Clean Bandit featuring Jess Glynne, then Sam Smith, and finally Route 94 featuring Jess Glynne?**

Legends

Ten questions inspired by the 2014 NOW compilation celebrating some of the biggest and best acts of the last sixty years.

1. *Legends* opens with a 1979 Queen single that gave them the seventh of twenty-five Top 10 hits, but only made number 86 in the US. What was that song?

2. **The Tourists, featuring future Eurythmics Annie Lennox and David A. Stewart, had four Top 40 hits, the biggest of which was their 1979 cover version of a 1963 hit for Dusty Springfield. What was that song?**

3. Which Isle of Man-born legends' glittering CV includes writing number 1 hits covered by Take That, Boyzone and Steps?

4. **The Police had their fifth and most recent number 1 with 'Every Breath You Take' in 1983. Which duo sampled the melody for their own number 1 'I'll Be Missing You' fourteen years later?**

5. Members of which legendary British band were previously in a group called The Garden Wall, a name that appears in the lyrics of their 1974 Top 40 debut?

6. **In 1983, Phil Collins played drums on and produced Adam Ant's most recent Top 10 single. What was that song?**

7. Which legends better known for 'The Fly' wrote the music and lyrics for the 2011 Broadway musical *Spider-Man: Turn Off the Dark*?

8. **In 1984, Madonna had her first hit when 'Holiday' peaked at number 6. Which Dutch duo also reached number 6 with their rap version two years later?**

9. In Dublin in 1988, which French-Canadian legend won the Eurovision Song Contest for Switzerland?

10. **George Michael had his fifth 'solo' hit with the 1987 number 2 'Faith'. The introduction of 'Faith' features a cathedral organ playing the melody of which other George Michael-penned hit?**

DID YOU KNOW?
In addition to the Bee Gees' own five number 1s, the songwriting Brothers Gibb can also take credit for chart toppers by Diana Ross ('Chain Reaction', *NOW Dance '86*), Boyzone ('Words', *NOW 35*), Steps ('Tragedy', *NOW 44)* and Vanessa Jenkins, Bryn West and Sir Tom Jones ('Islands In the Stream, *NOW 72*). The latter also featured a guest appearance by Robin Gibb.

NOW
THAT'S WHAT I CALL

Running

Ten questions on the theme of 'Running', a subject so popular there have been five editions of this compilation since the first *NOW Running* in 2012.

1. Dexys Midnight Runners had their most recent Top 40 hit with the 1986 number 13 'Because of You', the theme to which BBC TV sitcom?

2. **Which two artists collaborated with Jay-Z on the 2009 number 1 'Run This Town'?**

3. Which British rock group with six number 1 singles had their most recent Top 10 hit in 1984 with 'Run Runaway'?

4. **Which one-word title provided different Top 20 hits for Janet Jackson in 1995, The Corrs in 1999 and Devlin featuring Yasmin in 2010?**

5. Bryan Adams had his first UK hit in 1985 when 'Run to You' reached number 11, but who were the British dance act who took their version to number 3 in 1992?

DID YOU KNOW?
The five volumes of *NOW... Running* contain more than three hundred inspirational, motivational songs, but so far the word 'run' only appears on them four times on the track listings: Frankie Goes To Hollywood 'Born To Run', Spencer Davis Group 'Keep On Running', Rage 'Run To You' and Galantis 'Runaway (U & I)'.

6. **In 2008, Leona Lewis had her third number 1 single with her version of 'Run' – but who originally took the song to number 5 in 2004?**

7. What was the subtitle of Kate Bush's 1983 number 3 single 'Running Up That Hill'?

8. **By what group name were Joseph Simmons, Darryl McDaniels and Jason Mizell better known?**

9. Name the Swedish dance duo who had their first hit in 2015 with 'Runaway (U & I)'.

10. **The Stray Cats' first two singles both peaked at number 9. 'Rock This Town' in 1981 was one, name the other.**

Drive

Readers should ensure that their car is safely parked and their engine turned off before they attempt these ten questions on the theme of 'Drive'.

1. Which one-word song title has provided different Top 20 hits for both the Cars and R.E.M?

2. **Which American rock band with three Top 40 hits between 1981 and 1985 are named after a type of pickup truck?**

3. Which Bruce Springsteen song provided Natalie Cole with a 1988 number 5 hit?

4. **Which 1989 number 7 single for Cyndi Lauper also reached number 7 for Roy Orbison in 1992?**

5. Which two female singers recorded a 2004 version of Rose Royce's 1976 hit 'Car Wash' for the soundtrack of the film *Shark Tale*?

6. **Different songs called 'You Drive Me Crazy' provided Top 10 hits in 1981 and 1999 for which two artists?**

7. Which 'other' form of transport had their biggest hit with the 2012 number 6 'Drive By'?

8. **Who had a 2016 number 2 with a dance version of Tracy Chapman's 1988 single 'Fast Car?**

9. Which American singer had her third and most recent Top 40 hit with a 1995 cover of 'Big Yellow Taxi'?

10. **Where did The Hollies 'wait' in 1966 and the Fatback Band 'wait' in 1975?**

NOW

THAT'S WHAT I CALL

Love

The romantic people at NOW are so passionate about this subject that they have released three *Love* compilations. Here are ten questions inspired by those albums.

1. What five-word song title has provided different Top 10 hits for Take That, Dru Hill and Calvin Harris & Disciples?

2. **Which 1997 film soundtrack gave Swedish band The Cardigans their biggest hit with the number 2 single 'Lovefool'?**

3. In 1994, Terence Trent D'Arby had his sixth Top 40 hit courtesy of 'Delicate', a duet recorded with which British R&B singer?

4. **Phil Collins had his third number 1 in 1988 with 'Groovy Kind of Love' – but who originally took the song to number 2 in 1966?**

5. In 1994, what did Big Mountain, All-4-One, Let Loose, Red Dragon with Brian and Tony Gold and Kylie Minogue have in common?

6. **Which romantic rockers had Top 40 hits with 'Fool for Your Loving', 'Guilty of Love', 'Is This Love', 'Give Me All Your Love' and 'The Deeper the Love'?**

7. In 1985, which singer had her biggest solo hit with a cover of a love song originally recorded by jazz singer Billie Holiday in 1945?

8. **Which 1992 number 1 single contains the lyrics 'If you stay I would only be in your way, so I'll go but I know I'll think of you every step of the way'?**

9. Which actor, singer and radio presenter made his chart debut with the 1989 number 2 'Love Changes Everything', from the musical *Aspects of Love*?

10. **In 1984, which chart-topping artist had his fifth Top 40 hit with a song subtitled '(No More Love on the Run)'?**

DID YOU KNOW?
The very first number 1 on the very first chart was the love song 'Here In My Heart' by American singer Al Martino. It spent nine consecutive weeks at number 1 between November 1952 and January 1953, a record broken by another love song, 'Cara Mia' by David Whitfield, which spent ten weeks at the top in 1954.

Football Anthems

Ten questions inspired by the 2018 NOW compilation album and the sport they call 'the beautiful game'. Sadly, the same adjective can't be applied to most of these singles.

1. Name the actor and TV personality who collaborated with Dizzee Rascal on the 2010 number 1 'Shout for England'.

2. **Dario G scored the second of three Top 10 hits with a song recorded for the 1998 FIFA World Cup in France. What was the song called?**

3. The Scottish World Cup squad reached number 4 in 1978 with the song 'Ole Ola (Mulher Brasileira)', featuring a singer born in Highgate, north London. Who is he?

4. **'We Are One (Ole Ola)' was the official song of the 2014 FIFA World Cup. It featured Jennifer Lopez, Brazilian singer Claudia Leitte and which male American rapper?**

5. The December 1998 number 21 'Naughty Christmas (Goblin in the Office)' was the follow-up to which act's number 2 football anthem from earlier that year?

6. **In 2000, England Supporters Band reached number 26 with their version of the theme to a 1963 American Second World War film. Name the film.**

7. 'This Time (We'll Get It Right)' by the 1982 England World Cup squad was written by Chris Norman and Pete Spencer of Smokie, who also wrote a 1979 Top 40 hit for which former England captain?

8. **In 1998, '(How Does It Feel to Be) On Top of the World' reached number 9 for England United, comprising of Echo & the Bunnymen, Ocean Colour Scene, Space and which girl band?**

9. England footballer John Barnes rapped on the 1990 number 1 'World in Motion' by England New Order. In 1988 he did the same for his club side Liverpool – what was their number 3 single called?

10. **In 2010, a third version of 'Three Lions' peaked at number 21. Credited to the Squad, the usual line-up of David Baddiel, Frank Skinner and the Lightning Seeds was joined by which chart-topping singer?**

Christmas

Ten Yule-themed questions based on one of the most popular and successful NOW albums, first released in 1985 and updated several times since.

1. Who sang the opening line on the original 1984 version of the Band Aid single 'Do They Know It's Christmas'?

2. **What 'double disappointment' links Mariah Carey's 'All I Want for Christmas Is You' in 1994 and 2018, and Wham!'s 'Last Christmas' in 1984 and 2017?**

3. 'Happy Xmas (War Is Over)' is credited to John & Yoko, the Plastic Ono Band and which third act?

4. **Cliff Richard has spent Christmas at number 1 four times; in 1960 with the Shadows, as a solo artist in 1988 and 1990, and as part of which act in 1989?**

5. Twenty years before the department store became a regular contributor to the Christmas chart race,

how was another John Lewis responsible for a 1980 Christmas number 3, a festive favourite ever since?

6. **What did Patty Donahue, singer with the Waitresses, 'forget' according to the lyrics of their 1982 single 'Christmas Wrapping'?**

7. Which Christmas favourite has provided a Top 10 hit for Bing Crosby and for Bros?

8. **One-hit wonders Michael Andrews featuring Gary Jules had the Christmas number 1 in 2003 with their version of 'Mad World'. Which cult film soundtrack was their song originally recorded for?**

9. In 2009, following a social-media campaign, which *X Factor* winner was kept off the Christmas number 1 spot by 'Killing in the Name' by Rage Against the Machine?

10. **Spice Girls held the Christmas top spot each year from 1996 to 1998, and in two of those years kept TV characters at number 2. Name either of them.**

DID YOU KNOW?
Sir Paul McCartney is the singles chart King of Christmas, appearing on four Christmas number 1s for The Beatles between 1963 and 1967, one each with Wings in 1977, Band Aid 20 in 2004 and The Justice Collective in 2012. He also recorded a message for the B-Side of the original 1984 Band Aid single, Christmas number 1 in 1984.

Disney

First released in 2011, NOW's collection of Disney songs has been updated four times, with songs from new blockbusters added alongside existing family favourites. Ten questions to test your knowledge of Disney's movie melodies.

1. Who had her first Top 40 hit in 2008 with 'See You Again' from *Hannah Montana 2*?

2. **In 1994, Elton John had two Top 20 singles from *The Lion King* soundtrack. The number 14 hit 'Can You Feel the Love Tonight' was one; what was the other?**

3. Which 2013 Oscar-winning animation shares its title with a 1998 number 1 single for Madonna?

4. **Which three chart-topping artists combined on the theme to Walt Disney Pictures' 1993 version of *The Three Musketeers*?**

5. Which 1991 Disney animated film shares its title with a 1978 Top 40 hit for David Bowie?

DID YOU KNOW?
At the 1939 Academy Awards, Disney's S*now White and the Seven Dwarfs* received an Academy Honorary Award. Walt Disney received a full-size Oscar statuette and seven miniature ones, presented to him by 10-year-old actress Shirley Temple.

6. **Which singer-songwriter's credits include 'Simon Smith and the Amazing Dancing Bear', 'You Can Keep Your Hat On' as well as 'You've Got a Friend In Me' from *Toy Story*?**

7. Which former cast member of *The All New Mickey Mouse Club* began his solo career with the 2002 number 2 'Like I Love You'?

8. **Which song from *Pinocchio* became the first from a Disney film to win an Academy Award?**

9. Name the 1985 number 16 for Dionne Warwick and Friends that shares its title with a song performed by vultures in Disney's 1967 animation *The Jungle Book*.

10. **Which Disney title character's name also provided the title of a Top 40 hit for Otis Redding and Carla Thomas in 1967, and Salt-N-Pepa in 1988?**

Old Skool

It's time to dig out your old boom box and bust some moves as we present ten questions inspired by 'the biggest names and the coolest beats' on this 2017 NOW compilation.

1. Sugababes vs. Girls Aloud reached number 1 in 2007 with their version of 'Walk This Way', but who first took it to number 8 in 1986?

2. **What nationality are Wyclef Jean and Pras Michel of Fugees?**

3. Which Top 40 single by TLC shares its title with a hit single by Radiohead?

4. **By what name are Joseph Saddler and Nathaniel Glover, Melvin Glover, Eddie Morris, Robert Wiggins and Guy Williams better known?**

5. Who reached number 3 in 2003 when they urged Beyoncé and actress Lucy Liu to 'get on the floor' and 'shake it like a Polaroid picture'?

6. **Which English singer topped the chart in 2000 when she was featured on Eminem's number 1 single 'Stan'?**

7. Who do Ladies Love so much that he has made the Top 40 seventeen times since his 1987 chart debut 'I Need Love'?

8. **Whose 1991 number 15 single sampled Lou Reed, Ian Dury and the Blockheads, Sergei Prokofiev and Spotty from *SuperTed*, then earned a mention in Robbie Williams's 2000 number 1 'Rock DJ'?**

9. Which hugely successful hip-hop artist and producer has appeared on Top 10 singles alongside 2Pac, Blackstreet, Eminem, Snoop Dogg, Knoc-Turnal, 50 Cent and Skylar Grey?

10. **Which Phil Collins song gave Brandy and Ray J another Top 40 hit in 2001?**

DID YOU KNOW?
Rappers Jay-Z, The Notorious B.I.G., Busta Rhymes and DMX were all pupils at the George Westinghouse Career and Technical Education High School in Brooklyn, New York City. Between them they have more than sixty Top 40 singles.

NOW

THAT'S WHAT I CALL

Musicals

Ten questions inspired by the big show stoppers that had the crowds on their feet, brought the house down, and landed in the chart.

1. Who appeared with Peter Kay on the 2011 *Comic Relief* single, 'I Know Him So Well'?

2. **In 1998, which musical provided Boyzone with their fourth number 1 with 'No Matter What'?**

3. Which punk guitarist had a solo number 1 in 1982 with a song from *South Pacific*?

4. **In 1996, Madonna had her forty-fifth Top 40 hit when 'Don't Cry for Me Argentina' reached number 3. What was her forty-sixth Top 40 hit, also taken from the soundtrack of *Evita*?**

5. Which song from *The Rocky Horror Picture Show* gave Damian a number 7 hit in 1989?

6. **'You'll Never Walk Alone' was a number 1 hit for Gerry & the Pacemakers in 1963, and for**

the Crowd in 1985, but which Rodgers and Hammerstein musical was it written for?

7. In 2009, which former *American Idol* contestant had her third Top 40 hit with 'And I Am Telling You I'm Not Going' from the musical *Dreamgirls*?

8. **Songwriter Lionel Bart had his greatest successes with the musical *Oliver!* and which song that was a number 1 hit twice for Cliff Richard?**

9. Which rapper made number 2 in 1998 when he sampled a tale of hard times in the orphanage from the musical *Annie*?

10. **In 1991, Jason Donovan had his fourth number 1 single with a song from which Andrew Lloyd Webber and Tim Rice musical?**

NOW

THAT'S WHAT I CALL

Mum

Inspired by the 2017 NOW compilation, here are ten questions on the theme of 'Mum'. Or 'Mummy', 'Mother', 'Mama', 'Ma' or 'Mater'…

1. Which American singer and songwriter had his first solo hit in 1972 with 'Mother and Child Reunion'?

2. **Which two-word song title connects a 2004 number 6 by Black Eyed Peas and a 2015 number 9 by David Guetta featuring Nicki Minaj and Afrojack?**

3. The Rolling Stones have had forty-three Top 40 singles, but one of them, a 1966 number 5, has the longest title with ten words. Name the song.

4. **American trio Wilson Phillips features Carnie and Wendy Wilson, the daughters of Brian Wilson of The Beach Boys, along with Chynna Phillips. Who was Chynna's famous singing mum?**

5. What did Rizzle Kicks suggest their 'mama do' on their 2011 number 2?

6. **Which British group's fifth Top 40 hit was the 1984 number 14 'Mothers Talk'?**

7. Who had a 1977 number 2 that begins with the line 'Freeze, I'm Ma Baker, put your hands in the air and gimme all your money'?

8. **Who partnered Tom Jones on his 2000 remake of the 1970 Three Dog Night single 'Mama Told Me Not to Come'?**

9. Whose 'Mom' gave Fountains of Wayne their biggest hit in 2004?

10. **Dr Hook shortened their name after their 1972 chart debut 'Sylvia's Mother'. What was the band originally called?**

NOW

Dad

Ten questions on the theme of Dads and Daddys, Pas and Papas, Fathers and Paters.

1. Who got to number 2 twice – once with a band, once as a 'solo' artist – with a cover of the Cat Stevens song 'Father and Son'?

2. **What two-word song title provided different number 6 hits for Boney M in 1976 and Darts in 1977?**

3. Which American soul singer had his only Top 40 hit with the 1975 number 4 hit 'Swing Your Daddy'?

4. **In 1995, which Manchester band had the second of four Top 40 hits with the number 8 single 'In The Name of The Father'?**

5. After nine consecutive Top 3 singles, who failed to crack the Top 10 when 'Father Figure' peaked at number 11 in 1988?

6. **Who had a number 3 hit in 1982 after they added some 'pig' to a 1965 James Brown song title?**

7. Which 1961 song by American doo-wop group Shep and the Limelites gave Cliff Richard his seventy-fourth Top 40 hit in 1981?

8. **In 1991 which American singer had her eighth Top 40 hit and won the Grammy 'Song of the Year' Award after she recorded a new duet with her father, who died in 1965?**

9. Which 'Father' had three Top 20 hits in 1978, including the number 13 single 'Dippety Day'? Clue: the other two hits include the name of his companions.

10. **In 2001 which American rock band's first Top 40 hit was a last resort?**

NOW

THAT'S WHAT I CALL

Smash Hits

In 1987, *NOW* teamed up with the utterly amazing *Smash Hits* magazine to bring you '32 Swingorilliant Hits of the 80s'. Here are ten poptastic questions about some of the featured artists.

1. Whose run of fifteen Top 40 hits began with the 1985 number 15 'All Fall Down' and ended with 'Rock My World', at number 28 in 1988?

2. **In 1985, who had their ninth Top 40 single with 'Don't Mess with Doctor Dream' and appeared onstage with Madonna at Live Aid?**

3. In 1992, Curiosity Killed the Cat shortened their name to Curiosity and had a number 3 single with a cover of which 1974 Johnny Bristol hit?

4. **In 2002, a singer who had previously topped the charts with different bands in 1986 and 1990 released an album under the name Biscuit Boy. Who was he?**

DID YOU KNOW?
The 1987 *NOW... Smash Hits* album included Depeche Mode's number 9 hit, 'Master And Servant'. Since they made their Top 40 debut in 1981 with 'New Life' the band have had forty-three Top 40 hits – fourteen of them in the Top 10 – but never got higher than number 4.

5. Which American act followed up their first two number 1s in 1979 with another three in 1980, then waited nineteen years for their sixth chart-topper?

6. **In 1998, Robbie Williams reached number four with a double A-side single featuring 'No Regrets' and a cover of which 1981 number 2 by Adam and the Ants?**

7. Which songwriter, whose band spent four weeks at number 1 in 1983, started his acting career in the 1971 public information film *Never Go with Strangers*?

8. **After four consecutive Top 40 hits, which British trio replaced their original singer with John 'Jon' Foster for their next three?**

9. Which sisters' short but respectable chart career consisted of four Top 10 singles between 1986 and 1988?

10. **Name the two female former backing singers who had a 1987 number 2 with 'Heartache'.**

Chilled

Kick back and relax with ten cool, calm and collected questions inspired by the 2014 *Chilled* album.

1. Which country was singer Katie Melua born in?

2. **Jakatta had their biggest hit in 2001 with 'American Dream', which sampled Thomas Newman's score to which 1999 Academy Award-winning film?**

3. In 2011, Slow Moving Millie had her only Top 40 hit with a cover of which song by The Smiths?

4. **Which 1999 number 19 hit includes the lyric 'If you're fond of sand dunes and salty air, quaint little villages here and there'?**

5. Which American singer was the featured vocalist on 'Lazy', the 2002 number 2 for X-Press 2?

6. **Which three-word song title that provided Sam Smith with his third number 1 in 2014 also provided different Top 40 hits for The Faces in**

the seventies, The Mission in the eighties and Erasure in the nineties?

7. The sister of Rollo Armstrong of Faithless is also a Top 40 artist, and featured on that group's 2002 single 'One Step Too Far'. Who is she?

8. **Which chart-topping British artist had her eleventh Top 40 hit with a cover of a 1990 single by The Waterboys?**

9. Name the female artist who duetted with Senegalese singer Youssou N'Dour on the 1994 number 3 single '7 Seconds'.

10. **In 2014, MNEK, Laura Welsh, Zak Abel and Jennifer Hudson all featured on different Top 40 singles by which English dance act?**

DID YOU KNOW?
Swedish guitarist José Gonzàlez made his chart debut with 'Heartbeats' after the song was used in a TV advert for Sony featuring 250,000 coloured balls bouncing in the streets of San Francisco. The 2006 number 9 single was a cover of a song originally recorded by another Swedish act, The Knife.

NOW
THAT'S WHAT I CALL

A Party

Ten questions on the theme of 'Party', inspired by the 2014 NOW album. Because everyone loves a party, right?

1. Which American band consisting of brothers Charlie, Robert and Ronnie Wilson had eight Top 40 hits between 1980 and 2004, including 'Party Lights' and 'Big Fun'?

2. **In 2012, which Kosovo-born singer had three consecutive number 1 hits, including 'How We Do (Party)'?**

3. Dave Stewart and Barbara Gaskin reached number 1 in 1981 with 'It's My Party', but who originally had a number 9 hit with the song in 1963?

4. **What historic party did the Sensational Alex Harvey Band invite listeners to in 1976?**

5. In 1999 the Vengaboys had the second of nine Top 40 hits with a song subtitled '(The Vengabus)'. What was the full title of this number 3 single?

6. **In 2004, Mark McGrath, singer with US rock band Sugar Ray, had his only 'solo' hit when he duetted on the number 10 single 'Party for Two' with which hugely successful female singer?**

7. Which British rock group had the fifty-fourth of their fifty-seven Top 40 hits with the prophetically titled 'The Party Ain't Over Yet'?

8. **Which former member of R&B trio TLC made her last Top 40 appearance with the 2001 number 16 'The Block Party'?**

9. More than fifty years before Nicki Minaj made her chart debut, which other Trinidadian artist had Top 10 hits with 'Let's Have a Party', 'Let's Have Another Party', 'Make It a Party' and 'Piano Party'?

10. **Which relatives' parties did Paul Nicholas and Monie Love attend on their respective 1976 and 1989 Top 20 hits?**

NOW

THAT'S WHAT I CALL

A GOOD YEAR

Answers from page 247

NOW

THAT'S WHAT I CALL

A Good Year

Ten questions presenting three number 1 singles that topped the chart in the same year – but what were those years?

1. 'Love Yourself' by Justin Bieber, '7 Years' by Lukas Graham and 'Shout Out to My Ex' by Little Mix.

2. **'My Old Man's a Dustman' by Lonnie Donegan, 'Three Steps to Heaven' by Eddie Cochran and 'Shakin' All Over' by Johnny Kidd & the Pirates.**

3. 'Bring Your Daughter … to the Slaughter' by Iron Maiden, 'Should I Stay or Should I Go' by the Clash and 'I Wanna Sex You Up' by Color Me Badd.

4. **'Cum on Feel the Noize' by Slade, 'Skweeze Me Pleeze Me' by Slade and 'Merry Xmas Everybody' by Slade.**

5. 'American Pie' by Madonna, 'We Will Rock You' by Five & Queen and 'Against All Odds' by Mariah Carey featuring Westlife.

6. **'Stand by Me' by Ben E. King, 'Star Trekkin" by the Firm and 'You Win Again' by Bee Gees.**

7. 'I'm a Believer' by The Monkees, 'Somethin' Stupid' by Nancy and Frank Sinatra, and 'The Last Waltz' by Engelbert Humperdinck.

8. **'Fireflies' by Owl City, 'Good Times' by Roll Deep and 'Start Without You' by Alexandra Burke featuring Laza Morgan.**

9. 'MMMBop' by Hanson, 'Barbie Girl' by Aqua and 'Teletubbies Say "Eh-oh!"' by Teletubbies.

10. **'Coward of the County' by Kenny Rogers, 'Theme from M*A*S*H (Suicide Is Painless)' by MASH and 'Xanadu' by Olivia Newton-John and Electric Light Orchestra.**

Summer Hits

Ten bright and sunny questions inspired by the 2016 *Summer Hits* compilation.

1. In 1982, which band had the third of their twenty-four Top 40 hits with 'Someone Somewhere (In Summertime)'?

2. **Disco singer Kelly Marie had a 1980 number 1 with 'Feels Like I'm in Love', written by Ray Dorset. In 1970, Ray spent seven weeks at number 1 with which British band?**

3. Which chart-topping American singer announced she was 'Cool for the Summer' in 2015?

4. **Which 1935 George and Ira Gershwin song gave Fun Boy Three their fifth Top 40 hit in August 1982?**

5. American singer Bobby Goldsboro had two summer-themed Top 20 singles, with the 1973 number 9 'Summer (The First Time)' and which other hit single in 1974?

DID YOU KNOW?
Soul music legend Marvin Gaye had his only number 1 in 1968 with 'I Heard It Through The Grapevine', but returned to the top of the chart in 2015 when Charlie Puth featuring Meghan Trainor spent one week at number 1 with 'Marvin Gaye'. In 2016 the song appeared on *NOW... Summer Hits*, *NOW... No. 1 Hits* and *NOW... Party Hits*.

6. **Who reached number 2 in 2003 with a cover of Don Henley's 1985 single 'The Boys of Summer'?**

7. Which two Welsh bands have had different Top 40 singles called 'Indian Summer'?

8. **Name the 1966 number 8 summer anthem that includes the sound of car horns and a pneumatic drill.**

9. Which chart-topping act reached number 8 in 1998 with a cover of the Bananarama single 'Cruel Summer'?

10. **Mike Batt has written Top 10 hits for Art Garfunkel, Katie Melua and The Wombles, but his only chart hit under his own name came in 1975 with which number 4 single?**

A Wedding

Ten lovey-dovey questions, surrounded by hearts and flowers, on the theme of weddings, inspired by the 2011 NOW compilation.

1. In November 2003, who had the second of four number 1s when they 'Crashed the Wedding'?

2. **Which American vocal trio made their chart debut with the 1964 number 22 single 'Chapel of Love'?**

3. Which 1985 Top 10 single by Billy Idol starts with the line 'Hey, little sister, what have you done?'?

4. **In the 1980s, duo Godley and Creme had Top 20 hits with 'Under Your Thumb', 'Cry' and which 1981 number 7 single?**

5. What tale of enforced matrimony has provided a Top 40 hit for both Roy C and Rod Stewart?

6. **Which 2014 single gave Irish band Hozier a number 2 chart debut?**

7. Which chart-topping American singer had her third consecutive Top 20 hit with the 2015 number 20 'Dear Future Husband'?

8. **Which British band's twenty-two Top 40 hits include the 1996 number 8 'Don't Marry Her'?**

9. Which chart-topping singer had his fourth Top 40 hit with the 1977 number 26 'I Knew the Bride (When She Used to Rock 'n' Roll)'?

10. **Which 1964 Chuck Berry single begins 'It was a teenage wedding, and the old folks wished them well'?**

DID YOU KNOW?
ABBA's 1976 number 1 'Dancing Queen' opens the 2004 'Wedding' album, one of six times it has appeared on a *NOW* collection so far. ABBA's second most popular *NOW* song is the 1980 album track 'Happy New Year', which has made five appearances – all of them on different volumes of *NOW Christmas*.

NOW

THAT'S WHAT I CALL

Weather

There is a forecast of furrowed brows and high scores for our meteorological-themed questions. Should you get one wrong, remember what B*Witched said: 'Don't Blame It on the Weatherman'.

1. In 1993 who had the first and biggest of his seven Top 40 hits with 'It Keeps Rainin' (Tears From My Eyes)'?

2. **Which British trio had their only Top 40 hit with the 1969 number 1 'Something In The Air'?**

3. What meteorological phenomenon provided different Top 10 hits for Liverpool Britpop band Cast in 1996 and Finnish DJ Darude in 2000?

4. **Who had their biggest hit with the 2003 number 16 single 'Nice Weather for Ducks', taken from their Mercury Music Prize-nominated album *Lost Horizons*?**

5. Which 1989 number 5 for Bette Midler also provided a Top 40 hit for *Coronation Street* actor Bill Tarmey

in 1994 and for *London's Burning* actor Steven Houghton in 1997?

6. **In 1972, which Birmingham beat group had their fifth and final Top 40 hit with 'Storm in a Teacup'?**

7. Which Welsh band had eight Top 40 singles, including 'Where Were You Hiding When the Storm Broke?' and 'Rain in the Summertime'?

8. **Who had their biggest hit in 1992 with a song that begins with the lyrics 'Walking round the room singing "Stormy Weather", at 57 Mount Pleasant Street'?**

9. Name the Italian dance group who made their chart debut in 1991 with a cover of the 1979 Christopher Cross single 'Ride Like the Wind'.

10. **Which 1993 Top 10 single sampled an interview with American singer Rickie Lee Jones, whose only other chart hit was the 1979 number 18, 'Chuck E.'s in Love'?**

NOW
THAT'S WHAT I CALL

A Summer Party

Ten sizzling hot questions on the theme of 'Summer Party', inspired by the 2016 NOW compilation.

1. Glenn Frey had his biggest solo hit, and one of just two Top 40 singles, with 'The Heat Is On' in 1985. He also has seven Top 40 singles and two of the biggest-selling albums ever with which band?

2. **Which 1999 number 4 single by Jamiroquai shares its title with the name of an American rock band who had their biggest hit with the 1970 number 2 'Let's Work Together'?**

3. What 'meteorological phenomenon' was responsible for seven Top 40 hits in the late seventies and early eighties, including 'Too Hot to Handle' and 'Boogie Nights'?

4. **Which three-word song title provided different Top 10 hits for The Style Council in 1983 and Girls Aloud in 2005?**

5. Name the Scottish singer who had his biggest hit with the 1966 number 2 'Sunshine Superman'.

6. **Which *X Factor* winner helped Rudimental to their ninth Top 40 hit in 2017 with 'Sun Comes Up'?**

7. Which British band had their third number 1 courtesy of a 'Sunny Afternoon' in 1966?

8. **In 1984, which comedienne's last visit to the Top 40 required 'Sunglasses'?**

9. Who had their biggest hit in 2000 with a dance version of Chris Rea's 1988 number 12 single 'On the Beach'?

10. **In 1977, which female singer had the second of her seven Top 40 hits with 'Sunshine After the Rain'?**

NOW

THAT'S WHAT I CALL

Halloween

Ten un-scary questions on the theme of 'Halloween', with no mention of The Darkness or of Usher's 2012 number 5 hit 'Scream'.

1. Which veteran horror actor provided the voiceover for Michael Jackson's 1983 number 10 single 'Thriller'?

2. **In 2015, which dark arts did Little Mix dabble in to get their third number 1 single?**

3. Which country-music act had their only Top 40 single with the 1979 number 14 'The Devil Went Down to Georgia'?

DID YOU KNOW?
Bobby 'Boris' Pickett and The Crypt Kickers originally released Halloween favourite 'Monster Mash' in 1962, but it first made the UK chart in 1973 when it reached number 3. The group also recorded a 'Monster Mash' album, including the songs 'Bloodbank Blues', 'Graveyard Shift', 'Sinister Stomp' and 'Irresistable Igor'.

4. **In 1994, which Irish group reached number 14 with their third Top 40 single 'Zombie'?**

5. Which stars of CITV made number 12 in 2001 with 'Things That Go Bump in the Night'?

6. **Whose second Top 40 hit was their 1981 homage to the protagonist of Alfred Hitchcock's *Psycho*, 'Norman Bates'?**

7. Who had a 1993 number 3 with 'Love Song for a Vampire', taken from the Francis Ford Coppola film *Bram Stoker's Dracula*?

8. **What were Madness waiting for in 1986?**

9. Six years before his number 2 hit with 'Ghostbusters', Ray Parker Jr. was singer with R&B group Raydio, who made number 11 with what nursery rhyme-themed single?

10. **American singer Rockwell had his only Top 40 hit with the 1984 number 6 'Somebody's Watching Me', but who reached number 3 with their 2006 cover version?**

NOW

THAT'S WHAT I CALL

Winter

Wrap up warm or throw another log on the fire as you prepare yourself for ten questions on the frosty theme of 'Winter'.

1. In 1998, which American singer spent one week 'Frozen' at number 1?

2. **Which song that was originally a 1978 number 24 for Foreigner gave New York hip-hop duo M.O.P. the first of their two Top 40 hits in 2001?**

3. Who had a run of four consecutive Top 10 hits beginning with the 1988 number 2 'Beat Dis' and ending with the 1991 number 7 'Winter in July'?

4. **Which one-word song title provided different Top 40 hits for George Benson in 1986, Coldplay in 2000 and Natalie Imbruglia in 2005?**

5. Which American group were number 1 in February 1976 with 'December, 1963'?

6. **Which number 17 single by Spandau Ballet, released in February 1981, was the follow-up to their 1980 chart debut 'To Cut a Long Story Short'?**

7. Which British band followed up an enduring Christmas favourite with the 1974 number 6 hit 'Rock 'n' Roll Winter'?

8. **Which 1996 number 6 single by Queen shares its title with a 1982 number 2 by David Essex?**

9. Name the Australian singer-songwriter who had her third Top 40 hit in 2008 with a version of Connie Francis's 1962 single 'Warm This Winter'.

10. **Which song originally recorded by Simon & Garfunkel gave The Bangles their fifth Top 40 hit in 1988?**

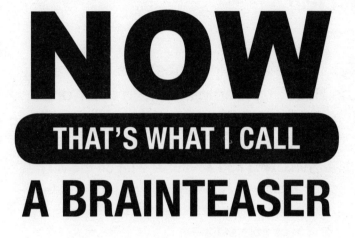

Answers from page 253

NOW!

Ten multiple-choice questions celebrating the Best Pop Compilations in the World ... Ever!

1. **In 1983, who had a number 2 hit on the very first volume of NOW Music and provided the voiceover for the television advert? Was it:**
    a. Suggs from Madness
    b. Tracey Ullman
    c. Boy George from Culture Club

4. **Shania Twain, Amy Winehouse and Janet Jackson have all appeared on at least ten different *NOW* albums – numbered and themed volumes – but what else do they have in common?**
    a. They have all had a hit with a cover version of a song by The Beatles
    b. They have all recorded a duet with Tony Bennett
    c. They have never had a number one single

3. **What do 'Unchained Melody' by The Righteous Brothers (first appearance *NOW 18*), 'Bohemian**

Rhapsody' by Queen (*NOW 21*) and 'Blue Monday'
by New Order (*NOW 1983*) have in common?
a. They have all been number 1 on two separate
   occasions
b. The song title doesn't get mentioned in the lyrics
c. They have all been the Christmas number 1 single

4. **What links Liverpool band The Christians (first**
   appearance *NOW 13*), Australian band INXS
   (*NOW 14*) and American band Kings of Leon
   (*NOW 71*)?
   a. They have all had Top 40 hits with two different
      lead singers
   b. They were all originally called The Spectres before
      they changed the band name
   c. They all included three brothers in the band

5. **In 1984 and 1985, *NOW 3, 4* and *5* featured the**
   famous *NOW* pig on the cover. What slightly
   different item was he wearing on each cover?
   a. Different sunglasses
   b. Different baseball caps
   c. Different headphones

6. **What was unique about the 1986 release *NOW:***
   ***The Summer Album*?**
   a. It is the only *NOW* album that doesn't contain any
      number 1 singles
   b. It is the only *NOW* album to include any of The
      Beatles' singles
   c. It is the only *NOW* album that features
      instrumentals only

7. **What link with *NOW* is shared by the films *Titanic* (1997), *Star Wars: Episode I – The Phantom Menace* (1999), and *Paddington* (2014)?**
   a. One of the stars of each film has appeared on a *NOW* album
   b. The theme song from each film appeared on a *NOW* album
   c. Dialogue from each film was sampled for a dance hit that appeared on a *NOW* album

8. **What do reggae singer Bob Marley, country singer Billy Ray Cyrus and Beatle John Lennon all have in common?**
   a. They have appeared on a *NOW* album and so has one of their children
   b. They have all had a song including the word 'Peace' in the title on a *NOW* album
   c. A version of one of their songs was recorded for a Christmas TV advert and appeared on *NOW*

9. **What links the number 1 singles 'When the Going Gets Tough …' by Billy Ocean (*NOW 7*), 'Mambo No. 5' by Lou Bega (*NOW 44*) and 'The Power of Love' by Frankie Goes to Hollywood (*NOW 46*)?**
   a. It was the only *NOW* appearance by each of the artists
   b. They were also number 1 for a different artist, and on a different volume of *NOW*
   c. They were all knocked off the number 1 spot, only to return two weeks later

10. **German dance act Sash! made four consecutive appearances on *NOWs 36* to *39* with 'Encore Une Fois', 'Ecuador', 'Stay' and 'La Primavera'. What was different about the four songs?**
    a. They peaked at numbers 1, 2, 3 and 4 in the singles chart
    b. Each one featured a different singer
    c. They all included vocals in a different language

A Challenge

Ten demanding and tricky questions to identify the Dons of Dance, the Professors of Pop, the Titans of Tune and the Know Alls of NOW.

Can you name the three different artists who have a song on NOW called …

1. 'Human', a number 8 in 1986 on *NOW 8,* a number 3 in 2003 on *NOW 72* and a number 2 in 2016 on *NOW 96*.
2. 'Stop', a number 4 in 1988 on *NOW 14,* a number 2 in 1992 on *NOW 39* and a number 9 in 2004 on *NOW 59*.
3. 'Sing', a number 3 in 2001 on *NOW 50,* a number 1 in 2012 on *NOW 82* and a number 1 in 2014 on *NOW 88*.
4. 'Only You', a number 1 in 1983 on *NOW 2,* a number 4 in 1991 on *NOW 19* and a number 13 in 2018 on *NOW 100*.
5. 'Paradise', number 11 in 2001 on *NOW 48,* number 1 in 2001 on *NOW 81* and number 2 in 2018 on *NOW 99*.

6. 'Pray', number 8 in 1990 on *NOW 19,* number 1 in 1993 on *NOW 26* and number 17 in 2002 on *NOW 53*.

Can you name the four different artists who have a song on NOW called …

7. 'In Too Deep', a number 14 in 1985 on *NOW 5,* a number 19 in 1986 on *NOW 8,* a number 6 in 1996 on *NOW 34* and a number 13 in 2001 on *NOW 51*.

8. 'Stronger', a number 7 in 2000 on *NOW 48,* a number 7 in 2002 on *NOW 54,* a number 1 in 2007 on *NOW 68* and a number 4 in 2015 on *NOW 91*.

Can you name the five different artists who have a song on NOW called …

9. 'Shine', number 5 in 1994 on *NOW 28,* number 6 in 2005 on *NOW 60*, a number 1 and a number 10 in 2007, both on *NOW 67*, and a number 2 in 2015 on *NOW 91*.

10. 'Stay', a number 1 in 1992 on *NOW 21,* a number 4 in 1993 on *NOW 26,* a number 2 in 1997 on *NOW 38*, a number 20 in 2015 on *NOW 93* and a number 8 in 2017 on *NOW 96*.

NOW

You know them by the name that's listed in the charts, printed on the single or comes up on your phone's music player. But what does it say on their birth certificate? Who was born …

1. Timothy Mosley in Norfolk, Virginia, in 1972? He produced albums for Ginuwine, Aaliyah and Missy Elliott before he made his Top 40 debut in 1999.

2. **Richard Melville Hall in Harlem, New York, in 1965? He played guitar for hardcore punk band Vatican Commandos before he had his first Top 40 hit in 1991.**

3. Henry Olusegun Adeola Samuel in Paddington, London, in 1963? He made his first Top 40 debut with a killer hit in 1990.

4. **Thomas Callaway in Atlanta, Georgia, in 1975? He was in Atlanta hip-hop group Goodie Mob before he made his Top 40 debut in 2007.**

5. Eilleen Edwards in Windsor, Ontario, in 1965? Her third album spent eleven weeks at number 1 in 1999 and has sold 3.5 million copies.

6. **Elizabeth Woolridge Grant in New York City in 1985? She once described her own music as 'gangsta Nancy Sinatra'.**

7. Michael Owuo Jr. in Thornton Heath, London, in 1993? He was the first artist to sing on the 2017 Artists for Grenfell charity single.

8. **William Adams Jr. in Los Angeles, California, in 1975? He had already topped the charts with an R&B group before making his solo debut in 2006.**

9. Katheryn Hudson in Santa Barbara, California, in 1984? A year before her debut she appeared in the video for Gym Class Heroes' number 3 hit, 'Cupid's Chokehold'.

10. **Thomas Woodward in Pontypridd, Wales, in 1940? He had his first two number 1 hits in the 1960s but had to wait until 2009 for his third.**

NOW

THAT'S WHAT I CALL

A Number 1

Ten questions to test your knowledge of the biggest hits, the bestsellers, the hottest items, or what John Lennon called 'the topper-most of the popper-most'.

1. Who had a gap of twenty-nine years between his first number 1, 'When I Need You' in 1977, and his second, 'Thunder in My Heart Again' in 2006?

2. **What remarkable achievement do The Beatles, John Lennon (solo), Elvis Presley, Ed Sheeran and Justin Bieber share?**

3. Which song by a Yorkshire-born singer first entered the Top 40 in November 1971 and finally made number 1 in March 2005, thirty-three years and four months later?

4. **Which song, originally written as a film theme, has been a number 1 single for four different artists in three different decades?**

5. In January 1976, Queen's 'Bohemian Rhapsody' was knocked off number 1 by a song that is mentioned in its lyrics. What was that song?

6. **Who are the only father and son to have each topped the chart as solo artists? Clue: the father reached number 1 in 1981, his son in 2002.**

7. In 2013, who became the first female solo artist to have number 1 singles in seven consecutive years?

8. **What distinction do Emile Ford & the Checkmates, Rolf Harris, Pink Floyd, Band Aid II, Westlife and Joe McElderry share?**

9. Which American actor can claim to have the shortest number 1 song title ever, for his 1975 hit 'If'?

10. **Which British band had forty-three Top 40 hits between 1981 and 2009, including fourteen in the Top 10, but have yet to have a number 1?**

DID YOU KNOW?
Black Eyed Peas' 2009 number 1 'I Gotta Feeling' and Pharrell Williams' 2013 number 1 'Happy' can claim to be the most featured songs on NOW, having both appeared on seventeen different NOW titles.

NOW

THAT'S WHAT I CALL

First and Last

Can you identify the artists who began and ended their Top 40 singles-chart stories with the following titles?

1. 'Love Song' (number 20 in 1979) and 'Alone Again Or' (number 27 in 1987).

2. **'Donna' (number 2 in 1972) and 'I'm Not in Love' (number 29 in 1995).**

3. 'King' (number 4 in 1980) and 'Kiss and Say Goodbye' (number 19 in 2005).

4. **'The Banana Boat Song' (number 8 in 1957) and 'The Living Tree' (number 37 in 2007).**

5. 'Do You Remember The First Time?' (number 33 in 1994) and 'Bad Cover Version' (number 27 in 2002).

6. **'Swear It Again' (number 1 in 1999) and 'Better Man' (number 26 in 2019).**

7. 'Endless Love' (number 7 in 1981) and 'Just for You' (number 20 in 2004).

DID YOU KNOW?
The very first UK singles chart was published on 14 November 1952. It featured twelve songs by thirteen different artists though none of the artists were making their last appearance. Nat 'King' Cole was the most successful of the historic debutants, returning with another thirty Top 40 hits.

8. **'What Makes You Beautiful' (number 1 in 2011) and 'History' (number 6 in 2015).**

9. 'If This Is Love' (number 8 in 2008) and 'What Are You Waiting For?' (number 38 in 2014).

10. **'Butterfly' (number 1 in 1957) and 'It's the Most Wonderful Time of the Year' (number 17 in 2007).**

NOW

THAT'S WHAT I CALL

A Band

Can you guess the name of these ten bands from the first names of the band members? We've added some details of their first NOW appearance to help you along.

1. Tom & Harry & Danny & Dougie (first appearance *NOW 58* in 2004).

2. **Tony & Brian & John & Terry (first appearance *NOW Dance 92* in 1992).**

3. Jean-Paul & Phil & Ray & Anita (first appearance *NOW 20* in 1991).

4. **Piers & Amir & Kesi & Leon (first appearance *NOW 82* in 2012).**

5. Lee & Jimmy & Spike (first appearance *NOW 35* in 1996).

6. **Danny & Glen & Mark (first appearance *NOW 70* in 2008).**

7. Célena & Heavenli & Naima (first appearance *NOW 41* in 1998).

8. **Lene & Réne & Søren & Claus (first appearance** *NOW 39* **in 1998).**

9. Liam & Keith & Keith & Leeroy (first appearance *NOW Dance 91* in 1991).

10. **Bob & Peter & Neville & Aston & Carlton (first appearance** *NOW 3* **in 1984).**

NOW

THAT'S WHAT I CALL

A Top Ten

Ten questions on the theme of numbers. Each question or answer will relate to an artist or song that includes the number of the relevant question, one to ten.

1. In 2006, which American singer teamed up with U2 for a re-recording of the band's 1992 single 'One'?

2. **Which British band had two Top 40 hits in 1980 with 'Two Pints of Lager and a Packet of Crisps Please' and 'Two Little Boys'?**

3. Which chart-topping American vocal trio had ten Top 40 hits in the seventies, including the 1979 Top 10 hits 'Woman in Love' and 'The Runner'?

4. **Name the chart-topping artist who in 2003 reached number four with his fourth solo single, 'Four Minute Warning'.**

5. Which American trio claimed to be a quintet and had the first of five Top 40 singles with a subterranean hit in 1996?

6. **Name the Hartlepool band whose biggest hit was originally released as '6 Underground' in 1996, when it reached number 15, then as 'Six Underground' in 1997, when it peaked at number 9?**

7. Which singer finished runner-up to Little Mix in the 2011 series of *The X Factor* and had his only Top 40 hit with a cover of the White Stripes' 'Seven Nation Army'?

8. **Name the 1986 number 13 single by Claire and Friends that includes the lyrics 'I got your picture on me wall, got your name upon me scarf'.**

9. Which American rock band had their biggest hit with the 2005 number 7 'The Hand That Feeds', and provided Johnny Cash with his last Top 40 single in his lifetime when he covered their song 'Hurt'?

10. **Whose '10' proved to be not quite perfect when it was kept off number 1 by B*Witched with 'Rollercoaster' in September 1998?**

NOW

THAT'S WHAT I CALL

Dance

Do you know your lindy hop from your lambada? Name the dance that featured in the title of the hits by these artists – award yourself a bonus point for each song or album title you can name.

1. Lou Bega (1999), Shaft (1999) and Bob the Builder (1999).

2. **Louis Armstrong (1952), The Shadows (1962) and Shakira (2002)**

3. Status Quo (1990), Rod Stewart (1992) and Toby Bourke with George Michael (1997).

DID YOU KNOW?
Detroit group DeBarge made their first appearance on *NOW Dance: The 12" Mixes*, the very first themed *NOW* album, released in May 1985. The quintet, featuring siblings Bunny, El, Marty, Randy and James DeBarge, had their only Top 40 hit with the number 4 single 'Rhythm of the Night'.

4. **Wizzard (1973), Bee Gees (1975) and Joe Jackson (1981).**

5. Scatman John (1995), Hanson (1997) and Westlife (2002).

6. **Public Image Limited (1979), Shed Seven (1999) and The Saturdays (2013).**

7. T. Rex (1976), Bamboo (1998) and Booty Luv (2006).

8. **Dire Straits (1983), Deacon Blue (1991) and Chaka Demus & Pliers featuring Jack Radics & Taxi Gang (1993).**

9. Van McCoy (1975), Hi Tension (1978) and Jay-Z featuring Mary J. Blige (1997).

10. **Los del Rio (1996), Los del Mar (1996) and Los del Chipmunks (1996).**

NOW

THAT'S WHAT I CALL

The Same Name

Ten questions on different songs that share the same title – and they all appeared on numbered volumes of NOW. Can you name the songs that provided hits for both acts?

1. A 1986 number 9 for Simple Minds and a 2003 number 3 for t.A.T.u.

2. **A 1985 number 8 for Mai Tai and a 2016 number 6 for One Direction.**

3. A 1989 number 4 for Belinda Carlisle and a 2018 number 7 for Tom Walker.

4. **A 1992 number 28 for Prince and the New Power Generation, and a 1995 number 4 for East 17.**

5. A 1998 number 10 for Chumbawamba and a 2014 number 7 for 5 Seconds of Summer.

6. **A 2000 number 1 for Gabrielle and a 2018 number 3 for Jonas Blue featuring Jack & Jack.**

7. A 2001 number 6 for Kate Winslet and a 2010 number 12 for Jason Derulo.

8. **A 2005 number 7 for Hilary Duff and a 2015 number 12 for the Vamps.**

9. A 2005 number 12 for The Magic Numbers and a 2015 number 11 for Little Mix.

10. **A 2009 number 4 for The Prodigy and a 2015 number 13 for Disclosure featuring Sam Smith.**

(Brackets)

Ten number 1 singles where part of the song title is in brackets. Can you identify the artist and the hit from the bracketed section only?

1. '... (But I Won't Do That)', number 1 for seven weeks in 1993.

2. **'... (My Lovely)', number 1 for four weeks in 1969.**

3. '... (If This Ain't Love)', number 1 for one week in 2000.

4. **'... (Lowry's Song)', number 1 for three weeks in 1978.**

5. '... (The Right Stuff)', number 1 for three weeks in 1989.

6. **'... (100%)', number 1 for two weeks in 2013.**

7. '... (P.S. I Love You)', number 1 for one week in 1998.

DID YOU KNOW?
In 2002, Icelandic band Sigur Rós released an album
simply called '( )'. All eight songs on the album were
untitled, while the accompanying booklet contained blank
pages so the listener could write their own interpretation of
the lyrics.

8. **'(Just Like) ...', number 1 for one week in 1980.**

9. '... (But My Love)', number 1 for three weeks in
    1975.

10. **'... (Exordium and Terminus)', number 1 for three
    weeks in 1969.**

NOW

THAT'S WHO I CALL...

Volume 2

You've been to their concerts, you bought their T-shirt and maybe you even screamed their name. Though probably not their real one. Who was born ...

1. Adam Wiles in Dumfries, Scotland, in 1984? Eight singles from his third album made the Top 10, breaking the record of seven on Michael Jackson's *Thriller*.

2. **Anna Mae Bullock in Nutbush, Tennessee, in 1939? Her autobiography was made into a film in 1993 and a West End musical in 2018.**

3. Orville Burrell in Kingston, Jamaica, in 1968? This former United States marine took his stage name from a character in a cartoon series.

4. **Patrick Okogwu in Plumstead, London, in 1988? In 2017, he launched his own What We Wear fashion label.**

5. Marvin Lee Aday in Dallas, Texas, in 1947? His debut album has spent more than ten years in the Top 100 of the album chart.

6. **Max Elliott in Lewisham, London, in 1961? He had his biggest hit in 1988 with a cover of a Cat Stevens song.**

7. Peter Hernandez in Honolulu, Hawaii, in 1985? At the age of six he appeared in the Nicolas Cage comedy *Honeymoon in Vegas* as Little Elvis.

8. **Alecia Moore in Doylestown, Pennsylvania, in 1979? She had her first number 1 in 2001 alongside Christina Aguilera, Lil' Kim and Mya.**

9. Cornell Haynes Jr. in Austin, Texas, in 1974? His Top 40 hits include collaborations with Janet Jackson and James Morrison.

10. **Charlotte Aitchison in Cambridge, England, in 1992? She had her first hit when she collaborated with a Swedish duo.**

DID YOU KNOW?
Between July and October 2016, Bryan Adams made chart history when '(Everything I Do) I Do It For You' spent sixteen consecutive weeks at number 1. During that time his follow-up single 'Can't Stop This Thing We Started' entered the chart at number 25, peaked at number 12 and dropped out of the Top 40 completely.

NOW

THAT'S WHAT I CALL

History

You may know your music and you may know your history, but how well do you know your music history? What artist and single were number 1 on these historic dates?

1. 30 August 1963, the day Philips launched the cassette tape? Born William Ashton in Lancashire, this singer and his group spent three weeks at number 1 with this second Top 40 hit, written by Lennon and McCartney.

2. **30 September 1967, the day BBC Radio 1 launched? Born Arnold Dorsey in Madras, India, this singer's second number 1 spent five weeks at the top. In 2012, he represented the UK at the Eurovision Song Contest.**

3. 1 July 1979, the day Sony launched the Walkman cassette player? This was the only number 1 and only Top 40 single for this London synthesiser band, whose frontman had a solo number 1 later the same year.

4. **1 October 1982, the day Sony launched the first compact-disc player? This British reggae band**

spent three weeks at number 1 with a single based on a song by Mighty Diamonds. It reached number 10 in the US.

5. 28 November 1983, the day the first volume of *Music* was released? A sixth Top 40 hit for this New York singer, the video starred supermodel Chrissie Brinkley, whom he married two years later.

6. **13 July 1985, the day Live Aid was staged at Wembley Stadium? Bernard Edwards and Nile Rodgers of Chic wrote five of these siblings' previous Top 40 hits. Their only number 1 stayed at the top for four weeks.**

7. 23 October 2001, the day Apple launched the first iPod? One of two Top 40 hits for the American rapper born Joseph Foreman, the song's success was helped when it featured in the film *Jay and Silent Bob Strike Back*.

8. **30 July 2006, the day the last weekly episode of *Top of the Pops* was broadcast? The fifth Top 40 hit for this Colombian singer featured a Haitian rapper and spent five weeks at the top of the chart.**

9. 21 June 2007, the day Apple launched the iPhone? The first of many number 1s for this singer, actress, businesswoman and diplomat, whose singles have spent a total of more than thirteen years in the Top 40.

10. **6 July 2014, the day music streaming first counted in the official singles chart? The first Top 40 single and a first number 1 for the girl from Boca Raton, Florida, made with a little help from an Australian jewel.**

NOW
THAT'S WHAT I CALL

A TV Theme

Here are ten songs that went on to become Top 40 hits after they were used as the theme music for TV shows. Can you name the shows?

1. 'California' by Phantom Planet, number 9 in 2002.

2. **'Falling' by Julee Cruise, number 7 in 1990.**

3. 'Galloping Home' by the London String Chorale, number 31 in 1973.

4. **'Midnight City' by M83, number 34 in 2012.**

5. 'On the Inside' by Lynne Hamilton, number 3 in 1989.

6. **'Searchin' My Soul' by Vonda Shepard, number 10 in 1998.**

7. 'Wish I' by Jem, number 24 in 2005.

8. **'Always There' by Marti Webb and the Simon May Orchestra, number 13 in 1986.**

9. 'Three Stars Will Shine Tonight' by Richard Chamberlain, number 12 in 1962.

10. **'The Wizard' by Paul Hardcastle, number 15 in 1986.**

NOW

THAT'S WHAT I CALL

Sing

Everyone step up to the microphone and sing along … if you know the words. Can you identify the ten party anthems these lyrics are taken from?

1. 'Everybody's got a bomb, we could all die any day, oh, but before I let that happen, I'll dance my life away.'

2. **'Be there 2 o'clock by the fountain down the road, I never knew that you'd get married.'**

3. 'My friends are all so cynical, refuse to keep the faith, we all enjoy the madness 'cause we know we're gonna fade away.'

4. **'He gives her a cuddle, glowing in a huddle, good night TV, you're all made up, and you're looking like me.'**

5. 'This song had gone multi-platinum, everybody bought our seventh album, it had outsold Michael Jackson.'

6. 'And so we're told this is the golden age, and gold is the reason for the wars we wage, though I want to be with you.'

7. 'Sleep in peace when day is done, that's what I mean, and this old world is a new world, and a bold world, for me.'

8. 'You're a teaser, you turn 'em on, leave 'em burning and then you're gone, looking out for another, anyone will do.'

9. 'You just gotta ignite the light, and let it shine, just own the night, like the Fourth of July.'

10. 'Some will win, some will lose, some were born to sing the blues, oh, the movie never ends, it goes on and on, and on, and on.'

DID YOU KNOW?
Blur's 1997 hit 'Song 2' was the second track on their album *Blur* and the second song from it released as a single. It is two minutes and two seconds long and peaked at number 2 in the chart.

NOW

Rock 'n' Roll

Pull on your 'Blue Suede Shoes' and join us for a trip back to the fifties, with ten questions inspired by the 2018 NOW compilation.

1. Name the American singer who had the first of sixteen Top 40 hits in 1959, and who co-wrote the English lyrics for ABBA's 1973 single 'Ring Ring'.

2. **On 3 February 1959, which other rock 'n' roll singer died in the plane crash that killed Buddy Holly and J.P. 'The Big Bopper' Richardson?**

3. Which British rock 'n' roll artist, with twenty-six Top 40 hits between 1959 and 1966, was born Ronald Wycherley?

4. **What shared three-word song title provided different Top 40 debuts for Little Richard in 1956 and Orange Juice in 1983?**

5. Whose stellar backing band featured Danny Cedrone on guitar, Billy Williamson on steel guitar, Johnny Grande on piano, Marshall Lytle on bass, Billy Gussak on drums and Joey D'Ambrosio on saxophone?

6. **In 1959, guitarist Duane Eddy had his third Top 40 hit when he reached number 6 with 'Peter Gunn'. Which British group accompanied him when he rerecorded it in 1986 for his twentieth Top 40 hit?**

7. Which 1958 song by Chuck Berry was included alongside music by Bach, Beethoven and Mozart on the Golden Record that was launched into space aboard the *Voyager 1* spacecraft in 1977?

8. **Who went one better than Bruce Channel when his version of the 1962 number 2 'Hey! Baby' topped the chart in 2001?**

9. Who had a run of twenty-two consecutive Top 40 hits, beginning with 'What Do You Want?' in 1959 and ending with 'Someone's Taken Maria Away' in 1965?

10. **Who became the first British male singer to have two Top 10 hits in the US when 'Does Your Chewing Gum Lose Its Flavour (On the Bedpost Overnight?)' peaked at number 5 in 1959?**

DID YOU KNOW?
Three of the original hits on *NOW… Rock 'n' Roll* later became chart-topping cover versions. Richie Valens' version of 'La Bamba' failed to chart in 1958 but made number 1 for Los Lobos in 1987. Brian Hyland's 'Sealed With A Kiss' reached number 3 in 1962 but number 1 for Jason Donovan in 1989, and Bruce Channel's 'Hey Baby' stalled at number 2 in 1962 but made number 1 for DJ Otzi in 2001.

NOW

THAT'S WHAT I CALL

A GENRE

Answers from page 264

Classic Rock

BIGGER! FASTER! LOUDER! LONGER!
Ten questions inspired by the 2015 NOW!
collection.

1. Name the rock royalty who started life as Smile.

2. **In 1978, who replaced Ronnie James Dio with Graham Bonnet and landed three Top 10 hits in the next three years?**

3. Who reached number 4 in 1992 with a cover of Argent's 1973 hit 'God Gave Rock and Roll to You'?

4. **Which 'space cowboy' reached number 1 in 1990 with a song that failed to chart when it was first released seventeen years earlier, despite being a US number 1 in early 1974?**

5. Who lent his distinctive voice to one-hit wonder Python Lee Jackson's 1972 number 3 'In a Broken Dream'?

6. **Who were the Canadian rock outfit originally named after brothers Randy, Robbie and Tim, and their friend Fred, who had a number 2 hit in 1974?**

7. Which rocker scored his only number 1 single when he rerecorded a thirty-year-old song with his daughter?

8. **In 2001, which American rock band got to number 2 and had 'two tickets to Iron Maiden, baby'?**

9. Thin Lizzy's biggest hit was their 1973 number 6 'Whiskey in the Jar'. Which two band members went one better with their 1985 number 5 duet 'Out in the Fields'?

10. **Which American rock group scored eighteen Top 10 singles between 1986 and 2006 but have yet to have a number 1 single?**

DID YOU KNOW?
Between 1968 and 2005, rock group Status Quo appeared on *Top of the Pops* more than any other band, notching up 106 performances. They were invited to play the 25th anniversary episode in December 1988 and the 2000th episode in September 2002.

NOW

THAT'S WHAT I CALL

Reggae

Ten questions on the theme of Jamaica's greatest export, inspired by the 2012 NOW compilation.

1. Whose 1978 number 1 single includes the line 'I don't like reggae, oh no, I love it'?

2. **Which chart-topping reggae duo's real names are John Taylor and Everton Bonner?**

3. Which hip-hop artist had his biggest hit with a cover of Bob Marley and the Wailers' song 'I Shot the Sheriff'?

4. **Which chart-topping reggae artist's Top 40 hits have featured guest vocalists including Grand Puba, Marsha and Rikrok?**

5. Who had his first Top 40 hit with 'Elizabethan Reggae' in 1970 but had to wait sixteen years for his second, 'I Want to Wake Up With You'?

6. **In 1983, Paul Young made number 2 with his version of 'Love of the Common People'.**

Which reggae singer first had a hit with this song in 1970?

7.   All three of UB40's number 1 singles have been cover versions. Who was the guest vocalist on the second of them in 1985?

8.   **Millie's 1964 number 2 single 'My Boy Lollipop' is one of the earliest reggae or ska hits, but who had a gender-changing Top 10 hit with 'My Girl Lollipop' in 1982?**

9.   The cast of the seventies' children's TV series *Here Come the Double Deckers* included Brinsley Forde as Spring. Which chart-topping reggae act did he later become singer for?

10. **Originally written by David Gates for the American rock band Bread, 'Everything I Own' was a number 1 hit for reggae legend Ken Boothe in 1974 and for which other solo artist in 1987?**

DID YOU KNOW?
Both ska legend Prince Buster, who had his biggest hit with the 1967 number 18 'Al Capone', and reggae singer Ini Kamoze, who reached number 4 in 1995 with 'Here Comes The Hotstepper', were born with the name Cecil Campbell.

NOW

THAT'S WHAT I CALL

Rhythm and Blues

It's one, maybe two or possibly even three of our favourite types of music. Here are ten questions on the theme of both 'Rhythm' and 'Blues'.

1. Whose 1989 album contained seven Top 40 singles, including 'Escapade', 'Black Cat' and 'Alright', along with the title track?

2. **In 1983, which British band added the number 9 hit 'Ol' Rag Blues' and the number 15 hit 'A Mess of Blues' to their total of fifty-seven Top 40 singles?**

3. Which Jamaican musician featured on Katy Perry's 2017 number 5 'Chained to the Rhythm'?

4. **Who was 'The Queen of the Blues' according to the subtitle of Ray Stevens's 1971 number 2 single?**

5. Which 1985 number 12 single begins with *Lovejoy, Deadwood* and *American Gods* actor Ian McShane saying, 'Ladies and gentlemen: Miss Grace Jones'?

6. **Which 'Blues' song by Elton John features Stevie Wonder on harmonica, and was the Top 40 follow-up to his 1982 number 8 'Blue Eyes'?**

7. What 1990 number 9 single for Jason Donovan was originally a 1963 number 5 hit for The Cascades?

8. **Who had his thirteenth Top 40 single with the 2000 number 11 'Natural Blues'?**

9. Which Italian dance group had the first of five Top 40 hits with the 1994 number 2 'The Rhythm of the Night'?

10. **In January 1956, American singer Guy Mitchell had a number 1 hit with 'Singing the Blues', which was knocked off the top spot by another version of the same song by which British singer and actor?**

NOW
THAT'S WHAT I CALL

Classic Soul

Ten questions about the Golden Age of American R&B, when the Motown, Stax and Philadelphia International labels ruled the charts and the dancefloors.

1. Which American vocal group had Top 20 hits in the sixties with 'Ain't Too Proud to Beg', 'Cloud Nine' and 'Get Ready'?

2. **Which US state was home to The Jacksons and gave Motown artist R. Dean Taylor his biggest hit in 1971?**

3. Who had five Top 10 hits between 1970 and 1972 with a line-up of Birdsong, Terrell and Wilson?

4. **Who recorded hit duets with Diana Ross, Tammi Terrell and Kim Weston?**

5. Which soul star co-wrote the 1975 number 12 'Your Kiss Is Sweet', the Top 40 debut for his ex-wife Syreeta?

6. **Who had his only Top 40 hit in 1969 with a song that paid tribute to Lou Rawls, Sam and Dave, Wilson Pickett, Otis Redding and James Brown?**

7. Which soul legend helped Annie Lennox get her first solo Top 40 hit when they duetted on a 1988 number 28 single?

8. **In 1961 the Marvelettes' 'Please Mr. Postman' was Motown Records first US number 1, but which duo had a UK number 2 hit with the same song in 1975?**

9. In 1987 which unlikely American singer reached number 30 when he duetted with Sam Moore on a new version of Sam and Dave's 1967 hit 'Soul Man'?

10. **Who left The Drifters in 1960, shortly before they had a number 2 hit with 'Save the Last Dance for Me', and had to wait twenty-seven years for his only solo number 1?**

DID YOU KNOW?
The first UK hit for Motown Records was Mary Wells' 1964 number 5, 'My Guy'. The song was written by Smokey Robinson, who had to wait until 1966 for his own Top 40 hit, when he and his group The Miracles reached number 37 with '(Come Round Here) I'm The One You Need'.

NOW

Remix

Ten questions celebrating songs in altered states, inspired by the 2018 NOW compilation.

1. Whose homage to Bollywood star Asha Bhosle reached number 1 in 1998 after Norman Cook remixed it?

2. **Which British band had their first Top 40 hit in 1990 when DJ Andrew Weatherall remixed their song originally titled 'I Am Losing More Than I'll Ever Have?'.**

3. In 1999, who had his biggest singles chart hit after a remix by Danish producer Funkstar De Luxe took 'Sun Is Shining' to number 3?

4. **'Despacito (Remix)' became Justin Bieber's sixth number 1 single in 2017, when he appeared alongside singer Luis Fonsi and rapper Daddy Yankee. What nationality are Luis and Daddy?**

5. What 1968 recording by Elvis Presley became his eighteenth number 1 single in 2002 when it was remixed by Dutch producer Junkie XL?

6. **Name the British husband-and-wife duo who had their biggest hit in November 1995 after American DJ Todd Terry remixed a single that had peaked at number 69 the previous year.**

7. In 1988, Israeli singer Ofra Haza had a number 15 hit with 'Im Nin Alu' after it was sampled for another number 15 hit, 'Paid in Full' by which American hip-hop duo?

8. **Which song gave Jamaican reggae singer Omi his chart debut and a number 1 hit in 2015 after German DJ Felix Jaehn remixed it?**

9. In 1989, Ben Liebrand's remix of the 'Eve of the War' reached number 3. Originally a 1978 number 36, the song is taken from one of the biggest-selling albums of all time. Name the album.

10. **In 1992, after an eight-year gap, Heaven 17 had their sixth Top 40 hit when Brothers in Rhythm remixed which 1982 hit single?**

NOW

THAT'S WHAT I CALL

Disco

The first disco hits appeared in the charts in 1975. Now, more than forty years later, here are ten questions to test your knowledge of this enduring dancefloor fashion.

1. Which chart-topping family outfit consisted of sisters Debbie, Joni, Kathy and Kim?

2. **In 1996 and 1997, two different number 1 hits sampled Patrice Rushen's biggest hit, the 1982 number 8 'Forget Me Nots'. George Michael's 'Fastlove' was one, what was the other?**

3. In 1997 who had the third of their seven number 1 singles with 'Discotheque'?

4. **One-hit wonders Lipps Inc. reached number 2 in 1980 with 'Funkytown'. Who covered it and also had their only chart hit in 1987?**

5. In 1977 The Trammps had their fifth Top 40 hit with 'Disco Inferno'. Who reached number 12 – and had her twenty-fourth Top 40 hit – with a 1993 cover version?

6. **Name the French disco act who collaborated with Chic for the 1979 number 18 'Spacer'.**

7. Dead or Alive had their first Top 40 hit with a cover of 'That's the Way (I Like It)', but who originally reached number 4 with this song in 1975?

8. **Which trio collaborated with Kool & the Gang on a remake of their 1979 single 'Ladies' Night'?**

9. Which family vocal group – who featured on the *Saturday Night Fever* soundtrack – began life as Chubby and the Turnpikes?

10. **In 1979 which Jackson followed up 'Blame It on the Boogie' with 'Weekend'?**

Power Ballads

Ten questions inspired by the anthemic, the epic, the heroic and the monumental songs that featured on the 2015 and 2019 NOW compilations.

1. Name the American Rock band who made their chart debut and had their biggest hit in 1993 with 'Runaway Train'.

2. **Which 1983 number 3 power ballad includes the lyrics 'As sure as Kilimanjaro rises like Olympus above the Serengeti'?**

3. Which American rock band's total of six Top 40 hits between 1970 and 1985 includes the power ballads 'Hard To Say I'm Sorry' and 'Hard Habit To Break'?

4. **In 1994, who reached number 5 with a dance version of Bonnie Tyler's chart-topping power ballad 'Total Eclipse of the Heart'?**

5. What optimistic power ballad gave an American band their only Top 40 hit, having first entered the chart at number 72 in 1982, and lived up to its title

when it finally reached number 6 twenty-eight years later?

6. **Cutting Crew had two Top 40 hits, both in 1986. One was the number 24 'I've Been in Love Before'. Can you name the other, which reached number 4 in September that year?**

7. Who gave up life as Beth Brennan to make her chart debut with the power ballad 'Torn'?

8. **Phil Collins had a 1984 number 2 hit with 'Against All Odds (Take a Look at Me Now)', but two other versions have topped the chart. Mariah Carey featuring Westlife in 2000 was one. Who had the other one?**

9. What power ballad was a Top 20 hit for John Waite in 1984 and Tina Turner in 1996?

10. **In 2013, Pink had a number 2 hit with 'Just Give Me a Reason', featuring Nate Ruess. With which chart-topping American indie band was Nate previously singer?**

DID YOU KNOW?
In 2004, when The Killers first released 'Mr. Brightside' it entered the chart at number 10 but dropped out of the Top 100 after just four weeks. Since then it has returned to the lower reaches of the chart on more than forty occasions, and spent a combined total of more than four years in the Top 100.

NOW

Rock

'Rock-a-billy', 'Rockabye', 'Rock Your Body', Rock DJ' … it's the solid foundation for the biggest hits. Here are ten questions on the theme of 'Rock', inspired by the 2014 NOW compilation.

1. Scottish pop/folk singer Sandi Thom had her only number 1 with a song stating that she wanted to be what other type of musician?

2. **Who had their only Top 20 hit in 1985 with 'Body Rock', the theme to a 1985 breakdancing film of the same name?**

3. Nine years after they released their debut single 'All Fall Down', which British band had their first Top 10 hit with the 1994 number 7 'Rocks'?

4. **What three-word title provided different Top 40 hits for Hues Corporation in 1974 and Aaliyah in 2002?**

5. Britney Spears had her thirteenth Top 40 hit in 2002 with 'I Love Rock 'n' Roll', but who had their only Top 40 entry in 1982 with the same song?

6. **After a five-year absence from the chart, which quartet scored their ninth consecutive Top 10 hit with 'Rock Steady' in 2006?**

7. In 2007, 'Party Rock Anthem' by LMFAO featuring Lauren Bennett and GoonRock spent four weeks at number 1. Which famous American musical dynasty do LMFAO members Redfoo and SkyBlu belong to?

8. **Kid Rock's only number 1 to date is the 2008 hit 'All Summer Long'. It samples and namechecks a 1976 Top 40 single by which other American rock band?**

9. Who did Amy Macdonald take to number 12 in 2007 for her first and biggest hit so far?

10. **Name the American rapper who featured on 'Rockstar', a 2017 number 1 for Post Malone.**

DID YOU KNOW?
The artist with the most Top 40 'rock' hits is Bill Haley and His Comets, who followed up his 1955 number 1, 'Rock Around The Clock', with 'Mambo Rock', 'Rock-A-Beatin' Boogie', 'The Saints Rock 'n' Roll', 'Rockin' Through The Rye', 'Rudy's Rock', 'Rock The Joint', and 'Don't Knock The Rock'.

Punk and New Wave

Punk and new-wave bands lit up the charts at the end of the seventies with attitude, energy and melody in equal measure. Here are ten questions inspired by one of pop's most exciting moments.

1. Which nine-year-old single gave The Clash their only number 1 after it was used in a 1991 TV commercial for Levi's jeans?

2. **Which British punk band had nine Top 40 hits, the biggest of which was a 1986 number 3 cover of a song that originally made number 2 for Barry Ryan in 1968?**

3. In 1977, Bob Marley and the Wailers reached number 9 with their fourth Top 40 hit, a double A-side release that featured 'Punky Reggae Party' and which other song?

4. **In August 1978, who made their *Top of the Pops* debut with 'Top of the Pops'?**

5. Who did Sex Pistols' singer John Lydon collaborate with for his only 'solo' Top 40 hit, 'Open Up', in 1993?

6. **Which Northern Irish punk band, with three Top 40 singles, were named after a song by an English punk band, who had just the one?**

7. What nationality was Plastic Bertrand, who made his chart debut when '*Ça Plane pour Moi*' reached number 8 in June 1978?

8. **In 1987, who followed up their Top 10 cover version of an Elvis Presley hit with another Top 10 cover, this time with a song that had originally been a hit for Buzzcocks in 1978?**

9. Which English sixties' band originally recorded the songs that provided Top 40 cover versions for The Fall, The Jam, The Pretenders and The Stranglers?

10. **Which punk singer's real identity is Marianne Elliott-Said?**

DID YOU KNOW?
The Ramones made their chart debut with the 1977 number 22 'Sheena Is a Punk Rocker'. The "Sheena" referred to in the title is the comic book character Sheena, Queen of the Jungle, first published in 1937.

NOW

THAT'S WHAT I CALL

Classical

Ten questions that explore and celebrate the links between big pop hits and celebrate the orchestral and operatic favourites of years gone by.

1. Which fellow Austrian took Mozart to number 1 in 1986 with 'Rock Me Amadeus'?

2. **Name the instrumental group who had a number 1 hit in 1962 with 'Nutrocker', a rock 'n' roll version of the march from Tchaikovsky's ballet, *The Nutcracker*?**

3. Most of Sarah Brightman's hits have been classical pieces or show tunes, but she had her first Top 10 single in 1978 with dance troupe Hot Gossip. What was it called?

4. **Name the English record producer who has worked with Madonna, Blur and All Saints, and had a number 4 hit in 1999 with his version of Barber's *Adagio for Strings*.**

DID YOU KNOW?
S Club 7's 2000 number 3 hit 'Natural' and Little Mix's 2013 number 14 hit 'Little Me' both sample 'Pavane In F Sharp Minor', composed by Frenchman Gabriel Faure in 1887.

5. In 1989 a figure usually associated with punk rock adapted Delibes's 'Flower Duet', from the 1883 opera *Lakmé*, as 'Aria' for use in a British Airways advert. Who was he?

6. **Liverpool band The Farm reached number 4 in 1990, and then number 5 in 2004, with their biggest hit, based on Johann Pachelbel's Canon in D Major. What was the song?**

7. Which German composer has featured in the title of Top 40 songs by Electric Light Orchestra in 1973, Walter Murphy in 1976 and Eurythmics in 1987?

8. **The bestselling single of 2008 shares its name with a chorus from Handel's 1741 oratorio *Messiah*. What is it called?**

9. 'You'll Never Walk Alone' has been a Top 40 hit on three occasions – originally for Gerry and the Pacemakers in 1963, and for The Three Tenors in 1998. But which act had a number 1 single with the song in 1985?

10. **Name the New Zealand-born soprano who had a number 5 hit with 'World in Union' in 1991.**

NOW

THAT'S WHAT I CALL

Pop

This abbreviation of 'popular' has 'popped' up lots of times since the first singles chart in 1952. Here are ten questions on bands and songs that mention our favourite subject.

1. In 2001, which American boy band had their ninth Top 40 hit with 'Pop'?

2. **According to The Divine Comedy's 1999 number 17 hit, what did 'The Pop Singer' fear?**

3. Which song gave the band M their biggest hit when it reached number 2 in 1979, and number 15 in 1989?

4. **Which chart-topping artist co-wrote Iggy Pop's 1996 number 26 hit 'Lust for Life'?**

5. Name the English pianist whose eighteen Top 40 hits between 1957 and 1962 included 'Party Pops', 'More Party Pops', 'More and More Party Pops' and 'Even More Party Pops'.

6. **Which Swedish band spent three weeks at number 1 with their 1994 debut single, then followed it up with the number 12 hit 'Old Pop in an Oak'?**

7. Which English indie band, with eleven Top 40 hits in the late eighties and early nineties, had their biggest hit with the 1993 number 9, 'Get the Girl! Kill the Baddies!'?

8. **Whose run of seven Top 40 hits began when they 'presented' Coati Mundi on the number 32 single 'Me No Pop I'?**

9. Charli XCX made her chart debut when she was a featured artist on the 2013 number 1 'I Love It'. Which Swedish duo partnered with Charli on the record?

10. **In 2005, the Crazy Frog had a second Top 40 hit with a cover of the instrumental 'Popcorn'. Who originally had a number 5 hit with the tune in 1972?**

NOW

THAT'S WHAT I CALL

Club Hits

A word of warning: your knowledge of dance anthems and floor fillers might not help you with these ten club-themed conundrums.

1. In 1983, Wham! had four Top 40 hits with 'Wham Rap', 'Bad Boys', 'Club Fantastic Megamix' and what other single, which reached number 4?

2. **After all eleven of their singles became Top 10 hits, including four number 1s, who decided to 'Say Goodbye' in 2003?**

3. Which 2003 number 3 single gave American rapper 50 Cent his chart debut?

4. **In 2010, who had the third of their five number 1 hits with 'The Club Is Alive'?**

5. Under what name did Scottish duo Billy Mackenzie and Alan Rankine have three Top 40 hits in 1982, including the number 13 single 'Club Country'?

6. **Which band had ten Top 40 hits in the eighties then returned to the charts in 1998 after a twelve-**

year absence with the number 4 hit 'I Wanna Be Loved'?

7. According to the subtitle of his 1982 number 12, what did David Essex say 'Me and My Girl' were up to?

8. **Who was the featured artist on Flo Rida's 2010 number 1 'Club Can't Handle Me'?**

9. Harry Wayne Casey and his band had the first of their ten Top 40 hits in 1974 with the number 7 'Queen of Clubs'. By what name are they better known?

10. **In 1981, 'Wordy Rappinghood' was a number 7 single for Chris Frantz and Tina Weymouth under the name Tom Tom Club. Which other Top 40 band did the pair play drums and bass for?**

DID YOU KNOW?
When South Korean singer Psy was promoting his 2013 number 10 hit 'Gentleman', the follow-up to 'Gangnam Style', he made an appearance on the final of *Britain's Got Talent*, and at the Stadio Olimpico in Rome, where football teams Roma and Lazio were contesting the Coppa Italia Final. Lazio won 1-0.

NOW

THAT'S WHAT I CALL

Country

Time for all you cowboys and cowgirls to get off your horse, take off your ten-gallon hat and hunker down for ten questions about good old country music.

1. Which country music star has never had a number 1 single in the UK but wrote 'I Will Always Love You', which spent ten weeks at number 1 in 1992 for Whitney Houston?

2. **In 1975, which Scottish comedian had a number 1 single with a parody of the Tammy Wynette single 'D.I.V.O.R.C.E.'?**

3. Which former professional footballer partnered with country singer Willie Nelson on the 1984 number 17 'To All the Girls I've Loved Before'?

4. **Which Scottish group had their third Top 40 hit in 1990, when their cover of Roger Miller's 1965 number 1 'King of the Road' reached number 9?**

5. By what name did brothers David and Howard have a number 3 hit in 1979 with 'If I Said You Had a Beautiful Body Would You Hold It Against Me'?

6. **Which chart-topping country artist has recorded Top 10 duets with Elton John and with Ronan Keating?**

7. What 1992 number 3 single by Miley Cyrus's father helped spark a craze for line dancing?

8. **Which country-music star had a number 1 single in 2005, when he partnered with rapper Nelly on 'Over and Over'?**

9. Who was born Henry John Deutschendorf Jr., had a number 1 single in 1974 and wrote Top 20 hits for Olivia Newton-John and for James Galway?

10. **Who was the featured artist on a rerecording of his own 1975 number 4 single, when it made number 12 for Rikki and Daz in 2002?**

DID YOU KNOW?
In 1979, band The Charlie Daniels reached number 14 with their only Top 40 hit, 'The Devil Went Down to Georgia'. Ten years prior to this success, Charlie was a session musician, playing on Leonard Cohen's single, 'Bird On A Wire', and Bob Dylan's single, 'Lay Lady Lay'.

Easy

That's 'Easy' as in 'Easy Listening', by the way. But if you know your Bacharach like the back of your hand then these ten questions will be a (summer) breeze.

1. Which actress partnered with Robbie Williams on his chart-topping version of Frank and Nancy Sinatra's 1967 number 1 'Somethin' Stupid'?

2. **The Oscar-winning song 'Raindrops Keep Fallin' on My Head' was a Top 40 hit in 1970 for Sacha Distel, B. J. Thomas and for Bobbie Gentry. But which film was the song originally written for?**

3. In 1993, Frank Sinatra had his last Top 40 hit with a duet version of 'I've Got You Under My Skin', recorded with which chart-topping rock singer?

4. **Which punk band had their sixth Top 40 single with their version of Dionne Warwick's 1964 number 9 hit 'Walk On By'?**

5. What nationality was the 'Flea' that gave Herb Alpert and the Tijuana Brass a number 3 hit in 1965?

6. **After a twenty-three-year chart absence, who had his sixth Top 40 hit in 1999, when he was featured vocalist on the single 'Walk Like a Panther' by All Seeing I?**

7. Which one-word song title has provided different Top 40 hits for Nat King Cole, David Essex and Menswear?

8. **Which trio had their first number 1 in September 1965 with 'Make It Easy on Yourself'?**

9. Name the theme song from the 1968 film *The Thomas Crown Affair* that provided actor and singer Noel Harrison with his only Top 40 hit.

10. **Which British singer was credited on comedian Peter Sellers's 1960 album *Songs for Swingin' Sellers* as crooner Fred Flange?**

NOW

THAT'S WHAT I CALL

House

Ed Sheeran had a 'Lego' one, Blur had one in the 'Country' and R. Dean Taylor had a ghost in his. Time to open the doors to our ten questions on the theme of 'House'.

1. Which band, with thirty-one Top 40 singles, had their only number 1 in 1982 with a song that begins with the lyrics, 'Good morning, Miss / Can I help you, son?'

2. **What five-word song title provided different Top 10 hits for Alan Price Set in 1967, Tracie in 1983 and Jack 'n' Chill in 1987?**

3. Which composer's 'House' did Clean Bandit pay homage to on their 2013 Top 40 debut?

4. **Name the indie band that had their biggest hit in 1990 with 'Shine On' and share their name with East 17's 1992 chart debut.**

5. In 1970, American rock band Frijid Pink had a number 4 hit with which song that had been number 1 for The Animals in 1964?

6. **Which American band, with six Top 40 singles, had their biggest hit in 1997 with 'Susan's House'?**

7. Name the house music 'super group' that features DJs Axwell, Steve Angello and Sebastian Ingrosso.

8. **Seven years after he wrote Split Enz's only Top 40 hit, the 1980 number 12 'I Got You', Neil Finn returned to the charts as a singer fronting which band?**

9. Name the dance trio that collaborated with the Cookie Crew for the 1988 number 5 'Rok da House', and with Merlin for the 1989 number 8 'Who's in the House?'

10. **In 1981, Shakin' Stevens had his first number 1 with a song that had given Rosemary Clooney her first number 1 in 1954. What was that song?**

DID YOU KNOW?
In 2015, the Official Chart Company decreed that the new chart would be announced on a Friday, rather than a Sunday. The first number 1 of the new era was English DJ David Zowie with 'House Every Weekend' – an ironic title, given that his chart total contained no sales from the previous Friday or Saturday.

NOW

THAT'S WHAT I CALL

A GEOGRAPHY LESSON

Answers from page 276

NOW

THAT'S WHAT I CALL

Geography

Ten questions on the theme of 'geography'. The only chart required to find your way around these questions is the Top 40 singles chart.

1. Name the South Holland city that gave a chart-topping 'South' band their thirteenth Top 40 hit?

2. **What was the number 2 single named after an ancient Roman city, by an English quartet who share their name with a Paris Metro station?**

3. Who were the Californian band named after a European capital city who spent four weeks at number 1 in 1986 with an action-movie theme that won an Oscar for Best Original Song?

4. **Which American singer who topped the chart as part of a duo shares her surname with the largest city on the US–Canada border and had her biggest solo hit with the 1994 number 11 'I Believe'?**

5. What 1985 number 1 begins, 'Okay, talk to you, South America, Australia, France, UK, Africa'?

6. **Which town gave a Birmingham reggae band a number 4 single in 1990? Presumably this cover version was named after the town in Jamaica, not the one in southwest London...**

7. Which Alaskan band made their Top 40 debut in November 2017 with 'Feel It Still', but had to wait twenty weeks until it peaked at number 3 the following March?

8. **Who had their biggest hit in 1981 with a number 2 single named after a European capital that begins 'Walked in the cold air, freezing breath on a window pane, lying and waiting'?**

9. Which Tanzanian-born singer made the Top 10 twice when he partnered with a superb soprano in a homage to her native city?

10. **Which Georgian-born singer had a number five hit in 2005 in which she claimed to know how many bicycles were in the Chinese capital, and the size of the observable universe?**

NOW

THAT'S WHAT I CALL

Ireland

Time to test your knowledge of music from the Emerald Isle, with ten questions celebrating the rich contribution Irish musicians have made to the Top 40.

1. Which band's homage to the Big Apple and biggest hit spent two weeks at number 2 in December 1987, and has since been back in the Top 40 in fourteen separate years?

2. **Between 2000 and 2002 which singer had six consecutive Top 10 hits, beginning with 'Gotta Tell You' and ending with 'I'm Right Here'?**

3. Who had five Top 10 hits, including two number 1s, as the frontman of an Irish band in the late seventies, but peaked at number 15 with his biggest solo single, 'The Great Song of Indifference'?

4. **Which 1972 number 5 hit for Jamaican singer Johnny Nash gave Hothouse Flowers the third of their four Top 40 hits in 1990?**

5. In 2004, who featured on two Top 10 singles after her 1987 instrumental 'Boadicea' was sampled for Mario Winans's number 1 hit 'I Don't Wanna Know', as well as the number 8 'answer' song 'You Really Should Know' by The Pirates?

6. **Who did Cliff Richard help to get his biggest 'solo' hit, when they duetted on the 1989 number 20 single 'Whenever God Shines His Light'?**

7. In 1970, who became the first of seven Irish acts to win the Eurovision Song Contest, and had a number 1 single with 'All Kinds of Everything'?

8. **Who had their biggest hit in 1996 with 'To Win Just Once', written shortly before their accordion player won €1.7 million on the Irish National Lottery?**

9. Under what name did former Undertones singer Feargal Sharkey and future Erasure keyboard player Vince Clarke record the 1983 number 4 single 'Never Never'?

10. **Which chart-topping Irish artist has had eight Top 40 hits, including collaborations with Shane MacGowan and Ian Brown, plus a cover of a 1962 single by country singer Loretta Lynn?**

NOW
THAT'S WHAT I CALL

Scotland

Ten questions celebrating the contribution made to the pop charts by Caledonian composers and tartan troubadours.

1. Which Scottish band made a 'Perfect' start to their chart career when their debut single reached number 1 in May 1988?

2. **In 1969, who became the first Scottish group to have a number 1 single when they recorded a version of the Beatles song 'Ob-La-Di, Ob-La-Da'?**

3. Which chart-topping Edinburgh act began and ended their run of twelve Top 40 hits with 'Keep On Dancing' in 1971 and 'You Made Me Believe in Magic' in 1977?

4. **Name the Lennoxtown lass who made her chart debut in 1964 and added to her ten Top 10 hits with 'Boom, Bang a Bang', Bowie and Barlow?**

5. Which Top 10 single by Kilmarnock band Biffy Clyro did the 2010 *X Factor* winner Matt Cardle record under the new title 'When We Collide'?

6. **Which Lanarkshire-born singer had his first taste of chart success when Slik reached number 1 in 1976 with 'Forever and Ever'?**

7. Which two-word song title gave Glasgow-born B.A. Robertson a number 2 chart debut in 1979 and has provided different Top 3 hits for will.i.am, Cher and Jessie J with Ariana Grande and Nicki Minaj?

8. **What stage name did Edinburgh-born singer Mary Sandeman adopt for her 1981 number 1 'Japanese Boy'?**

9. Which chart-topping Glasgow-born artist had solo Top 10 hits in 1990 with covers of songs made famous by Sylvester and the Bee Gees?

10. **Emeli Sandé had a number 1 with Professor Green and 'Read All About It', and with Labrinth and 'Beneath Your Beautiful', and on each occasion she knocked which Scottish artist off the top spot?**

DID YOU KNOW?
In June 1971, Sally Carr became the first Scottish woman to have a number 1 single when her band, Middle of the Road, spent five weeks at the top with 'Chirpy Chirpy Cheep Cheep'. Kylie Minogue covered the song in 2017 for the soundtrack of the Australian film, *Swinging Safari*.

London

Ten questions on chart hits inspired by the sights and sounds of the nation's capital city.

1. Which London landmark gave The Black Eyed Peas singer Fergie her solo Top 40 debut in 2006?

2. **Name the east London quartet who named their 1993 debut album after their hometown borough, and took their own name from its postcode.**

3. In 1997, which extremely successful songwriter had the last of her eleven Top 40 hits with a cover of The Kinks' single 'Waterloo Sunset'?

4. **Name the trio who made their chart debut with 'Wasting My Young Years' in 2013, and had a number 16 hit the same year with 'Strong'.**

5. What song gave the Electric Light Orchestra their fourteenth Top 40 single when it was paired with 'Confusion' on a 1979 double A-side release?

6. Who had his biggest hit in January 1975 when 'Streets of London' spent two weeks at number 2?

7. In 1992, who had their biggest hit courtesy of London SE14 when 'The Only Living Boy in New Cross' reached number 7?

8. **Which central London location helped Morrissey land a seventh consecutive Top 20 single in 1990?**

9. Which west London district links Top 20 hits by The Fratellis in 2005, Jon Bon Jovi in 1997 and Elvis Costello and the Attractions in 1978?

10. **In July 1979, who had the second of two number 2 singles with a song that begins 'I never thought it would happen with me and a girl from Clapham'?**

USA

Inspired by the 2013 NOW collection, here are ten questions about big hits with a connection to 'the other side of the pond'.

1. Which American singer was 'French Kissin' in the USA' in 1986?

2. **Name the chart-topping British singer whose biggest solo hit begins 'There's a place where a kid without a cent, he can grow up to be president'?**

3. Which New York landmark did Jay-Z and Alicia Keys celebrate on their 2009 collaboration?

4. **Which US city provided a Top 20 hit for Elvis Presley in 1964 and ZZ Top in 1992?**

5. Which group had their only Top 40 hit with the 1971 number 3 'Horse With No Name'?

6. **Which chart-topping artist's 1989 Top 10 hit mentions US presidents Harry Truman, Richard Nixon, Dwight D. Eisenhower, John F. Kennedy and Ronald Reagan?**

DID YOU KNOW?
Artists who have appeared on NOW and share their name with an American state include country duo Florida Georgia Line, British singer Indiana, Rock group Kansas, rapper French Montana, Swedish DJ Nevada, Scottish band Texas, dance duo Utah Saints and Jazz diva Dinah Washington.

7. In 2006, which English indie quartet had their only number 1 single with 'America'?

8. **Which chart-topping singer had Top 10 'American' hits with 'Life' and 'Pie'?**

9. What 'United States' was Liam Lynch singing about in 2002?

10. **Which English rock group wanted 'kippers for breakfast' in 1979?**

Wales

In this section we celebrate Wales, a country with a passion for rugby and singing. As very few rugby songs feature on the NOW albums, here are ten questions inspired by artists from 'the land of song'.

1. Which two chart-topping Welsh solo artists got together on the 1984 number 5 'A Rockin' Good Way'?

2. **Name the singer from indie band Kosheen who partnered with DJ Fresh for the 2011 number 1 'Louder'.**

3. In 1959, who became the first Welsh artist to top the charts, and made her most recent appearance courtesy of Kanye West?

4. **Which Pontardawe-born singer had her chart-topping debut single produced by Paul McCartney, represented the UK at the Eurovision Song Contest and sang on David Bowie's 1977 number 3 'Sound and Vision'?**

5. Which science-fiction character gave Newport rock band Feeder their biggest hit in 2001?

6. **Which chart-topping Welsh singer was the subject of a 1998 number 4 single by Space with Cerys Matthews of Catatonia?**

7. Whose six Top 40 hits between 2004 and 2005 include the number 3 single 'Guns Don't Kill People, Rappers Do'?

8. **Name the one-hit wonders from the Rhondda Valley who reached number 14 in 1977 with 'They Shoot Horses, Don't They?'**

9. Who was the Llandaff-born vocalist who featured on the 2003 number 3 'The Opera Song (Brave New World)' by Jurgen Vries before she had her own number 2 hit with 'Crazy Chick' in 2005?

10. **Which group gave Jamaican singer Shabba Ranks his first Top 20 hit when he featured on their 1991 cover version of The Beatles' 'She's a Woman'?**

(Which) Country

Over the years, the NOW albums have featured artists from Argentina to Zambia*, and many countries in between, but can you identify the country that each of these artists has in common?

1. Iggy Azalea, Gabriella Cilmi, Madison Avenue and Sia.

2. **The Weeknd, Avril Lavigne, Carly Rae Jepsen and Appleton.**

3. Aqua, Alphabeat, MØ and Whigfield.

4. **Sash!, Scooter, Cascada and Crazy Frog.**

5. The Script, Kodaline, Hozier and Damien Rice.

6. **Darius, The Shamen, KT Tunstall and Hue and Cry.**

7. Neneh Cherry, Zara Larsson, Robyn and Eric Prydz.

8. **Nicki Minaj, Billy Ocean, Haddaway and the Mad Stuntman.**

9. Feeder, Lisa Scott-Lee, Marina and the Diamonds, and The Automatic.

10. **2 Unlimited, Technotronic, Lasgo and Gotye.**

*Chris de Burgh (first appearance: NOW Christmas, 1985) was born in Venada Tuerto, Argentina, while Rozalla (first appearance: NOW Dance '91) was born in Ndola, Zambia

NOW

THAT'S WHAT I CALL

A THEME

Answers from page 282

NOW

THAT'S WHAT I CALL

A Drink

Quench your thirst for pop knowledge with these ten refreshingly tricky 'drink'-themed questions.

1. Which chart-topping act's run of twenty-nine Top 40 hits began with the 1970 number 6 'Love Is Life' and ended with the 1998 number 18 'It Started with a Kiss'?

2. **What did Kelis claim 'brings all the boys to the yard' in 2004?**

3. Name the American R&B singer who had two number 2 hits in 1998, one in partnership with Monica and one featuring Mase.

4. **Which 1980 single by Rupert Holmes is subtitled '(The Piña Colada Song)'?**

5. Which British-Canadian female group have 'Black Coffee' to thank for their fifth number 1?

6. **Who had three number 1 singles in the eighties with a line-up of Jay Aston, Cheryl Baker, Bobby G and Mike Nolan?**

7. Which refreshment took Major Lazer featuring Justin Bieber and MØ to number 1 in 2016?

8. **Who had the first of thirty-one Top 40 hits when 'Orange Crush' peaked at number 28 in 1989?**

9. Which alcoholic drink provided Top 40 hits for Cypress Hill in 1998 and Terrorvision in 1999?

10. **In 1972, British quintet the New Seekers had their first number 1 with what song that began life as a TV advert for Coca-Cola?**

Fashion

Ten questions on the theme of fashion, skilfully designed to separate the trendy from the tragic, and the stylish from the stale.

1. Which British band's name translates as 'Fashion Update'?

2. **Which female-and-male duo had 'The Look' in 1989 and were 'Dressed for Success' in 1990?**

3. Which British band had a total of fifteen Top 40 hits beginning with 'Speak Like a Child' in 1983 and ending with 'Promised Land' in 1989?

4. **What one-word title provided different number 13 hits for Orbital in 1999 and Mis-Teeq in 2003?**

5. Which 1966 number 4 by a chart-topping British band includes the lyrics 'One week he's in polka-dots, the next week he's in stripes'?

6. **Name the Australian quartet who made their chart debut in 2013 with the number 1 single 'She Looks So Perfect'?**

7. In 1996, who had his fourteenth Top 40 single with 'The Only Thing That Looks Good on Me Is You'?

8. **Which 1981 number 1 hit for Kraftwerk was a double A-side single combined with 'Computer Love'?**

9. Which American trio comprised of Frank Beard, Billy Gibbons and Dusty Hill reached number 22 in 1983 with 'Sharp Dressed Man'?

10. **Six years after she had a Top 10 hit with a James Bond theme, which Scottish singer featured on Prince's 1987 number 11 hit 'U Got the Look'?**

Food

Your instructions for this next set of questions come from Mr. William Shakespeare of Stratford-upon-Avon, who once said, 'If music be the food of love, play on'.

1. Whose run of seventeen Top 40 hits began with the 1978 number 33 'You Took the Words Right Out of My Mouth' and ended with the 2006 number 6 'It's All Coming Back to Me Now'?

2. **What food did 10cc claim 'Life Is' in their 1975 number 7 hit?**

3. Who had the Christmas number 1 in 2018 with 'We Built This City… On Sausage Rolls'?

4. **After topping the charts with two different acts in 1986 and 1990, who had four Top 40 hits in the nineties as Pizzaman?**

5. Which American pop band had 'Cake by the Ocean' in 2016?

6. **Which fruit provided different number 8 hits for The Stranglers in 1977 and Presidents of the USA in 1996?**

7. Which ABBA song did Blancmange cover for the sixth of their seven Top 40 singles in 1984?

8. **In 2003, which group followed up an eponymous number 2 debut single with the number 10 hit 'Say Cheese (Smile Please)'?**

9. Name the British duo who remixed Suzanne Vega's 1987 single 'Tom's Diner' and took it to number 2 in 1990.

10. **'Everything I Own' was a number 1 hit for Ken Boothe in 1974 and for Boy George in 1987, but which American band originally recorded it and had a number 32 single in 1972?**

NOW

THAT'S WHAT I CALL

A Girl

Time to test your knowledge of what Space referred to on their 1996 hit as the 'Female of the Species', with ten questions on the theme of 'girl' artists and songs.

1. Which duo landed on TV show *The Big Breakfast* from the planet Zog and had a number 5 hit in 1994 with 'Them Girls Them Girls'?

2. **When the 2009 hit 'Untouchable' stalled at number 11, it became the only one of twenty-two Top 40 hits to peak outside of the Top 10 for which girl group?**

3. Which American vocal group had their biggest hit when 'Hey Girl Don't Bother Me' spent three weeks at number 1 in 1971?

4. **Which two-word song title links different Top 10 hits for Racey in 1979, Ultimate KAOS in 1994 and Rachel Stevens in 2004?**

5. UB40's 1989 number 6 hit 'Homely Girl' and Paul Young's 1990 number 25 single 'Oh Girl' were both cover versions of songs that were originally hits for which American soul group in the seventies?

6. **Which 'girls' had five Top 40 hits between 2002 and 2004, four of which included part of their name in the song title?**

7. In 1990, who had a second Top 20 hit when they followed up their number 1 chart debut with a version of the Avons' 1959 number 3 'Seven Little Girls Sitting in the Back Seat'?

8. **Name the British sextet who made their chart debut with a 1981 number 4 hit subtitled '(Boy Meets Girl)'.**

9. Which American singer's total of more than thirty Top 40 hits includes 'Most Girls' in 2000 and 'Stupid Girls' in 2006?

10. **Which star of the *Carry On* films had the first of four Top 40 hits with the 1957 number 2 single 'Be My Girl'?**

DID YOU KNOW?
The first volume of NOW included the 1983 number 1 'Candy Girl' by New Edition. The American quintet included Ricky Bell, Michael Bivins and Ronnie DeVoe (who, as Bell Biv DeVoe, reached number 19 in 1990 with 'Poison'), Ralph Tresvant (who reached number 18 in 1991 with 'Sensitivity') and Bobby Brown (who had fifteen Top 40 hits including 'Two Can Play That Game', number 3 in 1994.

An Animal

Presenting ten menagerie-tastic questions on the theme of animals.

1. Who mentions 'Eye of the Tiger', the title of Survivor's 1982 number 1, on her 2013 number 1 'Roar'?

2. **Who sang on the 1990 number 8 'Elephant Stone' and reached number 5 in 2000 with 'Dolphins Were Monkeys'?**

3. Which 1961 number 11 by The Tokens was covered by Tight Fit and gave them their only number 1 in March 1982?

4. **What 2014 reptilian number 1 for Oliver Heldens and Becky Hill was subtitled '(Overdrive)'?**

5. Whose run of twenty Top 40 hits between 1964 and 69 includes 'Pretty Flamingo' and 'Fox on the Run'?

6. **In 1975, which TV comedy trio had the biggest of their five Top 40 hits with 'The Funky Gibbon'?**

7. 'I'm a Believer' was a Top 40 hit for EMF featuring Reeves and Mortimer in 1995 and for Robert Wyatt in 1974, but who originally took the song to number 1 in 1967?

8. **In 1997, which chart-topping artist had his eighth Top 40 hit with a cover of Steve Miller Band's 1977 single 'Fly Like an Eagle'?**

9. Which reptile provided different Top 10 hits for Elton John in 1972 and Jimmy Nail in 1994?

10. **In 2009, who had Top 10 hits collaborating with Elton John, Emeli Sandé and Esmée Denters, and had his first number 1 with 'Oopsy Daisy'?**

NOW

THAT'S WHAT I CALL

Music

'Music' can 'soothe the savage breast' and 'gives a soul to the universe' – but here are ten questions to see if it can also make you scratch your head.

1. Who had her tenth number 1 single in 2000 thanks to 'Music'?

2. **Which four-word song title provided different Top 40 hits for Barry White in 1975 and Shannon in 1983?**

3. In 1989, which dance act featured singer Betty Boo on their number 7 single 'Hey DJ / I Can't Dance to The Music You're Playing'?

4. **In 1980, who had their fourth Top 40 hit when the theme to the film *Can't Stop the Music* reached number 11?**

5. Following a performance at the 1999 BRIT Awards, the medley 'Thank ABBA for the Music' reached number 4. It was performed by Steps, Tina Cousins, Billie Piper, Cleopatra and which Irish quartet?

6. Vanilla Ice followed his 1991 number 1 debut 'Ice Ice Baby' with a cover of which 1976 Wild Cherry song?

7. What did Blur say 'Music Is', according to their number 10 hit from 2000?

8. Name the English DJ who collaborated with Tinie Tempah and Katy B on the 2015 number 1 'Turn the Music Louder (Rumble)'?

9. In 1969, who had their eighteenth consecutive Top 40 hit with a cover of the Ronettes' 1966 single 'I Can Hear Music'?

10. Which successful American songwriting duo were responsible for Sister Sledge's three Top 40 hits 'Lost in Music', 'We Are Family' and 'He's the Greatest Dancer'?

NOW

THAT'S WHAT I CALL

Science

Ten questions on the theme of 'Science', which is either the systematic study of the structure and behaviour of the physical and natural world, or a rich source of inspiration for pop singles.

1. Which chart-topping group had their tenth consecutive Top 10 hit with the 2005 number 4 'Biology'?

2. **Which one-word title provided different Top 40 hits for Embrace in 2004 and Pixie Lott in 2010?**

3. Which duo had fifteen Top 40 hits between 1995 and 2005, including two number 1s, one of which featured Noel Gallagher on vocals?

4. **Which song by McFly shared a double A-side single with 'The Ballad of Paul K' and gave them a number 9 hit in December 2005?**

5. Which Merseyside band had the sixth of their eighteen Top 40 hits with the 1983 number 20 'Genetic Engineering'?

6. **In 2002, which chart-topping British quartet had their fifth Top 40 single with 'The Scientist'?**

7. Which Manchester group partnered with rapper MC Tunes on two Top 40 hits in 1990, including the number 18 single 'Tunes Splits the Atom'?

8. **Who had their biggest hit in 1980 with a song that includes the lyrics 'He's got a Degree in Economics, Maths, Physics and Bionics'?**

9. Name the Californian sisters who had the seventh of their eight Top 40 hits with 'Neutron Dance'.

10. **Which British band named after a 1973 science-fiction film had their biggest hit with the 1987 number 11 single 'Sonic Boom Boy'?**

NOW

THAT'S WHAT I CALL

A Boy

As Deniece Williams sang on her 1984 number 2, 'Let's Hear It for the Boy'. Presenting ten questions on the theme of 'boy' artists and songs.

1. Which two-word song title provided different Top 40 hits for Marty Wilde in 1959, Miami Sound Machine in 1986 and Skepta in 2010?

2. **The 2005 Top 10 hits 'Falling Stars (Waiting for a Star to Fall)' by Sunset Strippers and 'Star to Fall' by Cabin Crew were both dance versions of the 1988 hit 'Waiting for a Star to Fall' by which American duo?**

3. Whose total of more than thirty Top 40 solo hits includes 'Last of the Famous International Playboys', 'The Boy Racer' and 'I Just Want to See the Boy Happy'?

4. **Name the other boy band who emerged from *Popstars: The Rivals*. Deemed not good enough for One True Voice, they still managed four Top 40 hits, including a cover of Duran Duran's 1984 number 2 'Wild Boys'.**

5. Which Manchester band reached number 24 in May 1999, when they had their seventh Top 40 hit with a cover of Thin Lizzy's 1976 number 8 single 'The Boys Are Back in Town'?

6. **Who spent five weeks at number 1 with his 1991 chart debut and followed it up with his only other Top 40 hit, 'I'm a Man Not a Boy'?**

7. In 1992, which chart-topping artist had his most recent solo Top 40 hit with a number 22 cover of a ballad that had originally given Dave Berry a number 5 hit in September 1964?

8. **Name the 1988 number 13 single for Scritti Politti subtitled '(Don't Feel Sorry for Loverboy)'.**

9. Which 1968 number 5 for Andy Williams provided San Francisco trio Boys Town Gang with their only Top 40 hit in 1982?

10. **In 1962, which song taken from the film *Summer Holiday* gave Cliff Richard his sixth number 1 when it was coupled with 'The Next Time' as a double A-side release?**

News

Some people listen to music to escape the news, but occasionally two worlds collide. We present ten questions on the theme of 'news'.

1. Which song gave both Professor Green and Emeli Sandé their first number 1 in November 2011, while 'Part 3' took Emeli back into the Top 10 three months later?

2. **Which British band made their chart debut and had the first of four Top 40 hits with the 1967 number 5 'Paper Sun'?**

3. What two-word song title provided different Top 20 hits for Madonna in 1989 and Labrinth in 2012?

4. **Between 1977 and 1982, who had eighteen Top 40 singles, including four number 1s, but could only get to number 27 with their 1978 single 'News of the World'?**

5. Which British duo had the sixth of ten Top 40 hits with the 1981 number 4 'Mirror Mirror (Mon Amour)'?

6. **After four number 1 hits as a member of a boy band, who launched his solo career with the 2017 number 1 'Sign of the Times'?**

7. Which 2000 number 1 single by Destiny's Child featured a daily newspaper in its title?

8. **Which chart-topping artist's total of five Top 40 solo hits began with the 1984 number 23 'Listen to Your Father' and ended with the number 12 single 'I've Got News for You' in 1991?**

9. Name the 2007 comeback single by the Spice Girls that was subtitled '(Friendship Never Ends)'.

10. **In 1997, which chart-topping artist had a number 7 single that promised 'Both Sides of the Story'?**

NOW

THAT'S WHAT I CALL

Red

Ten questions on the theme of 'Red' – will they have you seeing red, or feeling in the pink?

1. Who started life as the Frantic Elevators, before a name change heralded thirty-two Top 40 hits, including the 1995 number 1 'Fairground'?

2. **In 1964, who had the second of five consecutive number 1 singles with 'Little Red Rooster'?**

3. Which two-word song title connects different Top 10 hits for Alvin Stardust in 1974 and Sugababes in 2006?

4. **Name the Jamaican DJ who partnered with Brian and Tony Gold for the 1994 number 2 'Compliments on Your Kiss'.**

5. Who had twenty-one Top 40 hits between 1990 and 2007 but never managed a number 1 single, although All Saints topped the charts with one of their songs in 1998?

6. **Name the German band fronted by singer Gabriele Kerner, whose only Top 40 hit spent three weeks at number 1 in 1994.**

7. What song inspired by the American comic strip *Peanuts* was a Top 10 hit for the Royal Guardsmen in 1967 and The Hotshots in 1973?

8. **Which American vocal group had their eighteenth and most recent Top 40 hit with the 1976 number 5 'You're More Than a Number in My Little Red Book'?**

9. What nationality is singer Daniel Merriweather, who had a number 5 single in 2009 with 'Red'?

10. **Which American rapper featured on Christina Aguilera's 2002 number 1 'Dirrty'?**

The Planets

As Coldplay sang on *NOW 88*, 'You're a sky full of stars, such a heavenly view'. Here are ten questions on chart hits inspired by that very same subject.

1. Which British band's long and successful chart career started with 'Earth' in 1981 and took in the 'Moon' in 1984?

2. **Which American singer made his chart debut as featured artist on 'Nothin' on You', the 2010 number 1 by B.o.B?**

3. Which planet provided different number 4 hits for Mark Wynter in 1962 and Don Pablo's Animals in 1990?

4. **What celestial journey gave Savage Garden their biggest hit in August 1998?**

5. Which Manchester indie band's Top 40 hits include 'Two Worlds Collide' and 'Saturn 5'?

6. **Which band came from Athens, Georgia, to have a hit with 'Planet Claire' in 1986?**

7. In 1991, who had the nineteenth of her twenty-six Top 40 singles with a cover of Elton John's 1972 hit 'Rocket Man'?

8. **Name the San Francisco rock band who made their chart debut in 2001 with 'Drops of Jupiter (Tell Me)'.**

9. In 2007, who saw a 'Green Light' after The Neptunes had produced her twelfth Top 40 hit?

10. **Who had their biggest hit when they rocketed to number 4 in 1998 with the theme from the film version of 'Lost in Space'?**

NOW

THAT'S WHAT I CALL

Power

The English philosopher Francis Bacon once said 'knowledge is power'. Time to put your knowledge to the test with our ten questions on the theme of 'power'.

1. What kind of 'Power' took American hip-hop duo Partners in Kryme to number 1 in July 1990?

2. **Who were the eighties' supergroup featuring singer Robert Palmer, Chic drummer Tony Thompson, and Duran Duran members John Taylor on bass and Andy Taylor on guitar?**

3. Which four-word song title saw both Jennifer Rush and Huey Lewis and the News have different Top 10 hits in 1985?

4. **Name the American sextet whose run of four Top 40 hits began in 2003 with 'Danger! High Voltage' and ended in 2004 with a cover of the Queen single 'Radio Gaga'.**

5. What 1973 number 4 single gave Cliff Richard his sixtieth Top 40 hit after it was chosen as the UK entry for that year's Eurovision Song Contest?

6. **After the Electric Light Orchestra had their first hit with the 1972 number 9 single '10538 Overture', who decided to move on to something more magical?**

7. What name did DJ/producers Mark Ronson and Diplo adopt for 'Electricity', their 2018 number 4 single with Dua Lipa?

8. **Who had three number one singles between 2001 and 2002, including a cover of a number 1 single for The Bangles and a cover of a number 1 single for Blondie?**

9. Name the 1997 single by Texas that is also the subtitle of Nelly Furtado's 2003 number 13 hit 'Powerless'.

10. **Which instrumental rock classic gave American guitarist Mason Williams a number 9 single and his only Top 40 hit in 1968?**

Radio

Ten questions designed to see if you know which 'Radio' hits were also chart hits.

1. Who has a 'Rock DJ' and 'Radio' to thank for his third and sixth number 1 singles?

2. **Which British singer came via Milan and the East End of London to have five Top 40 hits, including her 2001 number 7 cover version of the Donna Summer single 'On My Radio'?**

3. Name the song that provided both Indeep in 1983 and Seamus Haji featuring KayJay in 2007 with their only Top 40 hit.

4. **Which one-word song title has provided different Top 20 hits for Kings of Leon in 2010, Imagine Dragons in 2012 and Rita Ora in 2013?**

5. Which chart-topping male duo had fourteen Top 40 singles, including the 1995 number 15 'Our Radio Rocks'?

6. **If it weren't for her appearance on 'Let It Be', the 1987 number 1 charity single by Ferry Aid, whose Top 40 career would be limited to the 1986 number 6 'I Love My Radio'?**

7. Which Motown soul star had his eighth and most recent Top 40 hit in 1979 with 'H.A.P.P.Y. Radio'?

8. **Name the 1992 number 14 single by Shakespears Sister that was subtitled '(Turn Your Radio On)'.**

9. What nationality are rock group Rush, who had their biggest hit in 1980 with 'The Spirit of Radio'?

10. **What name did British singer Anna Kumble go by when she had the first of five Top 40 hits with 'Viva La Radio'?**

NOW

THAT'S WHAT I CALL

The Blues

According to Chelsea FC in 1972, and The Beautiful South in 1996, 'Blue Is The Colour'. Here are ten questions to test your knowledge of this popular musical hue.

1. Who can count 'Blue Moon', 'Blue River' and 'Indescribably Blue' among his 139 Top 40 hits?

2. **Who sang 'The Blues' for Deacon Blue on their 1989 number 14 single?**

3. Which member of Fugees had two of their three solo hits in 1998, including the number 6 single 'Blue Angels'?

4. **Which two-word song title provided different Top 10 hits for Don Partridge in 1968 and Elton John in 1982?**

5. Justin Hayward and John Lodge managed just one Top 40 single with the 1975 number 8 'Blue Guitar' but had nine Top 40 singles, including a 1964 number 1, as members of which British band?

6. **In 2004 which former star of the TV series *Neighbours* had their fifth Top 40 single with 'Out of the Blue'?**

7. Prior to his solo success, Eddy Grant was singer with which chart-topping band whose Top 40 hits include the 1970 number 9 'Black Skin Blue Eyed Boys'?

8. **In 1990, ten years after the film in which it featured was released, who had their only Top 40 hit with a cover of Solomon Burke's 1964 single 'Everybody Needs Somebody to Love'?**

9. Which chart-topping artist had the twelfth of his fourteen Top 40 hits in 1993 with 'Now I Know What Made Otis Blue'?

10. **Who had a number 1 single in the US in 1963 but had to wait until 1990 before it charted in the UK, when the song was used as the title track of a David Lynch film?**

DID YOU KNOW?
In 2011, actor and comedian Hugh Laurie had the UK's best-selling Blues record with his number 2 album 'Let Them Talk'. The same year, his comedy partner Stephen Fry provided vocals for the title track of Kate Bush's number 5 album, '50 Words For Snow'.

NOW
THAT'S WHAT I CALL

Royal

Ten questions on the theme of 'Royal', to test your knowledge of the noble singers and regal songs that have graced the singles chart.

1. Whose total of more than fifty Top 40 hits includes collaborations with the Miami Project and the Muppets?

2. **Which 1976 number 1 single includes the lyrics 'Where they play the right music, getting in the swing, you come to look for a king'?**

3. Which four-word song title provided different Top 40 hits for the Thompson Twins in 1985 and Jamiroquai in 1999?

4. **In December 1990, the Proclaimers had their third Top 40 single when 'King of the Road' reached number 9, but who wrote the song and originally took it to number 1 in 1965?**

5. Whose chart career got the green light when her debut single 'Royals' entered at number 1 in November 2013?

6. **Name the British artist, born Desiree Heslop, who had four Top 40 hits including the 1984 number 7 'Say I'm Your Number One'.**

7. What alias did American DJ Chris Brann and singer Gaelle Adisson adopt for their 1999 number 1 single 'King of My Castle'?

8. **Which chart-topping act had the first of their ten Top 40 hits with the 1974 number 7 'Queen of Clubs'?**

9. Which American rock group made their chart debut in 2000 with 'The Lost Art of Keeping a Secret'?

10. **What was the only hit for Gary Byrd and the GB Experience? The song reached number 6 in 1983 and was the only single ever released on Stevie Wonder's WonDirection label.**

NOW

THAT'S WHAT I CALL

School

Ten questions on the subject of school to separate the top of the class from those who must try harder.

1. Which British trio made their chart debut with the 2002 number 3 single 'That's What I Go to School For'?

2. **Released in November 1979 and featuring the children of Islington Green School, what was the last number 1 single of the 1970s?**

3. In 1995, dance group Baby D had a number 3 hit with '(Everybody's Got to Learn Sometime) I Need Your Loving', but who originally had a hit with the song in 1980?

4. **Name the 1977 Christmas number 1 that was one half of a double A-side single along with 'Girls' School'.**

5. Which 1993 single by Madonna was the theme to the baseball film *A League of Their Own*?

6. **Which 1971 song by Alice Cooper provided American pop duo Daphne and Celeste with their third Top 40 hit in September 2000?**

7. Which British band had twenty Top 40 singles, the biggest of which was the 1986 number 3 'Lessons in Love'?

8. **Which 1980 number 3 single begins 'Naughty boys in nasty schools, headmasters breaking all the rules'?**

9. Name the country-music singer from Stamford, Texas, who had her only Top 40 hit with the 1968 number 12 'Harper Valley PTA'.

10. **Which female rock band had their biggest hit when they shared the *St. Valentine's Day Massacre* EP with Motörhead?**

DID YOU KNOW?
Art Garfunkel, Kris Kristofferson, Sheryl Crow, Kiss singer Gene Simmons, Brian May of Queen, Soul singer Roberta Flack, Ezra Koenig of Vampire Weekend and Sting all worked as teachers before they found fame in the pop charts.

NOW

THAT'S WHAT I CALL

THE
ANSWERS

NOW That's What I Call a Decade

NOW That's What I Call Sixties Answers

1. 'Michelle'. While The Overlanders' version spent three weeks at number 1 in February 1966 a 'rival' version by David & Jonathan peaked at number 11. The Beatles' original recording was never released as a UK single but reached number 1 in Belgium, France, Norway and the Netherlands.

2. The Equals, who spent three weeks at number 1 in 1968 with 'Baby, Come Back'. In 1994 it also provided another reggae singer, Pato Banton, with his only chart-topper.

3. Dusty Springfield, who appeared on *NOW Dance 901* with the 1989 number 14 'In Private'. She had her only number 1 with 'You Don't Have to Say You Love Me' in May 1966.

4. Marc Almond. Their version of 'Something's Gotten Hold of My Heart' spent four weeks at number 1 in February 1989.

5. Billy Idol. The former singer with Generation X had a number 7 hit with 'Mony Mony' in October 1987. Tommy James and the Shondells' only other hit was the 1966 number 38, 'Hanky Panky'.

6. Wet Wet Wet had a number 1 single in 1988 with 'With a Little Help from My Friends', a number 1 for Joe Cocker in 1968, and in 1994 with 'Love Is All Around', a number 5 for The Troggs in 1967.

7. Procol Harum. 'Homburg' was the follow-up to 'A Whiter Shade of Pale', which spent six weeks at number 1 in 1967, and re-charted in 1972 when it reached number 13. At the 1977 BRIT Awards 'A Whiter Shade of Pale' was declared the best British pop single of the last twenty-five years.

8. Actor and singer Bernard Cribbins, who had the second of three Top 40 hits with 'Right Said Fred' in 1962. He had his biggest hit in April that year when 'Hole in the Ground' spent two weeks at number 9.

9. Bonzo Dog Doo-Dah Band. Singer Neil Innes also had one Top 40 hit as frontman of 'the prefab four' The Rutles, who reached number 39 in 1978 with 'I Must Be in Love'.

10. Paul McCartney. In 1968 he also produced Mary Hopkin's chart debut 'Those Were the Days', which knocked The Beatles' 'Hey Jude' off the number 1 spot.

NOW That's What I Call Sixties Dance Answers

1. 'Simon Smith and the Amazing Dancing Bear' was the biggest hit for Alan Price Set, though Alan was the original keyboard player with The Animals and played on their 1964 number 1 'House of the Rising Sun'.

2. Martha and the Vandellas. It was the first of ten Top 40 hits for the Motown legends, and though it peaked at number 28 when first issued in 1964, it recharted in 1969, when it reached number 4.

3. The Drifters. They had their biggest hits with 'Save the Last Dance for Me', number 2 in 1960, and 'Kissin' in the Back Row', also a number 2 hit, in 1974.

4. 'Let's Dance'. Chris's tally of five Top 40 hits is topped and tailed by 'Let's Dance', which reached number 2 when it was first released in 1962, then number 9 when it recharted in 1972.

5. Duane Eddy. He had his first hit in 1958 with the number 19 single 'Rebel Rouser', which – like 'Dance with the Guitar Man' – was co-written with Lee Hazlewood. Lee made his own chart appearance alongside Nancy Sinatra on the 1967 number 11 'Jackson'.

6. The Shadows. Before their 'solo' hits they backed Cliff Richard on the number 1s 'Travellin' Light' and 'Living Doll', though they were credited as the Drifters on the latter before they changed their name.

7. Wilson Pickett. It was the fourth of seven Top 40 hits for the man dubbed the Wicked Pickett, the biggest of them being his 1965 number 12 chart debut 'In the Midnight Hour'.

8. 'Dance to the Music'. The first of five Top 40 hits, it reached number 7 in 1968. In 1974, frontman Sly Stone married actress Kathy Silva onstage during a sold-out concert at Madison Square Garden.

9. The Beach Boys. 'Dance, Dance, Dance' reached number 24 and was their fourth Top 40 hit, while a new version of their 1964 single 'Fun, Fun, Fun', recorded with Status Quo, was their twenty-eighth.

10. Dave Edmunds. In 1970 his first solo single, 'I Hear You Knocking', was the Christmas number 1, topping the charts for six weeks.

NOW That's What I Call Seventies Answers

1. The Who. Despite twenty-five Top 40 hits, The Who have yet to have a number 1 single. 'My Generation' (1965) and 'I'm a Boy' (1966) both stalled at number 2.

2. Gerry Rafferty. His biggest hit, 'Baker Street', peaked at number 3 in 1978. In the eighties *NME* journalist Stuart Maconie devised the urban myth that TV presenter Bob Holness was the saxophone player on 'Baker Street'.

3. T. Rex, The Beatles and the Rolling Stones. In 1971, David Bowie mentioned John Lennon in the lyrics of his number 3 hit 'Life on Mars?', and in 1975 the two of them co-wrote the number 17 single 'Fame'.

4. Hot Chocolate. Their debut single was a version of John Lennon's 'Give Peace a Chance', released on The Beatles' Apple label. The band had their only number 1 in July 1977 when 'So You Win Again' spent three weeks at the top.

5. 'Please turn me over.' The song also appeared at the end of side 3 of their 1977 number 4 album *Out of the Blue*, so the instruction appears on both the album and single versions.

6. 'I Will Survive'. Gloria Gaynor's version was originally released as the B-side of 'Substitute', her cover of the 1975 song by the Righteous Brothers, which also gave Dutch band Clout their only Top 40 hit in 1978.

7. Bad Company. The supergroup, which included Mick Ralphs, previously of Mott the Hoople, and Raymond 'Boz' Burrell of King Crimson, had their biggest hit with the 1974 number 15 'Can't Get Enough'.

8. Vanilla Ice. 'Play That Funky Music' was his follow-up to 'Ice Ice Baby', which spent four weeks at number 1. 'Ice Ice Baby' includes a co-writing credit for Queen and David Bowie, as it samples their 1981 number 1 'Under Pressure'.

9. Mud. Between 1973 and 1976 Mud spent 124 weeks in the Top 40 and had three number 1s – 'Tiger Feet', 'Lonely This Christmas' and 'Oh Boy', originally a number 3 for Buddy Holly and the Crickets in 1958.

10. Ram Jam. In 1990 a remix by Dutch DJ Ben Liebrand made number 13. In 2003 a version by Tom Jones could only make number 50.

NOW That's What I Call Seventies Dance Answers

1. 'The Floral Dance'. On his version the Hanwell Band backed Sir Terry, though an instrumental version of the song had previously been a number 2 hit for the Brighouse & Rastrick Brass Band in 1977.

2. Rod Stewart and the Faces. This was the only one of their four Top 40 singles to be credited to both Rod and the Faces. The others – including the 1973 number 2 'Cindy Incidentally' – all listed the Faces only.

3. Barry Blue. The 1973 number 2 hit 'Dancin' (on a Saturday Night)' was co-written by Barry and Lynsey de Paul, who had her own number 14 hit the same year with 'Won't Somebody Dance with Me'.

4. Chic. Dance is a common theme for Chic founder Nile Rodgers, who also played on or produced David Bowie's 'Let's Dance', Sister Sledge's 'He's the Greatest Dancer' and Daft Punk's 'Lose Yourself to Dance'.

5. Marshall Hain. Julian Marshall and Kit Hain had one more Top 40 hit with 'Coming Home', after which they split. Kit went on to write for Roger Daltrey and Fleetwood Mac while Julian joined The Flying Lizards.

6. The Nolan Sisters. The Irish siblings had eight Top 40 hits between 1979 and 1982. In 1990, Coleen married actor Shane Richie, who had a number 2 hit in 2003 with a cover of Wham!'s 'I'm Your Man'.

7. David Bowie with 'John, I'm Only Dancing'. In 1979 he released a new version, entitled 'John, I'm Only Dancing (Again)', originally recorded in 1974 during sessions for his *Young Americans* album.

8. Electric Light Orchestra. Mik was a member of the group between

1973 and 1979 and played on some of their biggest hits, including 'Evil Woman', 'Livin' Thing' and 'Mr. Blue Sky'.

9. Disco-Tex and the Sex-O-Lettes. The group were founded by Bob Crewe, who wrote many of the Four Seasons' biggest hits, and Monti Rock III, who played a nightclub DJ in the film *Saturday Night Fever*.

10. Cozy Powell, whose 'Dance with the Devil' peaked at number 3 and was the first of three solo Top 40 hits. He returned to the Top 40 in 1993 with Queen guitarist Brian May on the number 23 hit 'Resurrection'.

NOW That's What I Call Eighties Answers

1. 'Absolute Beginners'. The Jam got to number 4 in 1981, while David Bowie reached number 2 with his 1986 film theme. The film also included a song by Paul Weller's next band, The Style Council.

2. Red Box. The duo, made up of Julian Close and Simon Toulson-Clarke, had a second Top 40 hit in November 1986 when 'From America' spent two weeks at number 10.

3. Flash and the Pan. A follow-up single, 'And the Band Played On', got no higher than number 54, though it reached number 4 in Australia, where it was retitled 'Down Among the Dead Men'.

4. 'Never Can Say Goodbye'. Originally a minor hit for the Jackson 5 in 1971, it made number 2 for Gloria Gaynor in 1974, while The Communards' version peaked at number 4 in 1987.

5. 'See The Day'. Dee C. Lee first had chart success when she sang backing vocals on the Wham! hits 'Bad Boys' and 'Young Guns (Go For It!)'. In 1984 she joined The Style Council and was married to singer Paul Weller from 1987 to 1998.

6. Grace Jones, who made her chart debut in 1980 with a number 17 cover of The Pretenders' 'Private Life', and had her biggest hit in 1985 with the number 12 single 'Slave to the Rhythm'.

7. The Plastic Population, a.k.a. Matt Black and Jonathan More of the duo Coldcut. Yazz also worked with Coldcut on their 1988 number 6 'Doctorin' the House'.

8. *Star Trek*. T'Pau, a Vulcan elder, first appeared in the 1967 episode 'Amok Time'. The band T'Pau had their biggest hit in 1987, when 'China in Your Hand' spent five weeks at number 1.

9. Marilyn. 'Calling Your Name' made number 4 in December 1983 and was the first of three Top 40 singles, including 'Cry and Be Free' and 'You Don't Love Me'.

10. Terence Trent D'Arby with 'If You Let Me Stay'. The song made number 7 in April 1987 and was one of four Top 20 singles from his debut album *Introducing the Hardline According to Terence Trent D'Arby*.

NOW That's What I Call Eighties Party Answers

1. 'Our House'. 1982 was a good year for Madness, who also made number 14 with 'Cardiac Arrest' and number 4 with 'Driving in My Car'.

2. 'Garden Party'. The Marillion single was the second of their twenty-three Top 40 hits, while Icelandic group Mezzoforte reached number 17 in March 1983 with an instrumental featuring a flugelhorn solo.

3. 'Come On Eileen'. The single was credited to Dexys Midnight Runners with the Emerald Express. Máire Fahey, sister of Siobhan Fahey from Bananarama, plays the character of Eileen in the video.

4. Dead or Alive with 'You Spin Me Round (Like a Record)'. The song recharted and reached number 5 in 2006 after singer Pete Burns was a contestant on *Celebrity Big Brother.*

5. The Weather Girls, who reached number 2 in March 1984 with 'It's Raining Men'. The song finally made number 1 in 2001 when it was the third of four solo chart-toppers for Geri Halliwell.

6. Chaka Khan with 'I Feel for You'. The song originally appeared on Prince's 1979 self-titled album, and was reportedly written for singer Patrice Rushen, who rejected it.

7. Blondie. Their run of Top 20 singles began with 'Denis', number 2 in 1978, and ended with 'Island of Lost Souls', number 11 in 1982. In 1999 they had their sixth number 1 with 'Maria'.

8. Bananarama with 'Venus'. Their version made number 8, matching Shocking Blue's 1970 original. Despite twenty-five Top 40 hits, Bananarama's best chart placing is number 3, which they reached three times.

9. The Four Tops. 'Loco in Acapulco' was written for the soundtrack to the film *Buster*, starring Phil Collins in the title role.

10. Kim Wilde with 'Kids in America', written by her father Marty and her brother Ricky. Marty Wilde had his own number 2 single in 1959 with 'A Teenager in Love'.

NOW That's What I Call 1983 Answers

1. The Supremes. 'You Can't Hurry Love' was the seventh of thirty Top 40 hits for the trio, including their only number 1, 'Baby Love', which spent two weeks at the top in 1964.

2. Neil Diamond. 'I'm a Believer' was also a number 1 for The Monkees in 1967, and made number 29 in 1974 for Robert Wyatt. Neil's biggest hit as a singer was the 1970 number 3 'Cracklin' Rosie'.

3. Stephen 'Tin Tin' Duffy, whose biggest solo hit was the 1985 number 4 'Kiss Me'. In 2004 he co-wrote Robbie Williams's sixth number 1 single 'Radio', and the number 8 follow-up 'Misunderstood'.

4. 'Double Dutch' is all about skipping. DJ Jazzy Jeff and the Fresh Prince also mention 'girls playing Double Dutch' on their 1981 number 8 single 'Summertime'.

5. Limahl was born Christopher Hamill in Lancashire in 1958. Originally a member of Kajagoogoo, his only solo Top 40 hits – 'Only for Love' and 'The NeverEnding Story' – appeared on *NOW 1* and *NOW 4*.

6. Men Without Hats are from Canada. Notable Canucks who have since appeared on *NOW* include Justin Bieber, Nelly Furtado, Drake, Bryan Adams, Shania Twain and Michael Bublé.

7. Carol Kenyon. Carol was also the singer on Paul Hardcastle's 1986 number 8 'Don't Waste My Time'.

8. The Human League. Following their 1981 number 1 'Don't You Want Me', the 1978 single 'Being Boiled' – featuring the original line-up, with Ian and Martyn – was reissued and reached number 6.

9. Kirsty MacColl's version of 'Days' by The Kinks appeared on volumes *15* and *31*. Her other appearance was on *NOW 10*, as guest vocalist with The Pogues on their biggest hit 'Fairytale of New York'.

10. Maggie Reilly. Although this was Mike Oldfield's only *NOW* appearance, Maggie would receive a songwriting credit on *NOW 65* in 2006, when Cascada covered her song 'Everytime We Touch'.

NOW That's What I Call 1984 Answers

1. Eurythmics. 'Sex Crime (Nineteen Eighty-Four)' was taken from their soundtrack for the film *1984* and was the sixth of twenty-four Top 40 singles for the duo. 'Julia', a second single from the film, reached number 44.

2. John Waite. As singer and bass player with The Babys, John had a number 45 single in 1978 with 'Isn't It Time'. The single did better in the US, where it peaked at number 13.

3. *The Woman in Red*. Eighteen years after his chart debut, 'I Just Called To Say I Love You' became Stevie's first 'solo' number 1. He also topped the chart in 1982 with Paul McCartney on 'Ebony and Ivory'.

4. Elton John. The couple were married at Darling Point in Sydney, Australia, but divorced in 1988.

5. Sweden. The only 'hit' for the brothers Per, Richard and Louis Herrey, it peaked at number 46, though it did reach number 2 in their homeland.

6. *Purple Rain* by Prince. As a result of PMRC's efforts, record labels voluntarily agreed to place 'Parental Advisory' stickers on relevant albums.

7. *Chess*. Benny Andersson and Björn Ulvaeus of ABBA wrote the music, with lyrics by Tim Rice. An image of Murray from the 1966 film *The Family Way* was used on the front of a 1988 Japanese compilation of songs by The Smiths.

8. Jim Diamond, who also had a hit with the 1986 number 7 'Hi Ho Silver', the theme from the ITV series *Boon*. As singer with Ph.D he reached number 3 in 1982 with 'I Won't Let You Down'.

9. 'Let's Hear It for the Boy', which was denied the top spot by Wham!'s

'Wake Me Up Before You Go-Go'. It was the fifth and most recent Top 40 hit for Deniece, who had a number 1 single in 1977 with 'Free'.

10. Julian Lennon. 'Too Late for Goodbyes' and his 1991 single 'Saltwater' both peaked at number 6, just as John Lennon's 'Nobody Told Me' had in January 1984.

NOW That's What I Call 1985 Answers

1. Bryan Adams, who peaked at number 42 with his single 'Summer of '69'. He made his Top 40 debut in January 1985 with 'Run to You', which spent four weeks at number 11.

2. Earth, Wind & Fire. Philip sang on ten of their Top 40 hits, including the number 3 singles 'September' and 'Let's Groove'. His only other solo hit was the number 34 single 'Walking on the Chinese Wall'.

3. Jennifer Rush. 'The Power of Love' entered the Top 100 in June and took seventeen weeks before it reached the top of the chart in October 1985.

4. Elvis Costello. Due to perform with the Attractions, he opted to play a solo version of The Beatles' 'All You Need Is Love', which he introduced by asking the audience to 'help sing this old northern English folk song'.

5. 'So Far Away'. The others were 'Money for Nothing' (number 4), 'Brothers in Arms' (number 16), 'Walk of Life' (number 2) and 'Your Latest Trick' (number 26).

6. Madness. Their twenty-first single 'Uncle Sam' ended a run of twenty Top 20 hits that started when 'The Prince' reached number 16 in 1979, and included their only number 1 single, 'House of Fun' in 1982.

7. Neil, aka actor Nigel Planer, for his cover version of 'Hole in My Shoe', originally also a number 2 for Traffic in 1967. It spent three weeks at number 2, behind 'Two Tribes' by Frankie Goes to Hollywood.

8. John Parr. The single, subtitled '(Man In Motion)', reached number 6 in October 1985. The following year John made his only other Top 40 appearance on 'Rock 'n' Roll Mercenaries', a duet with Meat Loaf.

9. Paul Miles-Kingston. The then thirteen-year-old made his only chart appearance on the single taken from Andrew Lloyd Webber's *Requiem*.

10. Ventriloquist Keith Harris and his green feathered friend Orville, who made number 40 in the last chart of the year. In 1982 they reached number 4 with 'Orville's Song'.

NOW That's What I Call 1986 Answers

1. Su Pollard. Famous for the role of Peggy Ollerenshaw in *Hi-de-Hi!*, in 1974 she appeared on the TV talent show *Opportunity Knocks*, where she came second to a singing Jack Russell.

2. Cameo. 'Word Up!' was the fourth of their seven Top 40 hits. Gun's 1994 version reached number 8; Melanie G's 1999 version reached

number 13; while Little Mix got to number 6 with their 2014 version.

3. Sad Café, who had their biggest hit in 1979 with the number 3 'Every Day Hurts'. Fellow vocalist Paul Carrack was previously singer with Ace, who made number 20 in 1974 with 'How Long'.

4. Bob and Earl. The 1969 number 7 single was the only hit for the duo, but 'Harlem Shuffle' gave the Rolling Stones their twenty-eighth Top 40 single.

5. Doctor and the Medics with 'Spirit in the Sky'. It was the only Top 40 hit for Norman Greenbaum, though Doctor and the Medics would return once more with 'Burn', which reached number 29 in August 1986.

6. 'Open Your Heart'. The Human League song of that name reached number 6 in 1981, while the M People song reached number 9 in 1995.

7. 'World Shut Your Mouth'. In addition to Julian's seven Top 40 solo hits, he also had three with The Teardrop Explodes, including their 1982 number 6, Reward'.

8. Peter Cetera, who reached number 3 in September 1986 with 'Glory of Love'. He also wrote Chicago's biggest hit, 'If You Leave Me Now', which spent three weeks at number 1 in November 1976.

9. 'Reet Petite' by Jackie Wilson. It took twenty-nine years to get to number 1, a record that stood until 2005, when Tony Christie's 1971 single '(Is This the Way To) Amarillo' eventually topped the chart.

10. Prince. 'Christopher' was the name of the character Prince played in the 1986 film *Under the Cherry Moon*. The single reached number 2 in March but was kept off the top spot by Diana Ross with 'Chain Reaction'.

NOW That's What I Call 1987 Answers

1. Aretha Franklin, who spent two weeks at number 1 with 'I Knew You Were Waiting (For Me)'. Her first Top 40 hit of the eighties was a duet with Eurythmics, while her last saw her team up with Whitney Houston.

2. Shalamar. Their chart run began in 1977 with the number 30 single 'Uptown Festival' and peaked in 1982 when 'A Night to Remember' and 'There It Is' both made number 5.

3. 'Lean on Me'. Bill Withers's original version made number 18 in 1972, and the song has also been a Top 20 hit for Mud, who reached number 7 in 1976, and Michael Bolton, who reached number 14 in 1994.

4. Johnny Logan, who first won in 1980 with 'What's Another Year', then again in 1987 with 'Hold Me Now'. He also composed Ireland's 1992 winning song, 'Why Me?'

5. INXS. The Australian group, which included brothers Andrew, Jon and Tim Farriss in their ranks, had eighteen Top 40 hits, but never equalled the number 2 peak of 'Need You Tonight'.

6. The Chimes. They had one more Top 40 hit with 'Heaven' in 1989, though singer Pauline Henry had another five Top 40 entries, including her number 12 version of Bad Company's 1975 hit 'Feel Like Makin' Love'.

7. Bruce Willis with 'Under the Boardwalk'. It was his second hit in 1987, following his cover of the Staple Singers' 'Respect Yourself', which reached number 7 in March.

8. 'Full Metal Jacket (I Wanna Be Your Drill Instructor)', which used dialogue from the Stanley Kubrick film set to a dance beat. Abigail Mead was an alias for Kubrick's daughter Vivian.

9. John Farnham with 'You're the Voice'. Its parent album *Whispering Jack* spent twenty-five weeks at the top of the Australian album chart, but could only manage number 35 in the UK.

10. Pet Shop Boys. The synth-pop duo first recorded their song for a TV special to mark the tenth anniversary of Elvis's death. It was the band's third number 1 and spent four weeks at the top of the chart.

NOW That's What I Call 1988 Answers

1. Little Eva. The American singer, born Eva Narcissus Boyd, had two more hits the following year with the number 30 'Keep Your Hands Off My Baby' and the number 13 'Let's Turkey Trot'.

2. Robin Beck. In 1989 Robin sang backing vocals on Cher's number 6 hit 'If I Could Turn Back Time', and in 2006 she returned to the chart as vocalist on a dance version of 'First Time' by Swedish group Sunblock.

3. Billy Bragg (with pianist Cara Tivey). Both songs were taken from the charity album *Sgt. Pepper Knew My Father* produced by the *NME* music paper to raise money for Childline.

4. Taylor Dayne. 'Tell It to My Heart' was the first of five Top 40 hits, which included the 1993 number 14 'Can't Get Enough of Your Love', a cover of Barry White's 1974 number 8 single.

5. Eighth Wonder. The band, which also included Patsy's brother Jamie, had one more Top 40 hit with the number 13 single 'Cross My Heart'.

6. Enya. 'Orinoco Flow' was her chart debut and stayed at number 1 for three weeks. In 2004 Enya had a second number 1 when she was credited alongside rapper P. Diddy on 'I Don't Wanna Know' by Mario Winans.

7. Rose Tattoo. Their best UK chart effort was the 1981 number 60 'Rock 'n' Roll Outlaw'. 'Suddenly' was featured in the soap *Neighbours*, and played during the wedding of Scott Robinson (Jason Donovan) and Charlene Mitchell (Kylie Minogue).

8. Sabrina with 'Boys (Summertime Love)'. The singer, born Norma Sabrina Salerno, had one more Top 40 hit the following October with the number 25 single 'All of Me'.

9. Dollar. They had their tenth and last top 40 hit with 'Oh L'amour', originally a single for Erasure. Erasure's first three singles all failed

to make the Top 40, though the fourth, 'Sometimes', peaked at number 2.

10. Traveling Wilburys with 'Handle with Care'. They were the pseudonyms adopted by George Harrison (Nelson), Jeff Lynne (Otis), Roy Orbison (Lefty), Bob Dylan (Lucky) and Tom Petty (Charlie T. Jr.).

NOW That's What I Call 1989 Answers

1. Jive Bunny and the Mastermixers. Between August and Christmas, 'Swing the Mood', 'That's What I Like' and 'Let's Party' spent a combined total of nine weeks at number 1.

2. Will to Power. The band only made one more Top 40 appearance, when they reached number 29 in 1990 with a cover of 10cc's 1975 number 1 'I'm Not in Love'.

3. R.E.M. Although ten of their singles made the Top 10, the band from Athens, Georgia, reached their highest chart position in 2000 when 'The Great Beyond' peaked at number 3.

4. Technotronic. Felly appeared on the number 2 'Pump Up the Jam', Ya Kid K on the number 2 'Get Up (Before the Night Is Over)' and MC Eric on the number 14 'This Beat Is Technotronic'.

5. 'If You Don't Know Me By Now'. Between 1985 and 2005 Simply Red had thirty Top 40 singles, seven of which were cover versions, including their chart debut, 'Money's Too Tight to Mention'.

6. Black Box. 'Ride on Time' spent six weeks at number 1, but following a legal challenge Loleatta's vocal was removed and the song was rerecorded with future M People singer Heather Small.

7. Lisa Stansfield. She made her solo debut in August 1989 with the number 13 single 'This Is the Right Time' and would go on to have sixteen Top 40 singles, including two number 1s.

8. The Reynolds Girls. The single, 'I'd Rather Jack', produced by Stock, Aitken and Waterman, was the only chart entry for sisters Linda and Aisling Reynolds.

9. Bryan Hyland. His version also re-charted in 1975, when it reached number 7. Bryan's other big hit was his 1960 chart debut 'Itsy Bitsy Teenie Weenie Yellow Polka Dot Bikini', which reached number 8.

10. Transvision Vamp. A cover of 'Baby I Don't Care' aslo gave former *Brookside* actress Jenniefr Ellison her biggest hit when her version peaked at number 6 in 2003.

NOW That's What I Call 1990 Answers

1. Beats International featuring Lindy Layton. 'Dub Be Good to Me' spent four weeks at number 1 in March. In September, Lindy reached number 22 with a cover of Janet Kay's 1979 number 2 'Silly Games'.

2. The Wild Pair. In the promo video, Paula dances with the cartoon character MC Skat Kat, voiced by the Wild Pair (Bruce DeShazer and Marv Gunn).

3. 'Healing Hands'. Both songs had been released separately in 1989: 'Healing Hands' peaked at number 45, while 'Sacrifice' could only manage number 55.

4. Bobbie Gentry, with one of her four Top 40 hits. Deacon Blue were denied the top spot by Bombalurina and their version of 'Itsy Bitsy Teeny Weeny Yellow Polka Dot Bikini'.

5. Londonbeat. Band members Jimmy Chambers and George Chandler were 'in demand' backing singers in the eighties, including appearances on hits by Wham!, Paul Young, Tina Turner and Fine Young Cannibals.

6. Julee Cruise. 'Falling' was her only Top 40 hit, and featured lyrics written by *Twin Peaks* director David Lynch.

7. Candy Dulfer. Also Candy's only Top 40 hit, the instrumental 'Lily Was Here' reached number 6 and was taken from the soundtrack to the Dutch film *De Kassière*.

8. They Might Be Giants with 'Birdhouse in Your Soul'. Their only other Top 40 hit came in 2001 with the number 21 'Boss of Me', the theme to the TV series *Malcolm in the Middle*.

9. Lenny Kravitz. 'Justify My Love' made number 2 in December, while 'Rescue Me', the other new song on *Immaculate Collection*, made number 3 in April 1991.

10. Stefan Dennis. It was the only Top 40 hit for the actor who played ruthless businessman Paul Robinson. Later in 1990, Craig McLachlan, who played Henry Ramsay in *Neighbours*, made number 2 with his single 'Mona'.

NOW That's What I Call 1991 Answers

1. 'Sadeness (Part 1)' by Enigma. The song, which samples Gregorian chants by the German choir Capella Antiqua München, was the first and biggest of five Top 40 singles for the group.

2. *The Simpsons*. 'Do the Bartman' spent three weeks at number 1 in February 1991. While the Archies were one-hit wonders, The Simpsons had a second hit when 'Deep, Deep Trouble' made number 7 in April.

3. Kate Pierson of the B-52s. R.E.M.'s album *Out of Time* featured three more Top 40 singles – 'Losing My Religion', 'Near Wild Heaven' and 'Radio Song' – and was the sixth-bestselling album of the year.

4. Tammy Wynette, who was featured vocalist on 'Justified and Ancient (Stand by the JAMs)' by the KLF. The number 2 single was her biggest hit since she topped the chart with 'Stand by Your Man' in 1976.

5. P.M. Dawn. 'Set Adrift on Memory Bliss' spent two weeks at number 3 in August and sampled Spandau Ballet's 1983 number 1 'True'.

6. Massive Attack, who reached number 25 with 'Safe from Harm'. The song includes a co-writing credit for Panama-born jazz drummer Billy Cobham, whose 1973 composition 'Stratus' was sampled.

7. James with 'Sit Down'. The biggest of their nineteen Top 40 hits, it was denied the top spot by Chesney Hawkes's single 'The One and Only', written by Nik Kershaw and taken from the film *Buddy's Song*.

8. Zucchero. Adelmo 'Zucchero' Fornaciari had his first UK hit with '*Senza una Donna* (Without a Woman)' nine years after his Italian Top 40 debut with '*Una Notte Che Vola Via*'.

9. Scorpions. The German rock band had their biggest hit with 'Wind of Change', but were one of six different acts that had to settle for number 2 while Bryan Adams spent sixteen weeks at the top of the chart.

10. 'Bohemian Rhapsody'. The Queen single originally spent nine weeks at number 1 in 1975, but was reissued following the death of Freddie Mercury on 24 November 1991 and spent another five weeks at the top.

NOW That's What I Call 1992 Answers

1. Erasure. The EP included a version of 'Take a Chance on Me', with additional rap by MC Kinky, who had previously appeared on the 1989 number 15 'Everything Starts with an E' by E-Zee Possee.

2. Right Said Fred. The trio finally made number 1 with 'Deeply Dippy' in April 1992, having stalled at number 2 with their debut 'I'm Too Sexy' and made number 3 with the follow-up 'Don't Talk Just Kiss'.

3. Was (Not Was) with 'Shake Your Head'. Prior to this, their biggest hit was the 1987 number 10 'Walk the Dinosaur', which was included on the soundtrack to the 1994 live-action film version of *The Flintstones.*

4. 'Cloudbusting'. Utah Saints' original 1992 single used Kate Bush's vocal from her 1985 number 20 single, but their 2008 remix replaced this with a new vocal by former *Pop Idol* contestant Davina Perera.

5. 'Too Much Love Will Kill You'. The song was originally recorded by Queen in 1988, but the band version remained unreleased until it was rerecorded for their final studio album, *Made in Heaven*.

6. The Wedding Present, who released a limited-edition single each month in 1992, a campaign that peaked in May when 'Come Play with Me' reached number 10.

7. Jimmy Nail with 'Ain't No Doubt'. The lyrics quoted fellow Geordie Sting's 1985 number 26 single 'If You Love Somebody Set Them Free'.

8. Kris Kross. Chris 'Mac Daddy' Kelly and Chris 'Daddy Mac' Smith were held off the top spot by KWS with 'Please Don't Go', one of five Top 40 cover versions for the Nottingham dance trio.

9. Nick Berry. His version of Buddy Holly's 'Heartbeat' made number 2 in June, and was his only other Top 40 hit following the 1986 number 1 'Every Loser Wins'.

10. Undercover. They reached number 2 in September with their dance version of 'Baker Street', while Gerry Rafferty's original peaked at number 3 in 1978.

NOW That's What I Call 1993 Answers

1. Mr Blobby with 'Mr Blobby'. Anticipating a return by popular demand, Mr Blobby had another crack at the chart in 1995 with 'Christmas in Blobbyland', but could only get to number 36.

2. Lulu on 'Relight My Fire'. Take That also had number 1 hits in 1993 with 'Pray' and 'Babe'. Dan Hartman had his biggest hit in 1978 with the number 8 single 'Instant Replay'.

3. Doves. Both acts included twin brothers Andy and Jez Williams, along with Jimi Goodwin. Doves had their biggest hit in April 2002 with the number 3 single 'There Goes the Fear'.

4. Lisa Stansfield, who sang 'These Are the Days of Our Lives' with Queen and George. At the concert, held at Wembley Stadium on 20 April 1992, Queen and Lisa also performed 'I Want to Break Free'.

5. Aurora featuring Naimee Coleman. It was their only hit, while Duran Duran can boast thirty Top 40 singles, including the two number 1s 'Is There Something I Should Know?' and 'The Reflex'.

6. Darrin O'Brien went by the stage name of Snow. He had his only Top 40 hit with 'Informer', which reached number 2 in March 1993 but was kept off the top spot first by Shaggy, then by The Bluebells.

7. DJ Jazzy Jeff and the Fresh Prince, who had a number 1 with 'Boom! Shake the Room'. As Will Smith, his partner made number 1 in 1997 with 'Men in Black'.

8. Meat Loaf's 'I'd Do Anything for Love (But I Won't Do That)'. It spent seven weeks at number 1 and was the only chart appearance for Lorraine, who was credited as 'Mrs Loud'.

9. 'True Love'. Written by Cole Porter, it originally featured in the musical film *High Society*. Elton and Kiki topped the chart in 1976 with 'Don't Go Breaking My Heart', the first of Elton's seven number 1s.

10. 4 Non Blondes. 'What's Up?' was written by the band's singer, Linda Perry, whose other hits include Christina Aguilera's 'Beautiful' and Pink's 'Get the Party Started'.

NOW That's What I Call 1994 Answers

1. 'Without You'. The song was originally written and recorded by the group Badfinger. Harry Nilsson first charted in 1969 after his song 'Everybody's Talkin'' was featured in the film *Midnight Cowboy*.

2. Chaka Demus and Pliers, with 'Twist and Shout'. The third of six Top 40 hits but their only number 1, it spent two weeks at the top in January 1994.

3. Stiltskin. The group had just one more Top 40 hit, when 'Footsteps' reached number 34 in September 1994. In 1997, Stiltskin singer Ray Wilson joined Genesis and appeared on their album *Calling All Stations*.

4. Whigfield, whose debut single 'Saturday Night' spent four weeks at the top. Whigfield's last Top 40 hit came in December 1995, when she reached number 21 with a cover of Wham!'s 'Last Christmas'.

5. 'It's Alright'. East 17 had three more Top 10 hits in 1994, including their only chart-topper and the Christmas number 1, 'Stay Another Day'. Pet Shop Boys' 'It's Alright' peaked at number 5 in July 1989.

6. En Vogue. Their version of the 1968 song by soul singer Linda Lyndell gave Salt-N-Pepa the tenth of sixteen Top 40 hits, and En Vogue their sixth of nine.

7. Crash Test Dummies with 'Mmm Mmm Mmm Mmm'. The band had two more Top 40 singles, including a cover of XTC's 'The Ballad of Peter Pumpkinhead', which reached number 30 in 1995.

8. Boyzone. Their version of 'Love Me for a Reason' peaked at number 2, and though their next four singles all reached the Top 5, they would have to wait another two years for the first of their six number 1s.

9. 'Crocodile Shoes'. In 1996, a second series of the TV drama featured a new theme song, 'Country Boy', which reached number 25 and gave Jimmy his seventh and most recent Top 40 single.

10. Dina Carroll. Her version of 'The Perfect Year', from Andrew Lloyd Webber's musical *Sunset Boulevard*, reached number 5 in January, the eighth of her thirteen Top 40 hits.

NOW That's What I Call 1995 Answers

1. Everything But the Girl. Later in 1995, the duo reached number 3 with their single 'Missing', matching the previous best chart position of their 1988 cover of Rod Stewart's hit 'I Don't Want to Talk About It'.

2. Eric Clapton, who had his first Top 40 hit in 1965 with The Yardbirds' 'For Your Love'. His career includes hits with Cream and Derek and the Dominos, but 'Love Can Build a Bridge' is his only number 1 single.

3. Robson & Jerome. Their version of 'Unchained Melody', previously a number 1 for Jimmy Young in 1955 and the Righteous Brothers in 1990, was the bestselling single of 1995.

4. 'Don't Stop (Wiggle Wiggle)'. The American duo managed three further Top 40 entries, the biggest of them being 'La La La Hey Hey', which reached number 7 in September 1995.

5. 'Some Might Say'. Their chart-topping run ended in September 2005 with 'The Importance of Being Idle'; all eight of their number 1s spent just one week at the top.

6. The Boo Radleys. 'Wake Up Boo!' reached number 9 in March 1995, while *Wake Up!*, the album on which it featured, topped the chart the following month.

7. Damien Hirst. The video also featured appearances from comedian and Fat Les member Keith Allen, fellow comedian Matt Lucas, and models Sara Stockbridge and Jo Guest.

8. The Rembrandts. In America, 'I'll Be There for You' peaked at number 17, even though it was the most-played record on American radio for eight consecutive weeks.

9. Royston Vasey is the real name of stand-up comedian Roy 'Chubby' Brown. He was the featured vocalist on a new version of the Smokie song, 'Living Next Door to Alice', which reached number 3 in October 1995.

10. Pérez Prado. He made his chart debut with his orchestra with the 1955 number 1 'Cherry Pink and Apple Blossom White', a song revived by Modern Romance in 1982, when their version reached number 15.

NOW That's What I Call 1996 Answers

1. Gary Barlow. His first solo chart-topper came just three months after Take That bowed out (for the first time) with their number 1 cover of the Bee Gees' song 'How Deep Is Your Love'.

2. Gabrielle. As East 17 they had just one more Top 40 hit, with 'Hey Child', but following the departure of Tony Mortimer they renamed themselves E-17 and had two further hits, including the 1998 number 2 'Each Time'.

3. Paul Weller. His tally of hit singles includes twenty-four Top 40 hits with The Jam (four of them number 1s), another fifteen with The Style Council, plus a further thirty-two solo Top 40 singles so far …

4. New Zealand. OMC is an abbreviation of Otara Millionaires Club, named after a suburb of South Auckland. Their only Top 40 hit, 'How Bizarre' peaked at number 5 in August 1996.

5. *The X-Files*. The theme tune spent three weeks at number 2, and was only denied the top spot by The Prodigy's 'Firestarter', one of their two number 1s in 1996, along with 'Breathe'.

6. Spice Girls. 'Bumper to Bumper' was the B-side of 'Wannabe', 'Take Me Home' was the other side of 'Say You'll Be There', while 'One of These Girls' was coupled with '2 Become 1'.

7. Patti Smith. In 1978, the Patti Smith Group had their only Top 40 hit with 'Because the Night', a song Patti co-wrote with Bruce Springsteen, which peaked at number 5 in May.

8. Noel Gallagher, then still a member of Oasis. In 1999, Noel featured on another Chemical Brothers hit, the number 9 single 'Let Forever Be'.

9. The Woolpackers. They also managed a follow-up hit later the same month with the number 25 'Line Dance Party', while an *Emmerdance* album reached number 26 in December 1996.

10. Babylon Zoo, whose debut single 'Spaceman' spent five weeks at number 1 in 1996 following its use in an advert for Levi's jeans.

NOW That's What I Call 1997 Answers.

1. Hanson. When 'MMMBop' topped the chart, drummer Zac Hanson was just eleven years old and the three brothers had a combined age of forty-two.

2. Tori Amos with 'Professional Widow (It's Got to Be Big)'. Originally a harpsichord-based slow song on her 1996 album *Boys for Pele*, it was Tori's eleventh Top 40 single and only chart-topper to date.

3. 'Ecuador'. Sash! can boast ten Top 10 singles but have yet to reach number 1. Five of their hits – including 'Ecuador', which featured German trance DJ Rodriguez – had to settle for number 2.

4. 'On Her Majesty's Secret Service', which made number 7 in October. David Arnold made his chart debut with 'Play Dead', his 1993 number 12 collaboration with Björk.

5. Andrea Bocelli. In 1999 he had his second Top 40 single with '*Canto Della Terra*', and in 2017 Andrea recorded a version of Ed Sheeran's Christmas number 1 'Perfect', retitled 'Perfect Symphony'.

6. The Rolling Stones. The Verve sampled the distinctive melody in 'Bittersweet Symphony' from a 1965 version of the Rolling Stones song 'The Last Time' by Andrew Oldham Orchestra.

7. 'I'll Be Missing You' by Puff Daddy and Faith Evans featuring 112. The song had two three-week spells at the top of the chart, interrupted for one week in July by Oasis' third number 1 'D'You Know What I Mean?'

8. Chumbawamba with 'Tubthumping'. The Burnley anarchists spent three weeks at number 2, held off the top by Will Smith's 'Men in Black'. They had two more Top 40 hits, including the 1998 number 10 'Amnesia'.

9. 'Something About the Way You Look Tonight'. In Canada the single spent three years in the Top 20, including forty-six non-consecutive weeks at number 1.

10. 'Baby Can I Hold You'. Tracy Chapman's original version stalled at number 94, and her only Top 40 entry to date is the 1988 number 4 'Fast Car', also a number 2 hit for Jonas Blue in 2016.

NOW That's What I Call 1998 Answers

1. Ian Brown, who previously had twelve Top 40 hits with the Stone Roses. Number 5 remains his best chart placing, a position he matched in 2000 with his sixth Top 40 single, 'Dolphins Were Monkeys'.

2. Cher with 'Believe'. The bestselling single of the year in the UK, it also topped the charts in the US, where it won a Grammy Award for Best Dance Recording.

3. Spice Girls. Their seventh single 'Stop' entered the chart at number 2 but was kept off the summit by 'It's Like That' by Run-D.M.C. vs. Jason Nevins, the only number 1 for the New York hip-hop trio.

4. All Saints. Their original hits 'Never Ever' and 'Bootie Call' bookended covers of 'Under the Bridge', a 1992 number 13 for Red Hot Chili Peppers, and 'Lady Marmalade', a 1975 number 17 for Labelle.

5. Aaron Carter. Born December 1987, the younger brother of Backstreet Boys' Nick Carter reached number 18 in July 1998 with his version of the Beach Boys' 1963 chart debut 'Surfin' USA'.

6. Manic Street Preachers with 'If You Tolerate This Your Children Will Be Next'. They returned to the top in 2000 when 'The Masses Against the Classes' entered the chart at number 1.

7. Oasis with 'All Around the World'. At nine minutes and thirty-eight seconds, it is more than two minutes longer than The Beatles' 1968 hit 'Hey Jude', the previous longest number 1 single.

8. Cocteau Twins. The band, who scored five Top 40 hits between 1984 and 1996, were favourites of DJ John Peel, whose listeners voted their 1984 single 'Pearly-Dewdrops' Drops' the second-best song of that year.

9. Missy 'Misdemeanor' Elliott, who topped the chart in September 1998 with Melanie B with 'I Want You Back', and featured alongside Mocha on Nicole's only Top 40 hit, 'Make It Hot'.

10. 'Doo Wop (That Thing)'. Lauryn also made the Top 10 with her number 4 follow up 'Ex-Factor' but has yet to match the two number 1s – 'Killing Me Softly' and 'Ready or Not' – the Fugees had in 1996.

NOW That's What I Call 1999 Answers

1. Martine McCutcheon, who quit her role as Tiffany in *EastEnders* and had the first of five consecutive Top 10 singles with 'Perfect Moment', a song first recorded by Polish singer Edyta Górniak in 1997.

2. The Offspring, who spent a week at number 1 with 'Pretty Fly (For a White Guy)' but were denied a second chart-topper by Westlife, making their chart debut with 'Swear It Again'.

3. Barenaked Ladies. 'One Week' entered the chart at number 5 but slipped to number 11 the following week. The band had a second Top 40 hit later that year with the number 28 single 'It's All Been Done'.

4. Roxette. Marie Fredriksson and Per Gessle started their chart career with the 1989 number 7 'The Look' and had their biggest hit with 'It Must Have Been Love', which peaked at number 3 in June 1990.

5. Tatyana Ali, who played Ashley Banks in the American sitcom. Tatyana and Will had first charted with the number 6 single 'Daydreamin'' in 1998, and she would have one more Top 40 hit in 1999 with 'Everytime'.

6. Typically Tropical. Although they were one-hit wonders, band member Jeff Calvert also co-wrote Sarah Brightman and Hot Gossip's 1978 number 6 'I Lost My Heart to a Starship Trooper'.

7. '(Ba Da Bee)'. The Italian group's chart debut spent seventeen weeks in the Top 40 and was the second-bestselling single of 1999. They had one more hit in 2000 with the number 3 single 'Move Your Body'.

8. Mr Oizo. A follow-up single, 'Analog Worms Attack', failed to chart, and Mr Oizo remains a one-hit wonder.

9. 'Keep On Movin''. Five returned to the top of the chart in 2000 with a version of 'We Will Rock You' featuring Queen's Brian May and Roger Taylor, and again in 2001 with 'Let's Dance'.

10. 'Seasons in the Sun'. Canadian Terry Jacks originally recorded the song with The Beach Boys, who decided against releasing it. Terry then recorded his own version, which went to number 1 in the UK and the US.

NOW That's What I Call Twenty-first Century Answers

2001. Baha Men. The group from New Providence in the Bahamas returned to the chart in 2001 with the number 14 hit 'You All Dat', and had one more Top 40 single with 'Move It Like This', a number 16 hit in 2002.

2002. Gorillaz. The project created by Blur singer Damon Albarn and artist Jamie Hewlett had nine Top 40 hits, including the 2005 number 1 'DARE', featuring vocals by Happy Mondays' singer Shaun Ryder.

2003. Sugababes. Their version of 'Freak Like Me' used the lyrics of Adina Howard's original 1995 single, sung over the backing track of 'Are "Friends" Electric?', written by Gary Numan.

2004. Ms. Dynamite. Her debut album *A Little Deeper* included the Top 40 singles 'It Takes More', 'Dy-Na-Mi-Tee' and 'Put Him Out', and was also the winner of the 2002 Mercury Music Prize.

2005. Sam & Mark. Messers Nixon and Rhodes had finished second and third on the 2003 series of *Pop Idol*, behind Michelle McManus, who also topped the chart this year with 'All This Time'.

2006. Daniel Powter. 'Bad Day' spent twenty-five weeks in the Top 40, and was the eleventh-best-selling single of 2005, but was kept off the number 1 slot by James Blunt's 'You're Beautiful'.

2007. Lordi. Their 2006 victory made them the first Finnish act to win the competition, and it was the first time that a rock song took the prize.

2008. Eva Cassidy. While this was also Eva's only number 1 single, she has topped the album chart on three occasions. 'What a Wonderful World' was originally a number 1 for Louis Armstrong in 1968.

2009. 'Singin' in the Rain'. Mint Royale's version first charted in 2005, when it was used in a TV advert for Volkswagen, and recharted in 2008 after it featured on the TV show *Britain's Got Talent*.

2010. La Roux. 'In For The Kill' spent four weeks at number 2 in April but the duo went one better in July when 'Bulletproof' topped the chart for one week.

NOW That's What I Call a Compilation

NOW That's What I Call Movies Answers

1. John Travolta and Olivia Newton-John. 'You're the One That I Want' and 'Summer Nights' from *Grease* spent a combined total of sixteen weeks at number 1 in 1978.

2. *Days of Thunder*. 'Show Me Heaven' failed to make the US *Billboard* Hot 100 chart. Maria also wrote Feargal Sharkey's 1985 number 1 'A Good Heart'.

3. 'Burning Heart'. Survivor's only other chart entry was the 1986 number 80 'I Can't Hold Back'. In 2009 it featured in the film *Paul Blart: Mall Cop*, but sadly this didn't revive its prospects.

4. *Mannequin*. The film featured *Sex and the City* star Kim Cattrall in the title role. Starship's 1985 number 12 hit 'We Built This City' was co-written by Elton John's long-term collaborator Bernie Taupin.

5. Anne Hathaway. 'I Dreamed a Dream' was taken from the soundtrack to the 2012 film *Les Misérables*. The song has also been a Top 40 single for Susan Boyle in 2009 and Glee Cast in 2010.

6. 'Up Where We Belong' with Joe Cocker, which made number 7 in 1983. '(I've Had) The Time of My Life' has charted twice, reaching number 6 in 1987 and number 8 in 1990.

7. 'Choose Life' was the only hit for PF Project, though the same musicians also had a number 11 single in 1998 with 'Sounds of Wickedness' by Tzant featuring the Original ODC MC.

8. Peabo Bryson. All three of his Top 40 hits have been duets, including the 1983 number 2 'Tonight I Celebrate My Love' with Roberta Flack, which appeared on the very first *NOW That's What I Call Music* album.

9. *Mermaids*. The promo video also featured Winona Ryder and Christina Ricci, who played Cher's daughters in the film. Cher's previous number 1 was 'I Got You Babe' in 1965, with her then husband Sonny Bono.

10. Wendy Fraser. The song was originally written by Patrick Swayze for his 1984 film *Grandview, U.S.A.* but was not used, and finally saw the light of day in *Dirty Dancing*.

NOW That's What I Call Feel Good Answers

1. Shalamar. Comprised of Jody Watley, Jeffrey Daniels and Howard Hewett, the trio had eleven Top 40 singles between 1977 and 1983, including the 1982 number 5 'A Night to Remember'.

2. 'Happy Together', which reached number 10 in August 1991 and was the follow-up to Jason's fourth number 1, 'Any Dream Will Do'. The Turtles' biggest hit was the 1967 number 4 'She'd Rather Be with Me'.

3. Zambia. Born Rozalla Miller, she had eight Top 40 hits in total, including the 1991 number 11 'Faith (In the Power of Love)'. 'Everybody's Free …' was remixed in 1990, when it peaked at number 30.

4. Manfred Mann's Earth Band. 'Joybringer' reached number 9 in October 1973. The band also had two number 6 hits, with 'Blinded by the Light' in 1976 and 'Davy's on the Road Again' in 1978.

5. Helen Shapiro. Born in September 1946, she was fourteen when she first topped the charts in August 1961 with 'You Don't Know', then

spent three weeks at the top that November with 'Walkin' Back to Happiness'.

6. 'Reasons to Be Cheerful, Part 3'. The band first made the Top 10 in June 1978, when 'What a Waste' peaked at number 9, and had a number 1 single in January 1979 with 'Hit Me with Your Rhythm Stick'.

7. 'Have a Nice Day'. The Stereophonics' song was their twelfth Top 40 hit, while Bon Jovi were chalking up an impressive thirty-first.

8. Pink. In addition to his own 1999 number 4 single with 'Barber's Adagio for Strings', William co-wrote All Saints' fourth number 1, 'Pure Shores', and Madonna's Top 10 hits 'Ray of Light' and 'Beautiful Stranger'.

9. 'Milk and Alcohol', which reached number 9 in February 1979. It was one of just three Top 40 hits for the Essex R&B group, who topped the album chart in 1976 with their third album, *Stupidity*.

10. Pharrell Williams with 'Happy'. His total of four non-consecutive weeks was interrupted twice, with five weeks between his second and third spell at the top, though 'Happy' went on to spend fifty weeks in the Top 40.

NOW That's What I Call Legends Answers

1. 'Don't Stop Me Now'. Despite the low US chart position, readers of *Rolling Stone* magazine voted it Queen's third-greatest song in 2014. Unsurprisingly, 'Bohemian Rhapsody' was the number one choice.

2. 'I Only Want to Be with You', a number 4 for The Tourists in 1979, and for Dusty Springfield in 1963. Eurythmics had their only number 1 in July 1985 with 'There Must Be an Angel (Playing with My Heart)'.

3. Bee Gees. Take That had their eighth number 1 with 'How Deep Is Your Love', 'Words' gave Boyzone the first of six number 1s, and 'Tragedy' was the first of two chart-toppers for Steps.

4. Puff Daddy and Faith Evans, who spent six weeks at number 1 with their tribute to the late rapper Notorious B.I.G. Puff and Faith had a second hit duet with the number 23 single 'All Night Long'.

5. Genesis. Founding members Peter Gabriel, Tony Banks and Chris Stewart were all in The Garden Wall. By the time of their 1974 Top 40 debut 'I Know What I Like (In Your Wardrobe)', Stewart had been replaced by Phil Collins.

6. 'Puss in Boots'. The song appeared on Adam's album *Strip*, on which Phil also co-produced the title track, featuring a vocal contribution from Anni-Frid Lyngstad of ABBA.

7. Bono and the Edge of U2, who had their second number 1 with 'The Fly' in 1991. Despite technical difficulties and poor reviews, the *Spider-Man* musical ran for almost two and a half years.

8. MC Miker G and DJ Sven, aka Lucien Witteveen and Sven van Veen. 'Holiday Rap', their only Top 40 hit, also included a snippet of Cliff Richard's 1963 number 1 'Summer Holiday'.

9. Celine Dion with the song *'Ne Partez Pas Sans Moi'*. It won with 137

points, beating the UK entry – 'Go' by Scott Fitzgerald – by one point. 'Go' was written by Julie Forsyth, daughter of the late Sir Bruce.

10. 'Faith' begins with a melody from Wham!'s 1984 number 1 'Freedom', played by pianist Chris Cameron. Both songs appear on the 2014 *NOW ... Legends* compilation.

NOW That's What I Call Running Answers

1. 'Because of You' was the theme to *Brush Strokes*, which ran on BBC 1 from 1986 to 1991. It was Dexys' ninth Top 40 single, a run that included the number 1 hits 'Geno' and 'Come On Eileen'.

2. Rihanna and Kanye West. The third number 1 single for each of the three artists, it spent one week at the top in September 2009, before Pixie Lott's 'Boys and Girls' replaced it.

3. Slade. Their impressive run of twenty-four Top 40 hits began with the 1971 number 16 'Get Down and Get with It', previously a 1967 single for the American rock 'n' roll star Little Richard.

4. 'Runaway'. Janet Jackson's single made number 6, while Devlin featuring Yasmin made number 15, and The Corrs reached number 2 at the third attempt after the same song peaked at number 49 in 1996, and number 62 in 1997.

5. Rage, who had their only Top 40 hit with 'Run to You'. In some European countries they were obliged to call themselves En-Rage to avoid confusion with a German heavy-metal band called Rage.

6. Snow Patrol. It was the second cover version to give Leona a number 1 hit, following her 2006 chart debut with 'A Moment Like This', originally a US number 1 for Kelly Clarkson in 2002.

7. '(A Deal with God)'. A 2012 remix featured at the closing ceremony of the London Olympic Games, and charted at number 6, giving Kate her first Top 40 hit for seven years.

8. Run-DMC, featuring Joseph 'Run' Simmons, Darryl 'DMC' McDaniels and Jason 'Jam Master Jay' Mizell. Their five Top 40 hits include the 1998 number 1 'It's Like That'.

9. Galantis. The duo's Linus Eklöw co-wrote 'I Love It', the 2013 number 1 for Icona Pop featuring Charli XCX, while partner Christian Karlsson co-wrote Britney Spears's 2004 number 1 'Toxic'.

10. 'Runaway Boys', which peaked at number 9 in December 1980. The Stray Cats had two more Top 40 hits with 'Stray Cat Strut', a number 11 in 1981, and '(She's) Sexy + 17', number 29 in 1983.

NOW That's What I Call Drive Answers

1. 'Drive'. The Cars' song originally reached number 5 in 1984, but it recharted and made number 4 in 1985 following its use at Live Aid. R.E.M. made number 11 in 1992, the eighth of thirty-one Top 40 hits.

2. REO Speedwagon. The band from Champaign, Illinois, had their biggest hit with the 1981 number 7 power ballad 'Keep on Loving You'. The pickup truck ceased production in 1936.

3. 'Pink Cadillac'. Bruce's original was the B-side of his 1984 number 4 single 'Dancing in the Dark'. Natalie's version was one of eight Top 40 hits, the biggest being 'Miss You Like Crazy', number 2 in 1989.

4. 'I Drove All Night'. Although Cyndi's version made the charts three years earlier, Roy actually recorded it first but his version remained unreleased until after his death, when it was remixed by Jeff Lynne.

5. Christina Aguilera and Missy Elliott, whose version got to number 4. The original by Rose Royce (a group, not a person) reached number 9, while a 1988 reissue made number 20 and a 1998 remix reached number 18.

6. Shakin' Stevens, who spent four weeks at number 2 in 1981, and Britney Spears, who made number 5 in 1999.

7. Train. The Californian rock group have three additional Top 40 hits, including their 2001 number 10 chart debut 'Drops of Jupiter (Tell Me)'.

8. Jonas Blue featuring Dakota. Tracy Chapman's version peaked at number 5 in 1988 but recharted in 2011, when it reached number 4 after Michael Collings performed the song on series 5 of *Britain's Got Talent*.

9. Amy Grant, whose 1995 version reached number 20, while Joni Mitchell's original made number 11 in 1970. Joni also appeared on Janet Jackson's 1996 number 6 'Got 'til It's Gone', which sampled 'Big Yellow Taxi'.

10. The bus stop. 'Bus Stop' by the Hollies reached number 5 in 1966, the twelfth of their thirty Top 40 hits. A 1975 number 18, '(Are You Ready) Do the Bus Stop' by the Fatback Band, was the second of six Top 40 hits for the group founded by Bill 'Fatback' Curtis.

NOW That's What I Call Love Answers

1. 'How Deep Is Your Love'. Calvin Harris & Disciples reached number 2 in 2015, Dru Hill made number 9 in 1998, while Take That had their eighth number 1 in 1996 with their version of the Bee Gees' 1977 number 3 hit..

2. *Romeo + Juliet*. 'Lovefool' peaked at number 21 when it was first released in 1996, but climbed to number 2 after its inclusion in the Baz Luhrmann film. It was denied the top spot by Olive with 'You're Not Alone'.

3. Des'ree. The ballad 'Delicate' peaked at number 14 and was one of seven Top 40 entries for Des'ree, though that includes the three times that 'You Gotta Be' charted in 1994, 95 and 99.

4. The Mindbenders. The Manchester outfit had been the backing band for singer Wayne Fontana, who left in 1965 to pursue a solo career. Their line-up included Eric Stewart, later a founder member of 10cc.

5. They all had to settle for the number 2 slot while Wet Wet Wet spent fifteen weeks at number 1 with 'Love Is All Around', from the *Four Weddings and a Funeral* soundtrack.

6. Whitesnake. In 1989 singer David Coverdale married actress Tawny Kitaen, who appeared in the videos for their two biggest hits, 'Is This Love' and 'Here I Go Again', which both peaked at number 9 in 1987.

7. Alison Moyet. 'That Ole Devil Called Love' stalled at number 2, held off the top by Philip Bailey and Phil Collins with 'Easy Lover'. Alison previously reached number 2 in 1982, with 'Don't Go' by Yazoo.

8. 'I Will Always Love You'. In addition to Whitney Houston's 1992 number 1, Sarah Washington and Rik Waller have both had Top 40 hit versions, but the original by Dolly Parton has never made the UK chart.

9. Michael Ball. The first of his four Top 40 hits, it was kept from the top first by Simple Minds' only number 1, 'Belfast Child', then by Jason Donovan's first solo number 1, 'Too Many Broken Hearts'.

10. Billy Ocean. 'Caribbean Queen (No More Love on the Run)' reached number 6 for the singer born Leslie Charles. His only number 1 came in 1986 with 'When the Going Gets Tough, the Tough Get Going'.

NOW That's What I Call Football Anthems Answers

1. James Corden, who joined Dizzee Rascal on 'Shout for England', a new version of Tears for Fears' 1984 number 4 hit 'Shout', and Dizzee's fifth number 1 single.

2. 'Carnaval de Paris', which reached number 5 in June 1998. Dario G's other Top 10 hits were 'Sunchyme', number 2 in 1997, and 'Dream to Me', number 9 in 2001.

3. Rod Stewart, who also sang with the Scotland Euro 96 squad on the number 16 single 'Purple Heather'. The Scotland World Cup squad made the Top 10 again in 1982 with 'We Have a Dream'.

4. Pitbull. 'We Are One (Ole Ola)' made number 29 in the UK but reached number 1 in Belgium, Hungary and Switzerland. The song features a co-writing credit for Australian singer Sia Furler.

5. 'Vindaloo' by Fat Les. They also made number 10 in 2000 with a version of 'Jerusalem', though their 2002 single 'Who Invented Fish and Chips?' could only manage a chart peak of number 86.

6. *The Great Escape*. England Supporters Band first released their version of the film theme in 1998, when it reached number 46.

7. Kevin Keegan, who made number 31 in 1979 with 'Head Over Heels in Love'. His England colleagues Glenn Hoddle and Chris Waddle fared better in 1987 when 'Diamond Lights' reached number 12.

8. Spice Girls. '(How Does It Feel to Be) On Top of the World' was the last Spice Girls single to feature Geri Halliwell until their reunion in 2007.

9. 'Anfield Rap (Red Machine in Full Effect)'. In 1996, Liverpool FC with the Boot Room Boyz reached number 4 with their single 'Pass & Move (It's the Liverpool Groove)'.

10. Robbie Williams. 'Three Lions 2010' also featured comedian Russell Brand, the ACM Gospel Choir, soprano Olivia Safe and football commentator John Motson.

NOW That's What I Call Christmas Answers

1. Paul Young. Paul his since stated that the lines were originally intended for David Bowie, who was unable to make the 25 November recording session.

2. Both Christmas classics peaked at number 2 twice. Mariah Carey was stuck behind East 17 in 1994 while Wham! were second best to Band Aid in 1984. In 2017 both songs made it to number 2 again, only to find Ed Sheeran blocking their way with 'Perfect'.

3. The Harlem Community Choir. An estimated thirty children, aged between four and twelve years old, they recorded their contribution on 31 October 1971.

4. Band Aid II. The second version featured Cliff alongside the likes of Bananarama, Big Fun, Bros, Jason Donovan, Kylie Minogue and Wet Wet Wet, and was recorded and produced by Stock, Aitken and Waterman.

5. John Lewis is the real name of Jona Lewie, who spent five weeks at number 3 in December 1980 and January 1981 with his song 'Stop the Cavalry'.

6. Cranberries. 'Christmas Wrapping' failed to chart when first released in 1981, and peaked at number 45 the following year. The Spice Girls recorded a version as the B-side of their 1998 number 1 'Goodbye'.

7. 'Silent Night'. Bing's version reached number 8 in 1952, while Bros made number 2 in 1988. They were denied the top slot by Robin Beck's power ballad 'First Time'.

8. *Donnie Darko*. In 2003 Michael and Gary's version of 'Mad World' kept the slightly more festive 'Christmas Time (Don't Let the Bells End)' by The Darkness at number 2.

9. Joe McElderry, though his debut single – a cover of 'The Climb' by Miley Cyrus – did eventually get to number 1 the week after Christmas.

10. In 1997, 'Too Much' kept the Teletubbies at number 2 with 'Teletubbies Say "Eh-oh!"'. In 1998, 'Goodbye' was number 1 while *South Park*'s Chef was number 2 with 'Chocolate Salty Balls (P.S. I Love You)'.

NOW That's What I Call Disney Answers

1. Miley Cyrus. It was co-written by Miley using her real name Destiny Hope Cyrus, and reached number 11, her best chart position until 'We Can't Stop' made number 1 in 2013.

2. 'Circle of Life', which reached number 11 and was Elton's fiftieth Top 40 hit. Elton wrote the music for five original songs featured in *The Lion King*, with lyrics by Tim Rice.

3. *Frozen*. The film won the Academy Award for Best Animated Feature and Best Original Song ('Let It Go'). In 1998 'Frozen' became Madonna's eighth number 1, after a gap of eight years since 'Vogue' in April 1990.

4. Bryan Adams, Rod Stewart and Sting. 'All for Love' reached number 2 in January 1994 but was beaten to the top spot by D:Ream's 'Things Can Only Get Better'.

5. 'Beauty and the Beast'. The film theme, sung by Celine Dion and Peabo Bryson, reached number 9 in 1992, while the David Bowie song peaked at number 39 in February 1978 and was his twentieth Top 40 hit.

6. Randy Newman. The acclaimed songwriter received the Academy Award for Best Original Song in 2001 for 'If I Didn't Have You' from *Monsters Inc.*, and in 2010 for 'We Belong Together' from *Toy Story 3*.

7. Justin Timberlake, who appeared on *The All New Mickey Mouse Club* between 1993 and 1994 in a cast that included Britney Spears, Ryan Gosling and Christina Aguilera.

8. 'When You Wish Upon a Star'. The original version was performed by American singer Cliff Edwards in the character of Jiminy Cricket. Disney's 1940 animation also won the Academy Award for Best Original Score.

9. 'That's What Friends Are For'. The 'friends' appearing with Dionne Warwick were Elton John, Gladys Knight and Stevie Wonder. Disney's four vultures all have 'mop-top' haircuts and Liverpudlian accents.

10. 'Tramp'. Otis and Carla reached number 18, while Salt-N-Pepa's version peaked at number 2. The cast of *Lady and the Tramp* included Peggy Lee, who had a number 5 hit in 1958 with 'Fever'.

NOW That's What I Call Old Skool Answers

1. Run-D.M.C. The single featured Steven Tyler and Joe Perry of Aerosmith, who wrote and originally recorded the song in 1975, though the Aerosmith version failed to chart in the UK.

2. Haitian. In 2010 Wyclef Jean attempted to run for president of Haiti, but his bid was rejected, as he hadn't been resident in the country for the previous five years.

3. 'Creep'. The TLC song made number 22 in 1995 and was the second of their ten Top 40 hits. Two years earlier Radiohead made their chart debut and reached number 7 with their song of the same name.

4. Grandmaster Flash and the Furious Five. The influential group had one of the first hip-hop hits with their 1982 number 8 'The Message', while 'White Lines (Don't Do It)' was a number 7 hit for Grandmaster Flash and Melle Mel in 1983.

5. OutKast with 'Hey Ya!' The second Top 40 hit for the duo from Atlanta, Georgia, it stalled one place short of their previous chart best, the 2001 number 2 'Ms. Jackson'.

6. Dido. Eminem's second number 1 sampled Dido's song 'Thank You', subsequently a number 3 single for her in February 2001. Rihanna also sampled 'Thank You' for her 2016 song 'Never Ending'.

7. LL Cool J, or Ladies Love Cool James – known to his mother as

James Smith. He had his biggest hit in 1997 with the number 1 single 'Ain't Nobody', originally a number 8 hit for Rufus and Chaka Khan in 1984.

8. A Tribe Called Quest and 'Can I Kick It?' The single uses the bass line from Lou Reed's 'Walk on the Wild Side' and dialogue from *SuperTed,* voiced by former *Doctor Who* and *Worzel Gummidge* actor Jon Pertwee.

9. Dr. Dre. The artist born Andre Young first had success with rap group N.W.A., and has since won six Grammy Awards, including Best Rap Performance for the 2000 number 7 with Eminem 'Forget About Dre'.

10. 'Another Day in Paradise'. It was Brandy's seventh Top 40 hit and the first for her brother Ray J. In 1990, German dance group Jam Tronik had their only Top 40 hit when their version reached number 19.

NOW That's What I Call Musicals Answers

1. Susan Boyle sang with Peter Kay, the latter as his alter ego Geraldine McQueen. 'I Know Him So Well' is from the 1984 musical *Chess*, and was a number 1 single that year for Elaine Paige and Barbara Dickson.

2. *Whistle Down the Wind*. The title song from the musical, written by Andrew Lloyd Webber with Jim Steinman, also gave Australian singer Tina Arena her fourth and most recent Top 40 hit.

3. Captain Sensible of the Damned with 'Happy Talk'. Born Raymond Burns, the good Captain had two more solo Top 40 hits, including the 1984 number 6 'Glad It's All Over'.

4. 'Another Suitcase in Another Hall', which reached number 7 in March 1997. It was originally a number 18 hit for Barbara Dickson in 1977, and the second of her four Top 40 hits.

5. 'The Time Warp'. In 1989 it was third time lucky for Damian – his version was originally released in 1987 when it peaked at number 51, and then stuck at number 64 the following year.

6. *Carousel*. 'You'll Never Walk Alone' also provided a number 35 hit for The Three Tenors in 1998, while Pink Floyd incorporated a rendition by Liverpool FC supporters on the song 'Fearless' from their 1971 album 'Meddle'.

7. Jennifer Hudson, who won the 2006 Academy Award for Best Supporting Actress for her role in *Dreamgirls*. She had her biggest hit in 2015 when she featured on the number 7 single 'Trouble' by Iggy Azalea.

8. 'Living Doll'. It first made number 1 for Cliff and the Drifters (as the Shadows were then known) in August 1959, and topped the chart again for Cliff and the Young Ones in 1986.

9. Jay-Z with 'Hard Knock Life (Ghetto Anthem)', which sampled 'It's the Hard Knock Life'. Mike Myers covered it in the 2002 movie *Austin Powers in Goldmember*, co-starring Beyoncé, Jay-Z's wife.

10. *Joseph and the Amazing Technicolor Dreamcoat*. In 2007 'Any Dream Will Do' also gave Lee Mead his only Top 40 hit after he won the BBC TV talent show named after the song.

NOW That's What I Call Mum Answers

1. Paul Simon. The first of ten Top 40 solo hits for Paul. Backing singers on this song included Cissy Houston, mother of Whitney Houston.

2. 'Hey Mama'. This was the fourth Top 40 hit for Black Eyed Peas and an extraordinary twenty-eighth for French DJ David Guetta.

3. 'Have You Seen Your Mother, Baby, Standing in the Shadow?' The song features a brass section, arranged by Mike Leander, who was responsible for orchestral arrangements on The Beatles' 'She's Leaving Home'.

4. Michelle Phillips of the Mamas and the Papas. Chynna's father John Phillips was also a member of the same group.

5. 'Mama Do the Hump'. The video for Rizzle Kicks' fourth Top 40 single featured Jordan 'Rizzle' Stephens's mother and aunt miming the rap, along with a cameo appearance by James Corden.

6. Tears for Fears. The band have seventeen Top 40 hits, including the 1985 number 2 'Everybody Wants to Rule the World', but have never had a number 1 single.

7. Boney M. 'Ma Baker' was the third of sixteen top 40 hits, a total that includes the 1978 number 1 singles 'Mary's Boy Child' and the double A-Side 'Rivers of Babylon' / 'Brown Girl in the Ring'.

8. Stereophonics. Their version with Tom made number 4 while the Three Dog Night version peaked at number 3. Three Dog Night's only other Top 40 entry was 'Joy to the World', which reached number 24 in 1971.

9. 'Stacy's Mom'. The single reached number 11 and was the band's third Top 40 hit. The video featured model Rachel Hunter, former wife of Rod Stewart, in the title role.

10. Dr Hook and the Medicine Show. 'Sylvia's Mother' reached number 2, as did their next hit, 'A Little Bit More' in 1976. They finally made number 1 in 1979 with 'When You're in Love with a Beautiful Woman'.

NOW That's What I Call Dad Answers

1. Ronan Keating. Boyzone's version of 'Father and Son' reached number 2 in 1995; Ronan then teamed up with the song's writer, now known as Yusuf, for a new version and another number 2 hit in 2004.

2. 'Daddy Cool'. It was the first of sixteen Top 40 singles for Boney M, including the 1978 Christmas number 1, 'Mary's Boy Child'. Darts had eight Top 40 hits, including three consecutive singles that stalled at number 2.

3. Jim Gilstrap. The Texan singer is also the first voice heard on Stevie Wonder's 1973 number 7, 'You Are The Sunshine of My Life', where

he sings the opening two lines.

4. Black Grape. The band featuring former Happy Mondays singer Shaun Ryder had their biggest hit in June 1996 when 'England's Irie' reached number 6.

5. George Michael. His run of Top 3 hits between 1984 and 1987 featured four number 1s with Wham! and three as a solo artist, including his 1984 solo debut 'Careless Whisper', which includes a co-writing credit for Andrew Ridgeley.

6. Pigbag with 'Papa's Got a Brand New Pigbag'. In 1965 'Papa's Got a Brand New Bag' was the first of eleven Top 40 hits for James Brown, the biggest being the 1986 number 5 'Living in America'.

7. 'Daddy's Home'. It was also the forty-seventh single by Cliff to make it into the Top 10, where it spent four weeks at number 2 in December 1981, stuck behind 'Don't You Want Me' by the Human League.

8. Natalie Cole, who reached number 19 with a version of 'Unforgettable', a song made famous by her father Nat 'King' Cole. Elements of his original vocal were added to a new recording to make a 'virtual duet'.

9. Father Abraham and the Smurfs. They made their chart debut in June 1978 with 'The Smurf Song', which spent six weeks at number 2, and they reached number 19 in December with 'Christmas in Smurfland'.

10. Papa Roach. The Californian rock quartet had their first and biggest hit with 'Last Resort' in February 2001, when it entered the chart at number 3.

NOW That's What I Call Smash Hits Answers

1. Five Star. Six of siblings Delroy, Denise, Doris, Lorraine and Stedman Preston's singles made the Top 10, including their biggest hit 'Rain or Shine', a 1986 number 2.

2. Thompson Twins. Their ten Top 40 singles include the 1984 number 2 'You Take Me Up'. On 13 July 1985 they joined Madonna onstage in Philadelphia for her song 'Love Makes the World Go Round'.

3. 'Hang On in There Baby'. It matched the chart peak of Johnny Bristol's original version, and equalled Curiosity Killed the Cat's previous best, the 1986 number 3 'Down to Earth'.

4. Paul Heaton. With The Housemartins ho had a December 1986 number 1 with 'Caravan of Love', and with The Beautiful South he topped the chart in October 1990 with 'A Little Time'.

5. Blondie. 'Heart of Glass' and 'Sunday Girl' in 1979 were followed by 'Atomic', 'Call Me' and 'The Tide Is High' in 1980. In February 1999 they returned to the top with 'Maria'.

6. 'Ant Music'. Adam and the Ants' original version spent two weeks at number 2 in January 1981, when it was kept off the top by John Lennon's 'Imagine', which recharted following his death on 8 December 1980.

7. Gary Kemp of Spandau Ballet. In 1990, Gary starred alongside brother Martin in *The Krays*, and in 1992 he featured in *The Bodyguard* with Whitney Houston and Kevin Costner.

8. Bronski Beat. They made their chart debut in 1984 with the number 3 hit 'Smalltown Boy', featuring original singer Jimmy Somerville. Following his departure they had a fifth Top 40 hit when 'Hit That Perfect Beat' also peaked at number 3.

9. Mel and Kim. The Appleby sisters spent one week at number 1 in March 1987 with 'Respectable', the first chart-topper both written and produced by Mike Stock, Matt Aitken and Pete Waterman.

10. Pepsi and Shirlie. The former Wham! singers had one more Top 40 hit with 'Goodbye Stranger', also in 1987. In 2000 the duo sang backing vocals on Geri Halliwell's third solo number 1, 'Bag It Up'.

NOW That's What I Call Chilled Answers

1. Georgia, or the Georgian Soviet Socialist Republic, as it was when Katie was born in Kutaisi in September 1984.

2. *American Beauty*. Jakatta, an alias for DJ Dave Lee, sampled 'American Dream' and 'Dead Again' from the film score, together with 'Two of Hearts', a 1986 dance single by Stacey Q that only made number 86.

3. 'Please, Please, Please, Let Me Get What I Want'. The version by Slow Moving Millie, aka Amelia Warner, made number 31 in December after it featured in the John Lewis Christmas advert.

4. 'At the River' by Groove Armada. The vocal is sampled from 'Old Cape Cod', a 1957 song by Patti Page. Patti's only UK Top 40 hit was the 1953 number 9 '(How Much Is) That Doggie in the Window?'.

5. David Byrne. It was the third of four Top 40 hits for X-Press 2 and the biggest hit for both them and David, whose previous best was Talking Heads' 1985 number 6 'Road to Nowhere'.

6. 'Stay with Me'. Sam Smith's song spent a week at number 1 in 2014, while The Faces reached number 6 in 1971, The Mission reached number 30 in 1985, and Erasure reached number 15 in 1995.

7. Dido, or Dido Florian Cloud de Bounevialle O'Malley Armstrong, to use her full name. 'One Step Too Far' peaked at number 6 in April 2002, and was the band's thirteenth Top 40 hit.

8. Ellie Goulding. 'How Long Will I Love You?' made number 3 for Ellie in November 2013, after it featured in the Richard Curtis film *About Time*. The Waterboys version didn't make the chart.

9. Neneh Cherry, whose first chart success was the 1988 number 3 'Buffalo Stance'. Youssou first made the chart when he partnered with Peter Gabriel on the 1989 number 57 single 'Shakin' the Tree'.

10. Gorgon City. Their 2013 debut single 'Intentions' featured chart-toppers Clean Bandit but failed to reach the Top 100, and they had their biggest hit with the 2014 number 4 'Ready For Your Love', featuring MNEK.

NOW That's What I Call a Party Answers

1. The Gap Band. They made their chart debut in 1980 with the number 6 hit 'Oops Upside Your Head', and the same song recharted and reached number 16 in 2004, when the trio featured on a new version by DJ Casper .

2. Rita Ora. In February 2012, she was the featured artist on the DJ Fresh number 1, 'Hot Right Now', and just three months later she was back on top with Tinie Tempa and 'R.I.P.'. That August, she had a third spell at the top when, 'How We Do (Party)' spent one week at number 1.

3. Lesley Gore. Her version of 'It's My Party' was produced by Quincy Jones, who was also responsible for Frank Sinatra's *Sinatra at the Sands* album and composed the soundtrack to the 1969 film *The Italian Job*.

4. 'The Boston Tea Party'. The third of three Top 40 singles, it peaked at number 13. The band made their chart debut in 1975 with a number 7 cover version of Tom Jones's 1968 number 2 'Delilah'.

5. 'We Like to Party! (The Vengabus)'. The exclamation-mark loving Dutch pop group followed this single with their two chart-toppers, 'Boom, Boom, Boom, Boom!!' and 'We're Going to Ibiza!'

6. Shania Twain, for whom it was the twelfth of thirteen consecutive Top 40 hits. Her biggest hits came in 1999, when 'That Don't Impress Me Much' and 'Man! I Feel Like a Woman!' both peaked at number 3.

7. Status Quo. They made their chart debut in 1968 with the number 7 single 'Pictures of Matchstick Men' and had Top 20 hits in the 1970s, 80s, 90s and 2000s, including their only number 1, 'Down Down' in 1974.

8. Lisa 'Left Eye' Lopes. Although 'The Block Party' was the only solo hit for the singer who died in 2001, she was a featured artist on Top 40 singles by Lil' Kim, Melanie C and Donell Jones.

9. Pianist Winifred Atwell, whose fifteen Top 40 hits include the two number 1 singles 'Let's Have Another Party' in 1954 and 'The Poor People of Paris' in 1956.

10. 'Grandma's Party' was a number 9 hit, and the second of four Top 40 singles, for Paul Nicholas, while 'Grandpa's Party' reached number 16 for Monie Love, the second of her nine Top 40 hits.

NOW That's What I Call a Good Year Answers

NOW That's What I Call a Good Year Answers

The year revealed (and weeks at number 1 in brackets).

1. 2016 – 'Love Yourself' by Justin Bieber (3 weeks), '7 Years' by Lukas Graham (5 weeks) and 'Shout Out to My Ex' by Little Mix (3 weeks).

2. 1960 – 'My Old Man's a Dustman' by Lonnie Donegan (4 weeks),

'Three Steps to Heaven' by Eddie Cochran (2 weeks) and 'Shakin' All Over' by Johnny Kidd & the Pirates (1 week).

3. 1991 – 'Bring Your Daughter ... to the Slaughter' by Iron Maiden (2 weeks), 'Should I Stay or Should I Go' by The Clash (2 weeks) and 'I Wanna Sex You Up' by Color Me Badd (3 weeks).

4. 1973 – 'Cum on Feel the Noize' (4 weeks), 'Skweeze Me Pleeze Me' (3 weeks) and 'Merry Xmas Everybody' (5 weeks), all by Slade.

5. 2000 – 'American Pie' by Madonna (1 week), 'We Will Rock You' by Five & Queen (1 week) and 'Against All Odds' by Mariah Carey featuring Westlife (2 weeks).

6. 1987 – 'Stand by Me' by Ben E. King (3 weeks), 'Star Trekkin'' by the Firm (2 weeks) and 'You Win Again' by Bee Gees (4 weeks).

7. 1967 – 'I'm a Believer' by The Monkees (4 weeks), 'Somethin' Stupid' by Nancy and Frank Sinatra (2 weeks), and 'The Last Waltz' by Engelbert Humperdinck (5 weeks).

8. 2010 – 'Fireflies' by Owl City (3 weeks), 'Good Times' by Roll Deep (3 weeks) and 'Start Without You' by Alexandra Burke featuring Laza Morgan (2 weeks).

9. 1997 – 'MMMBop' by Hanson (3 weeks), 'Barbie Girl' by Aqua (4 weeks) and 'Teletubbies Say "Eh-oh!"' by Teletubbies (2 weeks).

10. 1980 – 'Coward of the County' by Kenny Rogers (2 weeks), 'Theme from M*A*S*H (Suicide Is Painless)' by MASH (3 weeks) and 'Xanadu' by Olivia Newton-John and Electric Light Orchestra (2 weeks).

NOW That's What I Call Summer Hits Answers

1. Simple Minds. The band had a number 1 single in the US in 1984 with 'Don't You (Forget About Me)' but had to wait another three years for their only UK number 1, 'Belfast Child'.

2. Mungo Jerry, with 'In the Summertime'. The band's name was inspired by the poem 'Mungojerrie and Rumpleteazer', from T.S. Eliot's *Old Possum's Book of Practical Cats.*

3. Demi Lovato. It gave the former *Barney & Friends* actor her seventh Top 40 hit when it peaked at number 7 in September 2015.

4. 'Summertime'. In 2012 the *New York Times* reported that the song has been recorded more than 25,000 times, though only Fun Boy Three and a 1966 soul rendition by Billy Stewart have made the UK Top 40.

5. 'Hello Summertime', which reached number 14 in August 1974. Bobby's biggest hit is the tearjerker 'Honey', which reached number 2 in 1967 and again in 1975.

6. DJ Sammy, whose four Top 40 hits include the 2002 number 1 'Heaven', with Yanou and featuring Do. Don Henley only has one other Top 40 solo hit, but he is co-writer of the Eagles' biggest hit, 'Hotel California'.

7. Manic Street Preachers, whose single reached number 22 in October 2007, and Stereophonics, whose single reached number 30 in March 2013.

8. 'Summer in the City' by Lovin' Spoonful. One of just three Top 40 singles for the New York band, the others were the 1966 number 2 'Daydream' and 'Nashville Cats, a number 26 hit in 1967.

9. Ace of Base. The Bananarama original also peaked at number 8, in August 1983, while their 1989 rerecording – renamed 'Cruel Summer '89' – reached number 19.

10. Summertime City'. Credited to Mike Batt with the New Edition, it was the theme to the BBC television series *Seaside Special*.

NOW That's What I Call a Wedding Answers

1. Busted. The pop trio's other chart-toppers were 'You Said No' in May 2003, 'Who's David' in February 2004 and the double A-side 'Thunderbirds'/'3AM' in August 2004.

2. The Dixie Cups. Elton John covered 'Chapel of Love' for the 1994 film *Four Weddings and a Funeral*, and in 1982 the Dixie Cups' only other hit, 'Iko Iko', made the Top 40 for both singer Natasha and all-female septet The Belle Stars.

3. 'White Wedding'. One of ten Top 40 solo singles for Billy Idol, it reached number 6 in 1985, as did the follow-up, a reissue of his 1984 single 'Rebel Yell', which had originally peaked at number 62.

4. 'Wedding Bells'. The former 10cc members also directed some high-profile music videos, including 'Girls on Film' by Duran Duran, 'Two Tribes' by Frankie Goes to Hollywood and 'Fade to Grey' by Visage.

5. 'Shotgun Wedding'. The original by one-hit wonder Roy C made number 6 in 1966, and number 8 when reissued in 1972. Rod's 1993 version made number 21 and was his thirty-ninth Top 40 single.

6. 'Take Me to Church'. The single spent four weeks at number 2, but was kept from the top spot first by Mark Ronson featuring Bruno Mars with 'Uptown Funk' and then by Ellie Goulding with 'Love Me Like You Do'.

7. Meghan Trainor. Her chart debut 'All About the Bass' spent four weeks at number 1 in October 2014, and she had a second chart-topper in August 2015 with the song 'Marvin Gaye', a duet with Charlie Puth.

8. The Beautiful South. The band made their chart debut with the 1989 number 2 'Song for Whoever', and had their only number 1 the following October when 'A Little Time' spent a week at the top.

9. Dave Edmunds, who made number 1 with his 1970 debut single 'I Hear You Knocking'. 'I Knew the Bride' was written by Nick Lowe, while Dave's 1979 number 4 hit 'Girls Talk' was written by Elvis Costello.

10. 'You Never Can Tell'. Chuck Berry's eighth Top 40 hit, it peaked at number 18 in 1964 and reached a new audience thirty years later when it was used in Quentin Tarantino's film *Pulp Fiction*.

NOW That's What I Call Weather Answers

1. Bitty McLean. His version of Fats Domino's 1961 single 'It Keeps Rainin'' spent two weeks at number 2 in September 1993 but was kept from the top spot by Culture Beat with 'Mr. Vain'.

2. Thunderclap Newman. The Who's Pete Townshend produced 'Something In The Air' for the trio that included guitarist Jimmy McCulloch, a member of Paul McCartney's band Wings between 1974 and 1977.

3. 'Sandstorm'. The Cast single reached number 8 in January 1996, the third of their eleven Top 40 singles. Darude made his chart debut with the instrumental 'Sandstorm' in June 2000, the first of three Top 40 hits.

4. Lemon Jelly. 'Nice Weather for Ducks' was the third of their five Top 40 hits. At the 2003 Mercury Music Prize, *Lost Horizons* lost out to *Boy in da Corner* by Dizzee Rascal.

5. 'Wind Beneath My Wings'. Bill Tarmey, *Coronation Street*'s Jack Duckworth, reached number 40 in 1994, while Steven Houghton, who played Gregg Blake in *London's Burning*, reached number 3 in 1997.

6. The Fortunes. They made their chart debut in 1965 with 'You've Got Your Troubles', which stalled at number 2 while the top spot was occupied by The Beatles with their eighth number 1, 'Help!'.

7. The Alarm. The band began life as a punk group called The Toilets, before a change of name and fortune saw them score their Top 40 debut and biggest hit with the 1983 number 17 'Sixty Eight Guns'.

8. Crowded House, who reached number 7 in March 1992 with 'Weather with You'. Their twelve Top 40 hits also include 'Four Seasons in One Day', number 26 in 1992, and 'Distant Sun', number 19 in 1993.

9. East Side Beat, whose version of 'Ride Like the Wind' reached number 3 in November 1991. The band had one more Top 40 hit the following year with a dance version of the Simple Minds song 'Alive and Kicking'.

10. 'Little Fluffy Clouds' by The Orb. It was the third of their eight Top 40 hits, the biggest of which was 'Toxygene', which peaked at number 4 in February 1997.

NOW That's What I Call a Summer Party Answers

1. The Eagles. Their biggest single was the 1977 number 8 'Hotel California', the title track of an album that has now sold over 32 million copies worldwide, while *Their Greatest Hits (1971–1975)* album has sold 40 million copies.

2. 'Canned Heat'. It was the fourteenth Top 40 hit for Jamiroquai, while the band Canned Heat had three Top 40 singles, including the 1968 number 8 'On the Road Again', and 'Going Up The Country', number 19 in 1969.

3. Heatwave, who had their biggest hit in March 1977, when 'Boogie

Nights' reached number 2. Songwriter Rod Temperton later wrote successfully for other musicians, including George Benson's biggest hit, the 1980 number 7 'Give Me The Night'.

4. 'Long Hot Summer'. It was the ninth of twenty-two Top 40 hits for Girls Aloud, twenty-one of which peaked in the Top 10. The Style Council song of the same name gave them their biggest hit in 1983, when it reached number 3.

5. Donovan. 'Sunshine Superman' spent one week at number 2 in December 1966 but was held off the top spot by Tom Jones's 'Green, Green Grass of Home', though it did reach number 1 for one week in the US.

6. James Arthur. 'Sun Comes Up' peaked at number 6 in August 2017 and was James's sixth Top 40 entry. Both he and Rudimental made number 1 with their debut singles, 'Impossible' and 'Feel the Love' respectively.

7. The Kinks. They made their 1964 chart debut with the number 1 hit 'You Really Got Me', topped the chart again in 1965 with 'Tired of Waiting for You', before 'Sunny Afternoon' completed the hat-trick in 1966.

8. Tracey Ullman. All five of Tracey's Top 40 hits were cover versions. Country singer Skeeter Davis originally recorded 'Sunglasses', while Tracey's biggest hit, 'They Don't Know', was a Kirsty MacColl song.

9. York. Despite the band name, the dance duo, brothers Torsten and Jörg Stenzel, actually came from Germany. Chris Rea first released 'On the Beach' in 1986, when it peaked at number 57.

10. Elkie Brooks, who had made her chart debut with the 1977 number 8 single 'Pearl's a Singer' and had her biggest hit in 1986 with the number 5 'No More the Fool'.

NOW That's What I Call Halloween Answers

1. Vincent Price. In 1975 Vincent provided a similar service to Alice Cooper, recording a vocal for his number 19 album *Welcome to My Nightmare*.

2. 'Black Magic'. Their 2015 single spent three weeks at the top, a position they previously held with their 2011 debut 'Cannonball' and its 2012 follow-up 'Wings'.

3. Charlie Daniels Band. The single made number 3 in the US, its popularity helped by its inclusion in the John Travolta film *Urban Cowboy*.

4. The Cranberries. The third of their nine Top 40 hits, in 2014 it was covered by A.D.A.M. featuring Amy, whose dance version reached number 16.

5. allSTARS*. Their second Top 40 single was a double A-side release combining 'Things That Go Bump In The Night' with their cover of Duran Duran's 1983 number 1 'Is There Something I Should Know?'.

6. Landscape. It was the follow-up to their number 5 hit 'Einstein a Go-

'Go'. Landscape's frontman Richard Burgess had a successful career as a producer, including Spandau Ballet's 1980 debut 'To Cut a Long Story Short'.

7. Annie Lennox. Her sixth Top 40 single as a solo artist, it was released as a double A-side with 'Little Bird'. The cover of Lennox's 1992 Album, 'Diva' pictured her wearing an extravagant headdress that was previously a costume for the James Bond film *Octopussy*.

8. '(Waiting For) The Ghost-Train'. Reaching number 18 in November 1986, this was the band's twenty-third consecutive Top 40 single.

9. 'Jack and Jill'. Raydio managed one further Top 40 hit in 1978 with the number 27 single 'Is This a Love Thing'.

10. Beatfreakz. The Dutch house-music group had one further Top 40 hit that year, when they made number 7 with a cover of the Rick James song 'Superfreak'.

NOW That's What I Call Winter Answers

1. Madonna. 'Frozen' was her eighth number 1 single, and her first since 'Vogue' in 1990. Madonna wrote 'Frozen' with Patrick Leonard, who helped out on her previous number 1s 'Like a Prayer' and 'Cherish'.

2. 'Cold As Ice', which peaked at number 4 in May 2001 for M.O.P., who also reached number 7 that August with 'Ante Up'. Foreigner had their biggest in 1984 when 'I Want to Know What Love Is' spent three weeks at number 1.

3. Bomb the Bass. The name was an alias for British DJ and producer Tim Simenon, who co-produced and is mentioned in the lyrics of Neneh Cherry's 1988 number 3 'Buffalo Stance'.

4. 'Shiver'. George Benson reached number 19 with his thirteenth Top 40 single, Natalie Imbruglia peaked at number 8 with her eighth, while Coldplay had their very first Top 40 hit when they reached number 35.

5. The Four Seasons. It was the only UK number 1 for the US quartet, who first charted in 1962 with the number 8 single 'Sherry'. Lead singer Frankie Valli had a solo number 3 in 1978 with the theme from *Grease*.

6. 'The Freeze'. It was the second of three singles taken from their debut album *Journeys to Glory*, along with 'Muscle Bound', which peaked at number 10 in May 1981.

7. Wizzard. 'Rock 'n' Roll Winter' was the follow-up to 'I Wish It Could Be Christmas Everyday', which spent four weeks at number 4 in December 1973, and re-entered the Top 40 in 1984 and 2007.

8. 'A Winter's Tale'. David Essex's sixteenth Top 40 single was only denied number 1 by Phil Collins's 'You Can't Hurry Love', famously the very first track on the very first NOW album, issued in November 1983.

9. Gabriella Cilmi. Her version reached number 22 in December 2008, while Connie Francis's original could only manage number 48,

though she did record versions in French and Japanese to improve international appeal.

10. 'A Hazy Shade of Winter'. The Bangles' version reached number 11 in March 1988. Simon & Garfunkel's version failed to chart when it was first released in 1966, but eventually reached number 30 in 1990.

NOW That's What I Call A Brainteaser Answers

NOW That's What I Call NOW! Answers

1. b) Tracey Ullman. Alongside the eleven number 1 singles on the first volume was Tracey's biggest hit, 'They Don't Know', written by Kirsty MacColl, who made her own first appearance as an artist on *NOW 10* in 1987.

2. c) They have never had a number 1 single. Shania's best showing to date is three weeks at number 3 with 'That Don't Impress Me Much'; Amy spent one week at number 2 when she featured on Mark Ronson's version of 'Valerie'; and Janet spent two weeks at number 2 with her duet with Luther Vandross, 'The Best Things in Life Are Free'.

3. b) The song title doesn't get mentioned in the lyrics. Other examples of this 'phenomenon' include Nirvana's 'Smells Like Teen Spirit', David Bowie's 'Space Oddity' and Blur's 'Song 2'.

4. c) They all had three brothers in the band. The Christians had Garry, Roger and Russell Christian; INXS had Andrew, Jon and Tim Farriss; while Kings of Leon have Jared, Nathan and Caleb Followill in their ranks.

5. a) Different sunglasses. The stylish individual wore grey sunglasses on *NOW 3*, green tints on *4* and pink wraparound shades on *5*. He (voiced by actor Brian Glover, so we will presume he was male) made occasional reappearances, notably on *NOW… 30 Years* in 2013 and *NOW 100* in 2018.

6. b) It is the only *NOW* album to include any of The Beatles' singles. *NOW: The Summer Album* included their 1967 single 'All You Need Is Love' plus 'Here Comes the Sun' from the 1969 *Abbey Road* album. There have been lots of cover versions of The Beatles' songs on *NOW*, including two for Wet Wet Wet – 'With a Little Help from My Friends' and 'Yesterday'.

7. a) One of the stars of each film has appeared on a *NOW* album. Kate Winslet appeared on *NOW 50* with 'What If', which made number 6 in December 2001; Ewan McGregor featured on the PF Project number 6 single 'Choose Life', which first appeared on *NOW Dance 97*; and Nicole Kidman had a number 1 hit when she duetted with Robbie Williams on 'Somethin' Stupid' on *NOW 51*.

8. a) They have all appeared on a *NOW* album and so has one of their children. Bob Marley and the Wailers made their first appearance on

NOW 3 with 'One Love/People Get Ready', while his son Damien 'Jr. Gong' Marley appeared on NOW 62 with 'Welcome to Jamrock', and his grandson Skip Marley featured on Katy Perry's single 'Chained to the Rhythm' on NOW 96. Billy Ray Cyrus's 'Achy Breaky Heart' made its first appearance on NOW 23, while daughter Miley first popped up on NOW 76 with 'Can't Be Tamed'. John Lennon's first solo appearance came on NOW 45 with 'Imagine', but son Julian appeared way back on NOW 4 with 'Too Late for Goodbyes'.

9. b) They were also number 1 for a different artist, on a different volume of NOW. Boyzone's version of 'When the Going Gets Tough ...' first appeared on NOW 42, Bob the Builder's version of 'Mambo No. 5' graced NOW 50, while Gabrielle Aplin's rendition of 'The Power of Love' was one of two songs by her on NOW 84.

10. b and c) They all included a different singer with vocals in a different language. 'Encore Une Fois' features Sabine Ohmes and includes French vocals; 'Ecuador' features Rodriguez with Spanish vocals; 'Stay' features La Trec with vocals in English; and 'La Primavera' features Patrizia Salvatore and includes Italian vocals.

NOW That's What I Call a Challenge Answers

1. 'Human'. A hit for the Human League on NOW 8, the Killers on NOW 72 and Rag'n'Bone Man on NOW 96. In 1986, 'Human' gave the Human League their second US number 1, following 'Don't You Want Me' in 1982.

2. 'Stop'. A hit for Sam Brown on NOW 14, Spice Girls on NOW 39 and Jamelia on NOW 59. Sam Brown had three Top 40 singles between 1986 and 1989; eight less than her father Joe between 1960 and 73 but one more than her mother Vicki, singer with The Vernons Girls, between 1962 and '63.

3. 'Sing'. A hit for Travis on NOW 50, Gary Barlow and the Commonwealth Band on NOW 82 and Ed Sheeran on NOW 88. 'Sing' gave Glasgow band Travis their biggest hit when it entered the chart at number 3 in July 2001.

4. 'Only You'. A hit for Flying Pickets on NOW 2, Praise on NOW 19, and Cheat Codes and Little Mix on NOW 100. Flying Pickets' founder Brian Hibbard also had a successful acting career, appearing in Coronation Street, Emmerdale and in the Doctor Who story 'Delta and the Bannermen'.

5. 'Paradise'. A hit for Kaci on NOW 48, Coldplay on NOW 81 and George Ezra on NOW 99. American singer Kaci Battaglia had two more Top 40 hits, including the 2002 number 10 'I Think I Love You', originally a 1971 number 18 for the Partridge Family.

6. 'Pray'. A hit for MC Hammer on NOW 19, Take That on NOW 26 and Lasgo on NOW 53. A 1990 number 8 hit, 'Pray' was the second of six

Top 40 hits for MC Hammer, and samples the 1984 Prince hit 'When Doves Cry' and Faith No More's 1988 single 'We Care a Lot'.

7. 'In Too Deep'. A hit for Dead or Alive on *NOW 5*, Genesis on *NOW 8*, Belinda Carlisle on *NOW 34* and Sum 41 on *NOW 51*. Genesis had twenty-one Top 40 hits, spending 118 weeks in the chart, but never got higher than the number 4 peak of their 1983 single 'Mama'.

8. 'Stronger'. A hit for Britney Spears on *NOW 48*, Sugababes on *NOW 54*, Kanye West on *NOW 68* and Clean Bandit on *NOW 91*. The Sugababes' 2002 number 7 was a double A-side release, coupled with 'Angels with Dirty Faces' – also the title of a 1978 number 19 single by punk band Sham 69.

9. 'Shine'. A hit for Aswad on *NOW 28*, the Lovefreekz on *NOW 60*, for Take That and for Booty Luv, both on *NOW 67*, and Years & Years on *NOW 91*. Aswad's 1994 number 8 single 'Shine' was remixed by the Beatmasters, who had four Top 40 singles and made their first NOW appearance on *NOW 11*.

10. 'Stay'. A hit for Shakespears Sister on *NOW 21*, Eternal on *NOW 26*, Sash! featuring La Trec on *NOW 38*, Kygo featuring Maty Noyes on *NOW 93* and Zedd & Alessia Cara on *NOW 96*. Shakespears Sister singer Siobhan Fahey co-wrote The Bluebells' 1993 number 1 single 'Young at Heart'.

NOW That's Who I Call ...? Answers

1. Timbaland was born Timothy Mosley in Norfolk, Virginia, on 10 March 1972. He made his Top 40 debut with 'Get on the Bus' by Destiny's Child featuring Timbaland, which reached number 15 in January 1999.

2. Moby was born Richard Melville Hall in Harlem, New York, on 11 September 1965. He made his Top 40 debut with 'Go', which reached number 10 in November 1991.

3. Seal was born Samuel Henry Adeola in Paddington, London, on 19 February 1963. He made his Top 40 debut with 'Killer' by Adamski (born Adam Tinley in 1967) featuring Seal, which spent four weeks at number 1 in May 1990.

4. Cee Lo Green was born Thomas Callaway in Atlanta, Georgia, on 30 May 1975. He made his Top 40 debut with 'Lil Star' by Kelis featuring Cee-Lo, which reached number 3 in March 2007.

5. Shania Twain was born Eilleen Edwards in Windsor, Ontario, on 28 August 1965. Taken from her chart-topping album *Come on Over*, 'You're Still the One' was her Top 40 debut, reaching number 10 in February 1998.

6. Lana Del Rey was born Elizabeth Woolridge Grant in New York City on 21 June 1985. She made her Top 40 debut with 'Video Games', which reached number 9 in October 2011.

7. Stormzy was born Michael Owuo Jr. in Thornton Heath, London, on 26 July 1993. He made his Top 40 debut with 'Shut Up', which reached number 8 in December 2015.

8. will.i.am was born William Adams Jr. in Los Angeles, California, on 15 March 1975. A founding member of the Black Eyed Peas, he

made his Top 40 solo debut with 'Beep' by Pussycat Dolls featuring will.i.am, which reached number 2 in March 2006.

9. Katy Perry was born Katheryn Hudson in Santa Barbara, California, on 25 October 1984. She made her Top 40 debut with 'I Kissed a Girl', which spent five weeks at number 1 in August 2008.

10. Tom Jones was born Thomas Woodward in Pontypridd, Wales, on 7 June 1940. He made his Top 40 debut with 'It's Not Unusual', which spent one week at number 1 in March 1965.

NOW That's What I Call A Number 1 Answers

1. Leo Sayer. 'Thunder in My Heart Again' was credited to Meck featuring Leo Sayer, and was a remix of a single that originally peaked at number 22 in 1977 for Leo, the same year as his first number 1.

2. They have all replaced themselves at number 1. The Shadows also deserve to be on this list as they knocked singles by Cliff Richard and The Shadows off the top spot three times between 1960 and 1963.

3. '(Is This the Way to) Amarillo' by Tony Christie. In 1971 it peaked at number 18, but it was rereleased in 2005 for *Comic Relief* and spent seven weeks at number 1.

4. 'Unchained Melody'. Originally written for the 1955 prison drama *Unchained*, it topped the chart that year for Jimmy Young, in 1990 for the Righteous Brothers, in 1995 for Robson & Jerome, and in 2002 for Gareth Gates.

5. 'Mamma Mia' by ABBA. Although 'Bohemian Rhapsody' has been number 1 twice, both instances spanned the New Year so it is the only record to be number 1 in four different years – 1975, 1976, 1991 and 1992.

6. Julio and Enrique Iglesias. Father Julio made number 1 for one week in 1981 with 'Begin the Beguine (*Volver a Empezar*)', while Enrique spent four weeks at number 1 in 2002 with 'Hero'.

7. Rihanna with 'Umbrella' (2007), 'Take a Bow' (2008), 'Run This Town' (2009), 'Only Girl (In the World)' and 'What's My Name?' (2010), 'We Found Love' (2011), 'Diamonds' (2012) and 'The Monster' (2013).

8. They had the first number 1 singles of the 1960s, 70s, 80s, 90s, 2000s and 10s.

9. Telly Savalas. The award for longest number 1 song title goes to Manic Street Preachers for 'If You Tolerate This Your Children Will Be Next', which topped the chart in September 1998.

10. Depeche Mode. The Basildon synth-pop act have yet to break into the Top 3, having stalled at number 4 three times with 'People Are People' in 1984, 'Barrel of a Gun' in 1997 and 'Precious' in 2005.

NOW That's What I Call First and Last Answers

1. The Damned. The punk veterans have nine Top 40 singles, the biggest of which was 'Eloise', a number 3 in 1986 and originally a number 2 hit for Barry Ryan in 1968.

2. 10cc. Their thirteen Top 40 hits include the number 1s 'Rubber Bullets' (1973), 'I'm Not in Love' (1975) and 'Dreadlock Holiday' (1978). 'I'm Not in Love' re-charted in 1995, when it reached number 29.

3. UB40. All three of their number 1s were cover versions – 'Red Red Wine' (originally a Neil Diamond song), 'I Got You Babe' (Sonny and Cher) and '(I Can't Help) Falling in Love With You' (Andy Williams).

4. Shirley Bassey, who has three James Bond film themes to her name – *Goldfinger* (1964), *Diamonds Are Forever* (1971) and *Moonraker* (1979) – though all three failed to crack the Top 20.

5. Pulp. The band never had a number 1 single but made number 2 twice in 1995, with 'Common People' and the double A-side 'Mis-Shapes' / 'Sorted For E's & Wizz'.

6. Westlife. Their tally of fourteen number 1 singles is the third-highest in UK chart history, equalled by Cliff Richard and only bettered by The Beatles (seventeen) and Elvis Presley (twenty-one).

7. Lionel Richie. Before his hugely successful solo career, Lionel had nine Top 40 hits with the Commodores, for whom he wrote their only number 1 single, 'Three Times a Lady' (1978).

8. One Direction, who were the first band to have their first four albums debut at number 1 in the US album chart. Their fifth, *Made in the A.M.*, stalled at number 2, beaten by Justin Bieber's *Purpose*.

9. The Saturdays. Prior to success with The Saturdays, Frankie Sandford and Rochelle Wiseman were both members of S Club Juniors, while Una Healy represented Ireland in the 2006 Eurovision Song Contest.

10. Andy Williams. Although he had twenty-one Top 40 hits, his only number 1 was his 1957 chart debut 'Butterfly'. Andy first recorded his Christmas classic 'The Most Wonderful Time of the Year' in 1963.

NOW That's What I Call a Band Answers

1. Tom Fletcher, Harry Judd, Danny Jones and Dougie Poynter are McFly. Their first NOW appearance was '5 Colours in Her Hair', number 1 for two weeks in April 2004.

2. Tony Mortimer, Brian Harvey, John Hendy and Terry Coldwell are East 17. Their first NOW appearance was 'House of Love', which reached number 10 in September 1992.

3. Jean-Paul DeCoster, Phil Wilde, Ray Slijngaard and Anita Doth are 2 Unlimited. Their first NOW appearance was 'Get Ready for This', which reached number 2 in October 1991.

4. Piers Agget, Amir Amor, Kesi Dryden and Leon 'DJ Lock' Rolle are Rudimental. Their first NOW appearance was 'Feel the Love',

featuring John Newman, number 1 for one week in June 2012.

5. Lee Brennan, Jimmy Constable and Spike Dawbarn are 911. Their first NOW appearance was 'Don't Make Me Wait', which reached number 10 in November 1996.

6. Danny O'Donoghue, Glen Power and Mark Sheehan are The Script. Their first NOW appearance was 'We Cry', which reached number 15 in May 2008.

7. Célena Cherry, Heavenli Denton and Naima Belkhiati are Honeyz. Their first NOW appearance was 'Finally Found', which reached number 4 in September 1998.

8. Lene Nystrøm, René Dif, Søren Rasted and Claus Norreen are Aqua. Their first NOW appearance was 'Barbie Girl', which spent four weeks at number 1 in November 1997.

9. Liam Howlett, Keith Flint, Keith 'Maxim' Palmer and Leeroy Thornhill are The Prodigy. Their first NOW appearance was 'Charly', which reached number 3 in September 1991.

10. Bob Marley, Peter Tosh, Neville 'Bunny Wailer' Livingston, Aston 'Family Man' Barrett and Carlton Barrett are Bob Marley and the Wailers. Their first NOW appearance was 'One Love/People Get Ready', which reached number 5 in May 1984.

NOW That's What I Call a Top Ten Answers

1. Mary J. Blige. Peaking at number 2 in April 2006, 'One' was the New York-born singer's biggest hit, though it failed to add to U2's tally of seven chart-toppers.

2. Splodgenessabounds. The number 7 single 'Two Pints of Lager ...', later adopted as the theme to a BBC TV sitcom, was officially a triple A-side single with 'Simon Templar' and 'Michael Booth's Talking Bum'.

3. The Three Degrees. In May 1974, they had their first UK hit with the number 13 single 'Year of Decision', and spent two weeks at the top that August with 'When Will I See You Again'.

4. Mark Owen. The Take That singer launched his solo career in 1996 with consecutive number 3 singles, 'Child' and 'Clementine', but is yet to add to the twelve number 1s he has racked up with his group.

5. Ben Folds Five. The trio from Chapel Hill, North Carolina – Ben Folds, Robert Sledge and Darren Jessee – made their Top 40 debut in September 1996 with 'Underground' and bowed out in April 1999 with 'Army'.

6. Sneaker Pimps. The band, who took their name from an article in the Beastie Boys' *Grand Royal* magazine about a 'footwear detective', had five Top 40 hits, including the 1997 number 21 'Spin Spin Sugar'.

7. Marcus Collins. His version of 'Seven Nation Army' peaked at number 9 in March 2012. The White Stripes' original version reached number 7 in May 2003, one of thirteen Top 40 hits for the Detroit duo.

8. 'It's 'Orrible Being in Love (When You're 8½)'. The Stockport school children's only Top 40 hit was written by Brian and Michael, responsible for the 1978 number 1 'Matchstalk Men and Matchstalk Cats and Dogs'.

9. Nine Inch Nails. 'The Hand That Feeds' was the fourth of their six Top 40 hits, while Johnny Cash reached number 39 in 2003 with 'Hurts'. He had his biggest hit in 1969 with the number 4 single 'A Boy Named Sue'.

10. Beautiful South with 'Perfect 10'. Their sixteenth Top 40 hit stalled at number 2 behind 'Rollercoaster', the second of four consecutive number 1 hits for Irish quartet B*witched.

NOW That's What I Call Dance Answers

1. Mambo: Lou Bega 'Mambo No. 5 (A Little Bit Of ...)', number 1 in September 1999, when it kept 'Sway (Mucho Mambo)' by Shaft at number 2. Bob the Builder had his second number 1 in September 1999 with his version of 'Mambo No. 5'. Bob's third single, 'Big Fish, Little Fish', could only make number 81 in 2008.

2. Tango: Louis Armstrong 'Takes Two to Tango', number 6 in 1952; The Shadows 'Guitar Tango', a 1962 number 4 and the thirteenth of their thirty-six Top 40 hits; and Shakira 'Objection (Tango)', number 17 in 2002.

3. Waltz: Status Quo 'The Anniversary Waltz Part One', number 2 in 1990; Rod Stewart 'Tom Traubert's Blues (Waltzing Matilda)', number 6 in 1992 and Toby Bourke with George Michael 'Waltz Away Dreaming', number 10 in 1997. 'Tom Traubert's Blues' was one of two Top 10 hits that Rod had in the nineties with songs written by Tom Waits – the other was 'Downtown Train', number 10 in 1990.

4. Jive: Wizzard 'See My Baby Jive', one of their two number 1s in 1973 – the other was 'Angel Fingers'; Bee Gees 'Jive Talkin'', a number 5 in 1975; and Joe Jackson 'Jumpin' Jive', the title of both a number 43 single and a number 14 album for Joe in 1981.

5. Bop: Scatman John 'Scatman (Ski-Ba-Bop-Ba-Dop-Bop)', number 3 in 1995; 'MMMBop' by Hanson, number 1 in 1997; and 'Bop Bop Baby', number 5 for Westlife in 2002. At the time this was Westlife's lowest peak chart position. Of their eleven previous singles, ten had made number 1, while 'What Makes a Man' stalled at number 2 – behind Bob the Builder's 'Can We Fix It?'.

6. Disco: Public Image Limited 'Death Disco', number 20 in 1979; Shed Seven 'Disco Down', number 13 in 1999; and The Saturdays 'Disco Love', a 2013 number 5. Public Image Limited's second single borrows a melody from Tchaikovsky's 1876 ballet *Swan Lake*.

7. Boogie: T. Rex 'I Love to Boogie', number 13 in 1976; Booty Luv 'Boogie 2nite', number 2 in 2006; and Bamboo 'Bamboogie' in 2006. In the late sixties T. Rex had three Top 40 singles as Tyrannosaurus Rex, before they shortened their name, scoring twenty-one Top 40 hits, including four number 1s.

8. Twist: Dire Straits 'Twisting by the Pool', number 14 in 1983; Deacon Blue 'Twist and Shout', number 10 in 1991; and Chaka Demus & Pliers 'Twist and Shout', number 1 in 1993. The Beatles' version of 'Twist and Shout' made number 2 in the US in 1964 but was kept off the top spot by ... The Beatles' 'Can't Buy Me Love'.

9. The Hustle: Van McCoy 'The Hustle', number 3 in 1975; Hi Tension 'British Hustle', number 8 in 1978; and Jay-Z featuring Mary J Blige 'Can't Knock the Hustle', number 30 in 1997.

10. Macarena: in 1996 all three acts charted with versions of 'Macarena'. A squeaky-voiced version by Los del Chipmunks reached number 65; Los del Mar managed number 43; while the original by Los del Rio peaked at number 2, behind 'Wannabe' by Spice Girls.

NOW That's What I Call the Same Name Answers

1. 'All the Things She Said' by Simple Minds is on *NOW 7* and by t.A.T.u. on *NOW 54*.

2. 'History' by Mai Tai is on *NOW 5* and by One Direction on *NOW 93*.

3. 'Leave a Light On' by Belinda Carlisle is on *NOW 16* and by Tom Walker on *NOW 99*.

4. 'Thunder' by Prince and the New Power Generation is on *NOW 22*, and by East 17 on *NOW 33*.

5. 'Amnesia' by Chumbawamba is on *NOW 39* and by 5 Seconds of Summer on *NOW 89*.

6. 'Rise' by Gabrielle is on *NOW 5* and by Jonas Blue featuring Jack & Jack on *NOW 100*.

7. 'What If' by Kate Winslet is on *NOW 50* and by Jason Derulo on *NOW 77*.

8. 'Wake Up' by Hilary Duff is on *NOW 62* and by the Vamps on *NOW 92*.

9. 'Love Me Like You' by the Magic Numbers is on *NOW 62* and by Little Mix on *NOW 92*.

10. 'Omen' by the Prodigy is on *NOW 72* and by Disclosure featuring Sam Smith on *NOW 92*.

NOW That's What I Call (Brackets) Answers

1. Meat Loaf, 'I'd Do Anything for Love (But I Won't Do That)'. The first single from *Bat Out of Hell II: Back into Hell*, the sequel to the 1978 original, which spent over 500 weeks in the album chart.

2. Peter Sarstedt, 'Where Do You Go To (My Lovely)'. As Eden Kane, Peter's brother Richard made number 1 in 1961 with 'Well I Ask You', and brother Robin made number 3 in 1976 with 'My Resistance Is Low'.

3. Spiller featuring Sophie Ellis-Bextor, 'Groovejet (If This Ain't Love)'. One of two Top 40 hits (just) for Italian DJ Cristano Spiller, who spent one week at number 40 in February 2002 with 'Cry Baby'.

4. Brian and Michael, 'Matchstalk Men and Matchstalk Cats and Dogs (Lowry's Song)'. The only Top 40 hit for Brian Burke and Michael Coleman, it featured Tintwistle Brass Band and St Winifred's School Choir.

5. New Kids on the Block, 'You Got It (The Right Stuff)'. NKOTB also successfully deployed brackets twice in 1990, on the number 5 'I'll Be Loving You (Forever)' and the number 8 'Didn't I (Blow Your Mind)'.

6. Duke Dumont featuring A*M*E, 'Need U (100%)'. Duke decided that it was the 'U', not the brackets, that made for a hit, so repeated the trick for his second number 1, 'I Got U' featuring Jax Jones.

7. Chef, 'Chocolate Salty Balls (P.S. I Love You)'. As voiced by soul-music legend Isaac Hayes, who first charted in 1971 when 'Theme from *Shaft*' reached number 4.

8. John Lennon, '(Just Like) Starting Over'. John Lennon's last single released in his lifetime, it entered the chart at number 30 on 8 November 1980 and climbed to the top on 20 December following his tragic death.

9. The Stylistics, 'Can't Give You Anything (But My Love)'. Although it only reached number 51 in the US, it was the tenth of sixteen UK Top 40 hits and the only number 1 for the Philadelphia soul quintet.

10. Zager and Evans, 'In The Year 2525 (Exordium and Terminus)'. The only hit for Denny Zager and Rick Evans; during the six weeks it was number 1 in the US, the first moon landing occurred, on 20 July 1969.

NOW That's Who I Call ...? Volume 2 Answers

1. Calvin Harris was born Adam Wiles in Dumfries, Scotland, on 17 January 1984. He made his Top 40 debut with 'Acceptable in the 80s', which reached number 10 in March 2007.

2. Tina Turner was born Anna Mae Bullock in Nutbush, Tennessee, on 26 November 1939. She made her Top 40 debut with Ike & Tina Turner's 'River Deep – Mountain High', which reached number 3 in July 1966.

3. Shaggy was born Orville Burrell in Kingston, Jamaica, on 22 October 1968. He made his Top 40 debut with 'Oh Carolina', which spent two weeks at number 1 in March 1993.

4. Tinie Tempah was born Patrick Okogwu in Plumstead, London, on 7 November 1988. He made his Top 40 debut with 'Pass Out', which spent two weeks at number 1 in March 2010.

5. Meat Loaf was born Marvin Lee Aday in Dallas, Texas, on 27 September 1947. He made his Top 40 debut with 'You Took the Words Right Out of My Mouth', which reached number 33 in June 1978.

6. Maxi Priest was born Max Elliott in Lewisham, London, on 10 June 1961. He made his Top 40 debut with 'Strollin' On', which reached number 32 in April 1986. In 1988, he reached number 5 with a cover of the Cat Stevens' song 'Wild World'.

7. Bruno Mars was born Peter Hernandez in Honolulu, Hawaii, on 8 October 1985. He made his Top 40 debut with 'Nothin' on You' by B.o.B. featuring Bruno Mars, which spent one week at number 1 in May 2010.

8. Pink was born Alecia Moore in Doylestown, Pennsylvania, on 8 September 1979. She made her Top 40 debut with 'There You Go', which reached number 6 in June 2000, and had her first number 1 in 2001 with 'Lady Marmalade' from the *Moulin Rouge!* soundtrack.

9. Nelly was born Cornell Haynes Jr. in Austin, Texas, on 2 November 1974. He made his Top 40 debut with 'Country Grammar', which reached number 7 in November 2000.

10. Charli XCX was born Charlotte Aitchison in Cambridge, England, on 2 August 1992. She made her Top 40 debut with 'I Love It' by Icona Pop featuring Charli XCX, which spent one week at number 1 in July 2013.

NOW That's What I Call History Answers

1. 'Bad to Me' by Billy J. Kramer and the Dakotas. They made their Top 40 debut with another Lennon and McCartney song 'Do You Wanna Know a Secret' and had a second number 1 in 1964 with 'Little Children'.

2. 'The Last Waltz' by Engelbert Humperdinck. His 1967 chart debut, 'Release Me', spent six weeks at number 1 and kept the Beatles' 'Penny Lane/Strawberry Fields Forever' at number 2.

3. 'Are "Friends" Electric' by Tubeway Army. It spent four weeks at number 1, while the album it came from, *Replicas*, also topped the chart. In September 1979 singer Gary Numan reached number 1 with 'Cars'.

4. 'Pass the Dutchie' by Musical Youth. They had an average age of thirteen, and their single was based on 'Pass the Kouchie' by Mighty Diamonds, changing it to 'Dutchie', patois for a cooking pot, to avoid drug references.

5. 'Uptown Girl' by Billy Joel. His only number 1, it spent five weeks at the top and was the second-best selling single of 1983. A 2001 version by Westlife was their eighth number 1 single.

6. 'Frankie' by Sister Sledge. Their previous hits 'Lost in Music' and 'We Are Family' both made the Top 40 three times, the former peaking at number 4 in September 1984, the latter at number 5 in January 1993.

7. 'Because I Got High' by Afroman. It was nominated for a Grammy for Best Rap Solo Performance but lost to 'Get Ur Freak On' by Missy Elliott. Afroman's only other Top 40 hit, 'Crazy Rap', reached number 10 in 2002.

8. 'Hips Don't Lie' by Shakira featuring Wyclef Jean. She returned to the top for three weeks in 2007 with 'Beautiful Liar' by Beyoncé and Shakira, and has two children with FC Barcelona footballer Gerard Piqué.

9. 'Umbrella' by Rihanna featuring Jay-Z. A chart-topper on both sides of the Atlantic for Barbados-born Rihanna, who was appointed Ambassador Extraordinary for her home country in 2018.

10. 'Problem' by Ariana Grande featuring Iggy Azalea. After three singles that failed to crack the Top 40, 'Problem' went straight in at number 1. Australian singer Iggy Azalea was born Amethyst Kelly.

NOW That's What I Call … a TV Theme Answers

1. *The O.C.* One of two Top 40 appearances for Phantom Planet, along with 'Just', their 2008 collaboration with Mark Ronson that reached number 31.

2. *Twin Peaks.* Singer Julee Cruise previously worked with composer Angelo Badalamenti and director David Lynch on the 1986 film *Blue Velvet*, which included her song 'Mysteries of Love'.

3. *The Adventures of Black Beauty.* Denis King, who was also responsible for the themes to *Lovejoy* and the prison drama *Within These Walls*, wrote the theme to this children's adventure series.

4. *Made in Chelsea.* The song was also used by BBC TV in the run-up to their coverage of the 2012 Olympic Games in London.

5. *Prisoner: Cell Block H.* 'On the Inside' was the only hit for Lancashire-born Lynne Hamilton, despite an attempted follow-up in 1989 with 'In Your Arms (Love Song from *Neighbours*)'.

6. *Ally McBeal.* In addition to singing the theme tune, Vonda Shepard frequently appeared in the programme as a musician performing at a local piano bar.

7. *Celebrity Love Island.* 'Wish I' was the third of three Top 40 singles in 2005 for the Welsh singer born Jemma Griffiths.

8. *Howard's Way.* Marti Webb had her first hit in 1980, when 'Take That Look off Your Face', from the Andrew Lloyd Webber and Don Black musical *Tell Me on a Sunday*, reached number 3.

9. *Dr. Kildare.* In addition to singing the theme tune, Richard Chamberlain played the title role in this successful medical drama. He also found time to have another three Top 40 singles.

10. *Top of the Pops.* Paul Hardcastle is best known for '19', which spent five weeks at number 1 in 1985. 'The Wizard' was adopted as the *Top of the Pops* theme in 1986, when it replaced Phil Lynott's 'Yellow Pearl'.

NOW That's What I Call Sing Answers

1. '1999' by Prince. Taken from his 1982 album of the same name, his first Top 40 hit originally stalled at number 25, though it made number 2 when it was rereleased in 1985.

2. 'Disco 2000' by Pulp. It peaked at number 7 in 1995 and was the third of four Top 10 singles taken from their number 1 album *Different Class*.

3. 'Millennium' by Robbie Williams. This was Robbie's first solo number 1, in 1998, and it sampled the theme to the 1967 James Bond film *You Only Live Twice*.

4. 'End of a Century' by Blur. It reached number 19 in 1994 and was the fourth Top 20 single from their number 1 album *Parklife*.

5. 'Year 3000' by Busted. Their second single, it reached number 2 in 2002 and was the second of eight consecutive Top 3 singles.

6. 'New Year's Day' by U2. Their first Top 10 single, in 1983, they have since had more than thirty others, including seven number 1s, beginning with 'Desire' in 1988.

7. 'Feeling Good' by Nina Simone. Nina recorded this song in 1965, but it took until 1994 to make the Top 40, after it was used on a TV advert for Volkswagen.

8. 'Dancing Queen' by ABBA. The fourth of nine number 1 singles, it spent six weeks at the top in 1976 and re-entered the chart in 1992, when it peaked at number 16.

9. 'Firework' by Katy Perry. Her ninth Top 40 hit, it peaked at number 3 in 2010 and stayed in the Top 40 for twenty-four weeks, but hung around in the Top 100 for over a year.

10. 'Don't Stop Believin'' by Journey. Although it is Journey's only Top 40 hit, singer Steve Perry was one of the twenty-one different soloists on the 1985 number 1, 'We Are The World' by USA For Africa.

NOW That's What I Call a Genre Answers

NOW That's What I Call Rock 'n' Roll Answers

1. Neil Sedaka, who first made the charts with the 1959 number 9 'I Go Ape', and had his biggest hits with 'Oh Carol' the same year, and 'Happy Birthday, Sweet Sixteen' in 1961, both of them peaking at number 3.

2. Ritchie Valens. He had his only Top 40 hit in 1959 with 'Donna', though Los Lobos had a number 1 single in 1987 with a cover of his song 'La Bamba', taken from the biopic of Ritchie's life and career.

3. Billy Fury. Born in Liverpool in 1940, he had three consecutive Top 10 hits in 1961 with 'Half Way to Paradise', 'Jealousy' and 'I'll Never Find Another You'.

4. 'Rip It Up'. The Little Richard number 30 was the first of sixteen Top 40 hits, while the Orange Juice number 8 single was their only Top 40 hit, though singer Edwyn Collins also had two solo Top 40 hits.

5. Bill Haley's Comets. While this line-up played on hits such as 'Rock Around the Clock' and 'Shake, Rattle and Roll', it is estimated that over a hundred musicians performed with the Comets between 1952 and 1981.

6. The Art of Noise. Duane Eddy had his biggest hit in 1960 with the number 2 single 'Because They're Young', the theme to a film of the same name, in which he also appeared.

7. 'Johnny B. Goode'. The single reached number 8 in the US but failed to chart in the UK, so didn't add to his eleven Top 40 hits, though a version by Jimi Hendrix peaked at number 35 in 1972.

8. DJ Ötzi, who recorded a cover version titled 'Hey Baby (Uhh, Ahh)'. The Austrian DJ's only other Top 40 hit was a number 9 cover of 'Do Wah Diddy', a song that gave Manfred Mann their first number 1 in 1964.

9. Adam Faith, whose first two hits, 'What Do You Want?' and the follow-up, 'Poor Me', both topped the chart. In the seventies Adam appeared alongside David Essex in the film *Stardust*, and with Roger Daltrey in *McVicar*.

10. Lonnie Donegan. The 'King of Skiffle' had thirty-one UK Top 40 singles, including his debut 'Rock Island Line', which reached number 8 in both the UK and US charts.

NOW That's What I Call Classic Rock Answers

1. Queen. Guitarist Brian May and drummer Roger Taylor formed Smile with singer-bassist Tim Staffell. In 1970 Tim left to join folk-rock outfit Humpy Bong, and up stepped replacement singer Freddie Mercury.

2. Rainbow. Their run of Top 10 hits began with 'Since You've Been Gone', number 6 in 1979, continued with 'All Night Long', number 5 in 1980, and ended with their biggest hit 'I Surrender', number 3 in 1981.

3. Kiss. The New York rockers also reached number 4 in 1987 with their only other Top 10 hit, 'Crazy Crazy Nights'. Argent's original version of 'God Gave Rock and Roll to You' peaked at number 18 in 1973.

4. Steve Miller Band with 'The Joker'. The 'Space Cowboy' referred to in the lyrics was a song on Steve's 1969 album *Brave New World*, while 'Gangster of Love' was a song on his 1968 album *Sailor*.

5. Rod Stewart. The song was recorded in 1969, two years before Rod had his debut solo number 1 with 'Maggie May'. Rod was reputedly paid a set of car-seat covers for recording the song.

6. Bachman–Turner Overdrive. Randy, Robbie and Tim Bachman along with Fred Turner founded the band, though the latter had left by the time they had their biggest hit, 'You Ain't Seen Nothing Yet'.

7. Ozzy Osbourne. In December 2003, Ozzy and Kelly Osbourne went straight in at number 1 with a version of Black Sabbath's 1972 album track 'Changes'.

8. Wheatus. Their debut single 'Teenage Dirtbag' spent two weeks at number 2, thwarted in its bid for the top by Atomic Kitten's 'Whole Again'.

9. Guitarist Gary Moore and singer Phil Lynott. The pair also collaborated on the 1979 number 8 'Parisienne Walkways', though only Gary's name appeared on the record sleeve.

10. Bon Jovi. Their best chart placing so far is the 1994 ballad 'Always', which spent three weeks at number 2. The band has the consolation of five consecutive number 1 albums, beginning with *New Jersey* in 1988.

NOW That's What I Call Reggae Answers

1. 10cc. 'Dreadlock Holiday' was the Manchester band's third number 1, following on from 'Rubber Bullets' in 1973 and 'I'm Not in Love' in 1975.

2. Chaka Demus & Pliers, whose run of six Top 40 singles began with the 1993 number 3 'Tease Me'. Their biggest hit, 'Twist and Shout', spent two weeks at number 1 in January 1994.

3. Warren G, who made number 2 with his version in 1997. Bob's original version was first released on the 1973 album *Burnin'* but wasn't released as a single until 2005, when it only made number 67.

4. Shaggy, whose four number 1s include 'It Wasn't Me' with Rikrok. His 1996 number 11 'Why You Treat Me So Bad' featured Grand Puba, while his 1997 number 7 'Piece of My Heart' featured Marsha.

5. Boris Gardiner. 'I Want to Wake Up With You' was the third best-selling single of 1986. The song was originally recorded by American country singer Con Hunley.

6. Nicky Thomas, a one-hit wonder who spent two weeks at number 9 in July 1970. 'Love of the Common People' was written by John Hurley and Ronnie Wilkins, whose chart successes include Dusty Springfield's 1968 number 9, 'Son of a Preacher Man'.

7. The Pretenders' Chrissie Hynde on 'I Got You Babe', originally number 1 for Sonny and Cher in 1965. UB40's other chart-toppers were 'Red Red Wine' in 1983 and '(I Can't Help) Falling in Love with You' in 1993.

8. Bad Manners, for whom 'My Girl Lollipop' made number 9, and was their ninth and last Top 40 hit. Their biggest chart success was a version of 'Can Can', which spent four weeks at number 3 in July 1981.

9. Aswad. Their biggest hit, the 1988 number 1 'Don't Turn Around', was originally recorded by Tina Turner as the B-side of her 1986 single 'Typical Male'. In 1994, Ace of Base reached number 5 with their version.

10. Boy George. 'Everything I Own' was his debut solo single and only solo number 1, spending two weeks at the top in March 1987. Ken Boothe's only other Top 40 hit was the 1974 number 11 'Crying Over You'.

NOW That's What I Call Rhythm and Blues Answers

1. Janet Jackson with *Rhythm Nation 1814*. The album's seven Top 40 hits included 'Miss You Much', 'Come Back to Me', 'Alright', 'Black Cat', 'Escapade' and 'Love Will Never Do (Without You)'.

2. Status Quo. Both 'Ol' Rag Blues' and 'A Mess of Blues' were taken from the album *Back to Back*, which also included one of their biggest hits, 'Marguerita Time', which reached number 3 in February 1984.

3. Skip Marley, the grandson of reggae legend Bob. His mother, Cedella, sang in the Melody Makers alongside his uncle, Ziggy Marley, while his grandmother, Rita, sang on many of Bob's most famous records.

4. 'Bridget the Midget (The Queen of the Blues)'. Singer and comedian Ray Stevens had seven Top 40 hits between 1970 and 1977, including his 1974 number 1, 'The Streak'.

5. 'Slave to the Rhythm', which reached number 12 in October 1985 for Grace Jones. In 2012, she performed the song at Queen Elizabeth II's Diamond Jubilee Concert, where she hula-hooped for the entire song.

6. 'I Guess That's Why They Call It the Blues', which reached number 5 for Elton in July 1983, the twenty-ninth of his Top 40 singles.

7. 'Rhythm of the Rain'. The only Top 40 hit in the UK and US for San Diego group The Cascades, their recording featured the renowned 'Wrecking Crew' session musicians, including Glen Campbell on guitar.

8. Moby. 'Natural Blues' was one of six Top 40 singles taken from his number 1 album '*Play*', and sampled 'Trouble So Hard', a 1937 record by American folk singer Vera Hall.

9. Corona. 'The Rhythm of the Night' was their biggest hit, spending two weeks at number 2 in September 1994, where it stuck behind 'Saturday Night' by Whigfield.

10. Tommy Steele. His version of 'Singing the Blues' was in turn knocked off the top spot after one week by Guy Mitchell. In 1957, both artists had a Top 20 hit with different versions of 'Knee Deep in the Blues'.

NOW That's What I Call Classic Soul Answers

1. The Temptations. Originally called The Primes, they managed nineteen Top 40 hits beginning with 'Ain't Too Proud to Beg' in 1965, and had their biggest hit in 1992 when a reissue of their 1964 single 'My Girl' made number 2.

2. Indiana. All of the Jackson 5, plus younger brother Randy and sisters Janet and La Toya, were born in Gary, Indiana. R. Dean Taylor's biggest hit was the 1971 number 2 'Indiana Wants Me'.

3. The Supremes with Cindy Birdsong, Jean Terrell and Mary Wilson. Cindy joined the group in 1967 and had previously been a member of Patti LaBelle & the Bluebells. Jean replaced Diana Ross in 1970.

4. Marvin Gaye. In 1967 Marvin and Kim made number 16 with 'It Takes Two'; 'The Onion Song', his 1969 duet with Tammi, made number 9; and 'You Are Everything', his 1974 duet with Diana, made number 5.

5. Stevie Wonder. The couple were married in 1970 but divorced eighteen months later. Syreeta's biggest hit was the 1979 duet with Billy Preston 'With You I'm Born Again', which made number 2.

6. Arthur Conley. 'Sweet Soul Music' was co-written by Arthur with his mentor Otis Redding, who died just six months after the single peaked at number 7.

7. Al Green. 'Put a Little Love in Your Heart' was written by Jackie DeShannon and had been a hit for the Dave Clark Five in 1969. The Al and Annie version was taken from the Bill Murray film *Scrooged*.

8. The Carpenters. It was the ninth of seventeen Top 40 hits for siblings Karen and Richard, while The Marvelettes had just one UK hit with the 1967 number 13 'When You're Young and in Love'.

9. Lou Reed. It was one of just three Top 40 hits for the former Velvet Underground singer, along with 'Walk on the Wild Side', number 10 in 1973, and 'Satellite of Love '04', number 10 in 2004.

10. Ben E. King. 'Stand by Me' peaked at number 27 when it was first released in 1961, but reached number 1 in 1987 after its use in a Levi's jeans commercial and as the theme to the 1986 film of the same name.

NOW That's What I Call Remix Answers

1. Cornershop. When 'Brimful of Asha' was first released in 1997 it peaked at number 60, but a Norman Cook remix saw it go straight in at number 1 when it was reissued in February 1998.

2. Primal Scream. The remix, retitled 'Loaded', reached number 16 in March 1990. It includes dialogue by Peter Fonda, sampled from the cult 1966 film *The Wild Angels*.

3. Bob Marley, who first recorded 'Sun Is Shining' in 1971. The remix by Funkstar De Luxe, a.k.a. Martin Ottesen, spent one week at number 3 in September 1999, just beating the number 4 peak of 'Buffalo Soldier' in 1983.

4. Puerto Rican. 'Despacito', which translates as 'Slowly', was the first Spanish-language single to hit number 1 since Sak Noel's 'Loca People' in 2005, the same year Daddy Yankee had a number 5 hit with 'Gasolina'.

5. 'A Little Less Conversation'. First recorded for the film *Live a Little, Love a Little,* the 1968 single reached number 69 in the US. The 2002 remix spent 4 weeks atop the UK chart but stopped at number 50 in the US.

6. Everything but the Girl with 'Missing'. The 1995 remix reached number 3 and spent 19 weeks in the Top 40. The duo also reached number 3 in 1988 with a cover of 'I Don't Want to Talk About It'.

7. Eric B. and Rakim. 'Paid in Full' was remixed by the English group Coldcut, who had four Top 40 hits of their own, including the 1988 number 6 'Doctorin' the House', featuring Yazz and the Plastic Population.

8. 'Cheerleader', which spent four weeks at number 1 in May 2015 for the singer born Omar Pasley. That's the longest consecutive stay at the top of the singles chart for a Jamaican artist.

9. *Jeff Wayne's Musical Version of The War of the Worlds*. Since it was first released in 1978, the album has sold almost 3 million copies and spawned a stage show, a 'live' tour, a DVD, a remix album and a video game.

10. 'Temptation'. The original 1983 version reached number 2 and gave Heaven 17 their biggest hit. The song was also their second-biggest

hit after the Brothers in Rhythm remix reached number 4 in November 1992.

NOW That's What I Call Disco Answers

1. Sister Sledge. Between 1975 and 1993 the sisters had twelve Top 40 hits, including 'Frankie', which spent four weeks at number 1 in July 1985.

2. Will Smith's 'Men in Black'. His first solo number 1, it spent four weeks at the summit and followed his 1993 chart-topper 'Boom! Shake the Room' by DJ Jazzy Jeff and the Fresh Prince.

3. U2. Six of U2's chart-toppers, including 'Discotheque', spent just one week at number 1. Only the 'With or Without You' sampling 'Take Me to the Clouds Above' by LMC vs. U2 held on for a second week.

4. Pseudo Echo. The Australian outfit made number 1 in their home country, while Lipps Inc., who hail from Minnesota, topped the US *Billboard* chart with their original version.

5. Tina Turner, who has thirty-four Top 40 hits, including 'River Deep Mountain High', 'What's Love Got to Do with It' and 'We Don't Need Another Hero (Thunderdome)' – which all peaked at number 3 – but has yet to have a number 1.

6. Sheila and B. Devotion, whose only other Top 40 hit was the 1978 number 11 'Singin' in the Rain'. 'Spacer' was sampled by Swedish dance act Alcazar for their 2001 number 13 'Crying at the Discotheque'.

7. KC and the Sunshine Band. 'That's the Way (I Like It)' also reached number 11 in 1998 for English dance act Clock, one of their thirteen Top 40 hits.

8. Atomic Kitten. Their 2003 version reached number 8, one better than Kool & the Gang's original version, which was the first of their eighteen Top 40 hits.

9. Tavares. Brothers Ralph, Arthur 'Pooch', Antone 'Chubby', Feliciano 'Butch' and Perry 'Tiny' Tavares had eight Top 40 hits, including the Bee Gees-penned 'More Than a Woman', a 1978 number 7.

10. Mick Jackson. The English singer had a number 15 hit with 'Blame It on the Boogie', which he co-wrote with his brother Dave and Elmar Krohn. In 1978, The Jacksons recorded the same song, their version reaching number 8.

NOW That's What I Call Power Ballads Answers

1. Soul Asylum. The band from Minneapolis were originally known as Loud Fast Rules. 'Runaway Train' won the 1994 Grammy Award for Best Rock Song.

2. Toto's 'Africa'. Doubts persist about the geographical accuracy of the song, as although Mount Kilimanjaro and the Serengeti National Park are both in Tanzania, they are some 180 miles apart.

3. Chicago. The power ballad specialists made their chart debut with an

uptempo cover of Spencer Davis Group's 1967 number 9 'I'm A Man', but had their biggest hit in 1976 when 'If You Leave Me Now' spent three weeks at number 1.

4. Nicki French. Her only other Top 40 hit was 'Don't Play That Song Again', a 2000 number 34 single and the UK entry in that year's Eurovision Song Contest, where it finished sixteenth.

5. Journey's 'Don't Stop Believin''. Although it quickly dropped out of the chart on its original release, it had a huge surge in popularity after it featured on both *The X Factor* and *Glee* in 2009.

6. '(I Just) Died in Your Arms'. The English band did better in the US, where 'I've Been in Love Before' reached number 9 and '(I Just) Died in Your Arms' topped the *Billboard* Hot 100 for two weeks.

7. Natalie Imbruglia, who played Beth Brennan in the Australian soap *Neighbours* in the early nineties, before her debut single 'Torn' made number 2 in 1997.

8. Steve Brookstein, who won the very first series of *The X Factor* in December 2004. His debut single and album both went to number 1 in 2005, but he is yet to appear in either chart again.

9. 'Missing You'. John Waite's original version peaked at number 9 and is his only Top 40 hit. Tina Turner's version made number 12 and was the twenty-ninth of her thirty-four Top 40 singles.

10. Fun. The New York band made number 1 in 2012 with 'We Are Young', featuring Janelle Monáe, and had one more Top 10 single that year with the number 7 'Some Nights'.

NOW That's What I Call Rock Answers

1. 'I Wish I Was a Punk Rocker (With Flowers in My Hair)'. The song originally peaked at number 55 in October 2005 before a rerelease saw it spend one week at number 1 in June 2006.

2. Maria Vidal. The American singer and songwriter also wrote Belinda Carlisle's 1990 Top 40 hit 'Summer Rain', and 'Every Time It Rains', a 1999 number 22 single and the last Top 40 hit for Ace of Base.

3. Primal Scream. 'Rocks' was a number 7 double-A-side release with 'Funky Jam'. The band have two further Top 10 singles – 'Kowalski', number 8 in May 1997, and 'Country Girl', number 5 in June 2006.

4. 'Rock The Boat'. Hues Corporation reached number 6 in August 1974, and had a second hit that year with the number 24 'Rock 'n' Soul'. Aaliyah's 2002 number 12 single was the follow-up to her only number 1, 'More Than A Woman'.

5. Joan Jett & the Blackhearts. Joan had previously been with the all-female rock group the Runaways and recorded a version of this song in 1979, accompanied by Paul Cook and Steve Jones of the Sex Pistols.

6. All Saints. 'Rock Steady' was written by the group's Shaznay Lewis, along with American Greg Kurstin, who also co-wrote Lily Allen's 2009 number 1 'The Fear' and Ellie Goulding's 2013 number 1 'Burn'.

7. Redfoo, a.k.a. Stefan Kendal Gordy, and SkyBlu, a.k.a. Skyler Austen Gordy, are the son and grandson of Berry Gordy, Motown Records' founder and co-writer of Jackie Wilson's 1986 number 1 'Reet Petite'.

8. Lynyrd Skynyrd. Despite their rock anthem 'Sweet Home Alabama' – sampled on 'All Summer Long' and originally a number 31 single in September 1976 – the band actually hail from Jacksonville in Florida.

9. 'Mr Rock & Roll'. Amy's first single and her number 28 hit 'This Is the Life' were both taken from her number 1 debut album, also called *This Is the Life*.

10. 21 Savage, a.k.a. Shéyaa Bin Abraham-Joseph. 'Rockstar' spent four weeks at number 1 and finished 2017 as that year's twenty-ninth-best selling single.

NOW That's What I Call Punk and New Wave Answers

1. 'Should I Stay or Should I Go?' It was first released as a double A-side single with 'Straight to Hell' in 1982, when it peaked at number 17 and became the thirteenth of the Clash's seventeen Top 40 hits.

2. The Damned. 'Eloise' was the only one of the band's singles to make the Top 10, with the 1979 number 20 'Love Song' being their next-best chart position.

3. 'Jamming'. The lyrics to 'Punky Reggae Party' mention several punk and reggae groups: 'The Wailers will be there, the Damned, the Jam, the Clash – Maytals will be there, Dr. Feelgood too'.

4. The Rezillos. It was the only Top 40 entry for the Scottish band, though their guitarist Jo Callis had greater success in 1981 as co-writer of the Human League's number 1 'Don't You Want Me'.

5. Leftfield, who reached number 13 with 'Open Up', the first of their six Top 40 hits. The Sex Pistols had twelve Top 40 singles, while Lydon's post-Pistols project Public Image Ltd had another seven.

6. Stiff Little Fingers, who had their biggest chart hit in 1980 with the number 15 'At The Edge'. They were named after a song on The Vibrators' debut album; they had their only Top 40 hit with the 1978 number 35 'Automatic Lover'.

7. Belgian. Born Roger François Jouret in Brussels, his only other Top 40 hit was a cover of the Small Faces' 1966 number 3 'Sha La La La Lee'.

8. Fine Young Cannibals, who followed up their number 8 version of 'Suspicious Minds' with a cover of 'Ever Fallen in Love (With Someone You Shouldn't've)', which peaked at number 9 in April 1987.

9. The Kinks. The Fall with 'Victoria'; The Jam with 'David Watts'; The Pretenders with 'Stop Your Sobbing' and 'I Go to Sleep'; and The Stranglers with 'All Day and All of the Night'.

10. Poly Styrene of X-Ray Spex, whose three Top 40 singles in 1978 were 'The Day the World Turned Dayglo', 'Identity' and 'Germ Free Adolescence'.

NOW That's What I Call Classical Answers

1. Falco. Born Johan Hölzel, he had his first Top 40 hit, and only number 1, when 'Rock Me Amadeus' topped the chart in May 1986.

2. B. Bumble and the Stingers, who adopted their name when they recorded a rock'n'roll version of Rimsky-Korsakov's 'Flight of the Bumble Bee'. 'Nut Rocker' re-charted in 1972 when it reached number 19.

3. 'I Lost My Heart to a Starship Trooper' made number 6 for Sarah Brightman and Hot Gossip in 1978. The follow up – 'Adventures of a Love Crusader' – could only manage number 53.

4. William Orbit had a number 4 with 'Barber's Adagio for Strings'. He also produced the hit singles 'Ray of Light' for Madonna, 'Tender' for Blur and 'Pure Shores' for All Saints.

5. Sex Pistols manager Malcolm McLaren, who collaborated with Greek new-age composer Yanni to adapt 'Flower Duet'. Malcolm had his biggest hit with the 1983 number 3 'Double Dutch'.

6. 'All Together Now' gave the Farm their biggest hit in 1990. In 2004 it reached number 5, credited to The Farm featuring S.F.X. Boys Choir, Liverpool. S.F.X. is short for St. Francis Xavier's College.

7. Beethoven. Electric Light Orchestra with 'Roll Over Beethoven' (a number 6 hit), Walter Murphy with 'A Fifth of Beethoven' (number 28) and Eurythmics with 'Beethoven (I Love to Listen To)' (number 25).

8. 'Hallelujah' by Alexandra Burke was the bestselling single of 2008. The original version by Leonard Cohen reached number 36 in December 2008, twenty-four years after it was first released.

9. The Crowd had a number 1 single with 'You'll Never Walk Alone' in 1985. The record was a charity project to raise funds for victims of the Bradford City stadium fire.

10. Kiri Te Kanawa, who had a number 5 hit in 1991 when the UK hosted the Rugby World Cup. Her compatriot Hayley Westenra also recorded a version which made number 70 in 2011, when New Zealand hosted the tournament.

NOW That's What I Call Pop Answers

1. NSYNC. The number 9 hit 'Pop' was written by Justin Timberlake with choreographer, musician and reality TV judge Wade Robson. The pair were also responsible for NSYNC's follow-up hit 'Gone'.

2. 'The Pop Singer's Fear of the Pollen Count' was the eighth of thirteen Top 40 hits for the band fronted by Neil Hannon. They had their biggest hit in 1999 with the number 8 single 'National Express'.

3. 'Pop Muzik'. Their chart debut, it spent two weeks at number 2 in 1979, and featured Wally Badarou on keyboards and Phil Gould on drums, both future members of Level 42.

4. David Bowie. The single failed to chart when it was first released in 1977, but gained a new audience in 1996 when it was used in Danny Boyle's film *Trainspotting*.

5. Russ Conway. His eighteen Top 40 hits spent 160 weeks in the chart and included two self-written number 1s in 1959: 'Side Saddle', which spent four weeks at the top, and 'Roulette', which stayed there for two weeks.

6. Rednex. 'Cotton Eye Joe' spent three weeks at number 1 in 1994, while 'Old Pop in an Oak' provided their only other Top 40 single the following year.

7. Pop Will Eat Itself. The band's singer Clint Mansell later had considerable success as a composer of film scores, including a Grammy Award nomination for his soundtrack for the 2010 film *Black Swan*.

8. Kid Creole and the Coconuts. In 1982 the band had three Top 10 singles, including their biggest hit 'Annie, I'm Not Your Daddy', which reached number 2 in October.

9. Icona Pop. The duo, Caroline Hjelt and Aino Jawo, attended the same music school in Stockholm. Their second Top 40 hit, 'All Night', was co-written with Australian duo Empire of the Sun.

10. Hot Butter. 'Popcorn' was the American band's only Top 40 hit, while Crazy Frog managed five, including a cover of 'Axel F', which spent four weeks at number 1 beginning in June 2005.

NOW That's What I Call Club Hits Answers

1. 'Club Tropicana'. In December 1983 Wham! reached number 15 with 'Club Fantastic Megamix', a medley of their songs 'A Ray of Sunshine' and 'Come On', and a cover of The Miracles' 1976 hit 'Love Machine'.

2. S Club 7. The double A-side single 'Say Goodbye' and 'Love Ain't Gonna Wait for You' reached number 2 in June 2003, the fifth of their eleven Top 10 singles to stall one place short of the summit.

3. 'In Da Club'. The song spent two weeks at number 3 and twenty-one weeks in the Top 40. Later in 2003 Beyoncé recorded a version which she retitled 'Sexy Little Thug'.

4. JLS. After the quartet split in 2014, Marvin Humes appeared on the number 13 hit 'Resonance' by LuvBug featuring Talay Riley, while Aston Merrygold reached number 28 in 2015 with 'Get Stupid'.

5. Associates. In 1982 they spent a total of twenty-three weeks in the Top 40, starting with the number 9 'Party Fears Two', followed by 'Club Country' and the number 21 double A-side '18 Carat Love Affair' / 'Love Hangover'.

6. Culture Club. Their hits included the number 1s 'Do You Really Want to Hurt Me' in 1982 and 'Kharma Chameleon', the bestselling single of 1983, which spent six weeks at the top in the UK and three in the US.

7. 'Night-Clubbing'. It was the fifteenth of nineteen Top 40 hits for the singer born David Cook, a run that included the number 1 singles 'Gonna Make You a Star' in 1974 and 'Hold Me Close' in 1975.

8. French DJ David Guetta. 'Club Can't Handle Me' was Flo Rida's third

number 1, following 'Right Round' featuring Kesha in 2009, and his turn as featured artist on Alexandra Burke's 2009 chart-topper 'Bad Boys'.

9. KC and the Sunshine Band. They had their biggest hit in 1983 when 'Give It Up' spent three weeks at number 1. In 1992, KWS topped the chart with a cover of KC's 1979 number 3 'Please Don't Go'.

10. Talking Heads, who had three Top 40 hits including the 1985 number 6 'Road to Nowhere'. Tom Tom Club's only other Top 40 hit was the 1982 number 22 'Under the Boardwalk'.

NOW That's What I Call Country Answers

1. Dolly Parton, who as a singer has yet to better the number 7 peak of her 1976 chart debut 'Jolene', a song which also gave The White Stripes their seventh Top 40 hit in 2004, when their version reached number 16.

2. Billy Connolly. In 1976, Billy was the opening act on Elton John's US tour. In 1979 he reached number 32 with his parody of the Village People single 'In the Navy', retitled 'In the Brownies'.

3. Julio Iglesias. Prior to his musical career Julio played in goal for Real Madrid Castilla. He also has a degree in law from the University of Madrid, in addition to six Top 40 hits between 1981 and 1988.

4. The Proclaimers. Their second Top 40 hit was 'I'm Gonna Be (500 Miles)', which peaked at number 11 in 1988 but topped the chart in 2007 when it was rerecorded with Brian Potter and Andy Pipkin, aka comedians Peter Kay and Matt Lucas.

5. The Bellamy Brothers. The song was written by David, who said the title was inspired by the comedian Groucho Marx. The Bellamy Brothers had one other Top 40 hit with 'Let Your Love Flow', a number 7 single in 1976.

6. LeAnn Rimes. In 1999 she reached number 10 with 'Written in the Stars', a duet with Elton John, while her duet with Ronan Keating, 'Last Thing on My Mind', peaked at number 5 in May 2004.

7. 'Achy Breaky Heart' by Billy Ray Cyrus, which spent two weeks at number 3 in August 1992. He returned to the Top 40 in October that year, when 'Could've Been Me' reached number 24.

8. Tim McGraw. It was the third number 1 for Nelly but the only Top 40 hit for Tim, though his wife – fellow country singer Faith Hill – has six Top 40 hits, including the 2001 number 3 'There You'll Be'.

9. John Denver, who reached number 1 with 'Annie's Song', also a number 3 hit for James Galway in 1978. In 1973, Olivia Newton-John had a number 15 hit with John's song 'Take Me Home, Country Roads'.

10. Glen Campbell on 'Rhinestone Cowboy (Giddy Up Giddy Up)' by Rikki and Daz. In 2006, Daz Sampson represented the UK in the Eurovision Song Contest with 'Teenage Life', where he finished in nineteenth place.

NOW That's What I Call Easy Answers

1. Nicole Kidman. In December 2001 'Somethin' Stupid' was Robbie's fifth solo number 1, while Nicole made her Top 40 debut that October with 'Come What May', from the Baz Luhrmann film *Moulin Rouge*.

2. *Butch Cassidy and the Sundance Kid*. B.J. Thomas originally recorded the song, written by Burt Bacharach and Hal David, for the film. His version reached number 1 in the US but only reached number 38 in the UK.

3. Bono of U2. Frank was never in the studio with his vocal partner for the 1993 *Duets* album. He recorded his part for 'I've Got You Under My Skin' in Los Angeles, while Bono completed his contribution in Dublin.

4. The Stranglers, whose version of 'Walk On By' reached number 21 in 1978. Yet another easy-listening classic from songwriters Bacharach and David, it was also a hit for Sybil in 1990 and Gabrielle in 1997.

5. 'Spanish Flea', which was the first of eight Top 40 hits for Herb, who is the only artist to hit number 1 in the US with both a song – 'This Guy's in Love with You' in 1968 – and an instrumental – 'Rise' in 1979.

6. Tony Christie. He made his chart debut in 1971 with the number 21 'Las Vegas', and his most recent appearance in 2006 with '(Is This the Way to) The World Cup', a record he later described as 'dreadful'.

7. 'Stardust'. Nat King Cole made number 24 in 1957 with a song based on a 1927 melody by Hoagy Carmichael. The David Essex song reached number 7 in 1974, while Menswear made number 16 in 1995.

8. The Walker Brothers. The unrelated threesome had their second number 1 six months later, when they spent four weeks in the top spot with 'The Sun Ain't Gonna Shine (Anymore)'.

9. 'The Windmills of Your Mind'. In 1968 it won an Oscar for Best Original Song, just twelve months after Noel's father, Rex Harrison, had won the 1967 Award with 'Talk to the Animals' from *Doctor Dolittle*.

10. Matt Monro, who had eleven Top 40 hits between 1960 and 1973, but is perhaps best remembered for the theme songs from the films *Born Free*, *From Russia with Love* and *The Italian Job*.

NOW That's What I Call House Answers

1. Madness with 'House of Fun', which reached number 1 in May 1982. They had three more singles in the Top 20 that year, including the number 5 hit 'Our House'.

2. 'The House That Jack Built'. Alan Price Set had five Top 40 hits between 1966 and 1968, Jack 'n' Chill had just the one, while Tracie's two Top 40 hits were released on Paul Weller's Respond label.

3. 'Mozart's House'. The single peaked at number 17 in April 2013 for the English trio, who had their first number 1 the following year with 'Rather Be', featuring Jess Glynne.

4. House of Love. The band, who had one more Top 40 hit in 1990 with 'The Beatles and the Stones', were no doubt frustrated in 1989 when two of their singles stalled at number 41.

5. 'House of the Rising Sun'. The song was the only chart entry for Frijid Pink, while The Animals had fifteen Top 40 hits. Their version of 'House of the Rising Sun' returned to the chart in 1972 and again in 1982.

6. Eels. The Californian band, fronted by Mark Everett, made their chart debut with the 1997 number 10 'Novocaine for the Soul', and had their biggest hit later that year when 'Susan's House' peaked at number 9.

7. Swedish House Mafia. The trio made their chart debut in 2010 with 'One (Your Name)' featuring Pharrell, and had their first number 1 in 2012 with 'Don't You Worry Child' featuring fellow Swede John Martin.

8. Crowded House. The band had the first of twelve Top 40 hits in 1987 with 'Don't Dream It's Over', and their biggest hit in 1992 with the number 7 single 'Weather with You'.

9. Beatmasters. The trio also had a number 14 hit in 1988 with 'Burn It Up', featuring P.P. Arnold, and a successful career remixing songs for other artists including Pet Shop Boys, Depeche Mode, Aswad and Tina Turner.

10. 'This Ole House'. American actress and singer Rosemary Clooney had one more number 1 with 'Mambo Italiano' in 1954, while Shaky managed another three, including his 1985 hit 'Merry Christmas Everyone'.

NOW That's What I Call a Geography Lesson Answers

NOW That's What I Call Geography Answers

1. 'Rotterdam' by the Beautiful South, which peaked at number 5 in October 1996. Their line-up included singer Jacqui Abbott, who became the second of three different front women when she replaced Briana Corrigan in 1994.

2. 'Pompeii' by Bastille. Their second hit stayed in the Top 40 for twenty-eight weeks after it entered the chart at number 2 in March 2013, but was kept off the top spot by Justin Timberlake's fourth number 1, 'Mirrors'.

3. Berlin with 'Take My Breath Away'. The second single released from the *Top Gun* soundtrack, after 'Danger Zone' by Kenny Loggins, the song recharted in November 1990 when it peaked at number 3.

4. Marcella Detroit, who spent eight weeks at number 1 in 1992 with Shakespears Sister and 'Stay'. Her second solo Top 40 hit was a duet with Elton John, a cover of the Motown classic 'Ain't Nothing Like the Real Thing'.

5. 'Dancing in the Street'by David Bowie and Mick Jagger. Their version of the 1964 Martha and the Vandellas single is a veritable 'pop atlas', also mentioning Chicago, New York, New Orleans, Philadelphia, Baltimore (Washington) D.C, Detroit ('the motor city') and L.A., along with Brazil, China and the U.S.S.R.

6. 'Kingston Town' by UB40. It was their twenty-third single to make the Top 40 and their tenth cover version, having originally been a single for Jamaican singer Lord Creator in 1970.

7. Portugal. The Man with 'Feel It Still'. The band's eleventh single was their first to chart in the UK and in the US Hot 100, where it peaked at number 4. In 2018 it won a Grammy Award for Best Group Performance.

8. Ultravox with 'Vienna'. The second of sixteen Top 40 hits, it spent four weeks at number 2 while 'Shaddap Your Face' by American-Australian act Joe Dolce Music Theatre had a five-week run at the top.

9. Freddie Mercury and Montserrat 'La Superba' Caballé with 'Barcelona'. It made number 8 when first released in 1987, and number 2 when it was a theme for the 1992 Barcelona Olympic Games.

10. Katie Melua with 'Nine Million Bicycles'. While she claimed that the quantity of bicycles in Beijing was 'a fact', she admitted that her statement that 'we are twelve billion light years from the edge' of the universe was a guess.

NOW That's What I Call Ireland Answers

1. The Pogues featuring Kirsty MacColl with 'Fairytale of New York'. In 1987 it was kept off the top spot by Pet Shop Boys' 'Always on My Mind', and has occupied every chart position in the Top 10 – except number 1.

2. Samantha Mumba. 'Gotta Tell You' was kept off the top spot by Eminem's first number 1, 'The Real Slim Shady', and her lowest peak position was the number 6 achieved by 'Lately' in 2001.

3. Bob Geldof, who twice topped the charts with the Boomtown Rats, first with 'Rat Trap' in November 1978, then with 'I Don't Like Mondays', which spent four weeks at number 1 in August 1979.

4. 'I Can See Clearly Now'. Hothouse Flowers' version reached number 23, as did a 1994 version by another Jamaican singer, Jimmy Cliff. The Irish band made their chart debut with the 1988 number 11 'Don't Go'.

5. Enya. 'I Don't Wanna Know' was credited to Mario Winans featuring Enya and P. Diddy, while 'You Really Should Know' was credited to The Pirates featuring Enya, Shola Ama, Naila Boss and Ishani.

6. Van Morrison. As the singer for Them, he had a number 2 hit in 1965 with 'Here Comes the Night', but despite forty Top 40 albums he has yet to better the singles chart peak of his 1989 collaboration with Cliff Richard.

7. Dana. Ireland is the most successful nation in the Eurovision Song Contest; those seven wins include three consecutive years between 1992 and 1994, while Irish singer Johnny Logan is the only singer to win twice.

8. The Saw Doctors. 'To Win Just Once' reached number 14 in July 1996 and was the last of the band's songs to feature lucky keyboard and accordion player Tony Lambert.

9. The Assembly. Vince Clarke wrote the first two top 40 hits for Depeche Mode before leaving to form Yazoo. He had planned for The Assembly to be his next long-term project, but instead formed Erasure with singer Andy Bell.

10. Sinéad O'Connor. She duetted with Shane MacGowan on the number 30 hit 'Haunted', with Ian Brown on the number 16 'Illegal Attacks' and had a number 18 hit with 'Success Has Made a Failure of Our Home'.

NOW That's What I Call Scotland Answers

1. Fairground Attraction, whose debut single 'Perfect' spent one week at number 1. They had one more Top 10 hit with 'Find My Love', before the band split and Glasgow-born singer Eddi Reader pursued a solo career.

2. Marmalade. The Glasgow group, who were originally called Dean Ford and the Gaylords, made their chart debut with the number 11 single 'Lovin' Things' and had eleven Top 40 hits between 1968 and 1976.

3. Bay City Rollers. The Edinburgh quintet had two number 1 singles in 1975, when 'Bye Bye Baby' spent six weeks at the top followed by three weeks for 'Give a Little Love'.

4. Lulu, who won the 1969 Eurovision Song Contest with 'Boom Bang-a-Bang', made number 3 with David Bowie's 'The Man Who Sold the World' and had a 1993 number 1 with Take That and 'Relight My Fire'.

5. 'Many of Horror', which originally peaked at number 20 for Biffy Clyro in January 2010 but reached number 8 that December after Matt Cardle's renamed version became the Christmas number 1.

6. Midge Ure, who had further Top 40 hits fronting Rich Kids and Ultravox before he had a solo number 1 with 'If I Was' in 1985, the year after he co-wrote 'Do They Know It's Christmas?' with Bob Geldof.

7. 'Bang Bang'. In addition to his five Top 40 hits as an artist, B.A. Robertson also co-wrote Cliff Richard's Top 10 hits 'Carrie' and 'Wired for Sound', and Mike and the Mechanics' biggest hit 'The Living Years'.

8. Aneka. 'Japanese Boy' spent one week at number 1 in August 1981, though the follow-up single 'Little Lady' peaked at number 50. A third single, 'Ooh Shooby Doo Doo Lang', failed to make the chart at all.

9. Jimmy Somerville. His version of 'You Make Me Feel (Mighty Real)' reached number 5, and was a number 8 hit for Sylvester in 1978.

Jimmy's 1990 version of 'To Love Somebody' reached number 8, having previously made number 41 for the Bee Gees in 1967.

10. Calvin Harris. 'Read All About It' replaced 'We Found Love' by Rihanna featuring Calvin Harris in 2011, while 'Beneath Your Beautiful' replaced 'Sweet Nothing' by Calvin Harris and Florence Welch in 2012.

NOW That's What I Call London Answers

1. 'London Bridge', which reached number 3 in September 2006. Fergie had her biggest solo hit the following year, when 'Big Girls Don't Cry' peaked at number 2.

2. East 17, who released their number 1 debut album *Walthamstow* in 1993. In another London reference, the album included their cover of the Pet Shop Boys' song 'West End Girls'.

3. Cathy Dennis, who reached number 11 with her version of a song that originally made number 2 for The Kinks in 1967. Her songwriting credits include Katy Perry's 'I Kissed a Girl' and Britney Spears's 'Toxic'.

4. London Grammar. The trio, who actually met at Nottingham University, had huge success with their debut album 'If You Wait', which peaked at number 2 and spent sixty-three weeks in the Top 40.

5. 'Last Train to London'. The single peaked at number 8 in December 1979, and was sampled by Atomic Kitten for their 2002 number 2 single 'Be With You'.

6. Ralph McTell. 'Streets of London' won an Ivor Novello Award for Best Song, and was re-recorded by Ralph and Annie Lennox in 2017, to raise funds for the homeless charity Crisis.

7. Carter the Unstoppable Sex Machine. The band had twelve Top 40 singles and made headlines in 1991 when Les 'Fruitbat' Carter rugby-tackled presenter Phillip Schofield at the *Smash Hits* Poll Winners Party.

8. 'Piccadilly Palare', which peaked at number 18 in October 1990. In 1995, Morrissey made reference to the eastern extremes of the District Line on his number 26 single 'Dagenham Dave'.

9. Chelsea. 'Chelsea Dagger' was a number 5 hit for the Fratellis, while Jon Bon Jovi reached number 4 with 'Midnight in Chelsea', and '(I Don't Want to Go to) Chelsea' was a number 16 hit for Elvis Costello and the Attractions.

10. Squeeze, whose number 2 hit 'Up the Junction' was denied the top spot by Tubeway Army's 'Are "Friends" Electric?'. In April 1979 'Cool for Cats' also peaked at number 2, behind Art Garfunkel's 'Bright Eyes'.

NOW That's What I Call USA Answers

1. Debbie Harry. The second of four Top 40 solo singles, 'French Kissin' in the USA' reached number 8 in December 1986, and was written by Chuck Lorre, writer of the US sitcoms *Roseanne*, *Cybill* and *The Big Bang Theory*.

2. Holly Johnson, for whom 'Americanos' reached number 4 in April 1989, as did his previous single, 'Love Train'. They followed his three number 1 hits with Frankie Goes to Hollywood between 1983 and 1984.

3. The Empire State Building. 'Empire State of Mind' made number 2 for Jay-Z and Alicia Keys, while a solo version by Alicia, 'Empire State of Mind (Part II) Broken Down' made number 4 in February 2010.

4. Las Vegas. The Elvis version of 'Viva Las Vegas' reached number 17 in 1964, then number 15 in 2007. ZZ Top's version reached number 10 in 1992, equalling their 1983 debut hit 'Gimme All Your Lovin''.

5. America. 'A Horse With No Name' topped the US chart, where the follow-up 'Ventura Highway' reached number 8, though it peaked at number 43 in the UK.

6. Billy Joel's number 7 single 'We Didn't Start the Fire'. In the US it was Billy's third number 1 single, while his only UK chart-topper is 'Uptown Girl', which spent five weeks at number 1 in 1983.

7. Razorlight. 'America' spent one week at number 1 in October 2006 before it was replaced by 'Welcome to the Black Parade', the only number 1 for My Chemical Romance.

8. Madonna. 'American Life' made number 2 in 2003, while her version of 'American Pie' topped the chart in 2000, going one better than the 1972 original by Don McLean, which stalled at number 2.

9. 'United States of Whatever'. The one-hit wonder reached number 10 in December 2002, though the talented Mr Lynch also directed the films *School of Rock* and *Tenacious D in the Pick of Destiny*.

10. Supertramp, according to their number 9 hit 'Breakfast in America'. Taken from the album of the same name, this song and 'The Logical Song', number 7 in April 1979, were the band's only Top 10 hits.

NOW That's What I Call Wales Answers

1. Bonnie Tyler and Shakin' Stevens. Bonnie topped the charts for two weeks in 1983 with 'Total Eclipse of the Heart', while 'Shaky' has spent ten weeks at number 1, including four weeks with 'Green Door' in 1981.

2. Sian Evans. 'Louder' spent one week at number 1 in July 2007. Caerphilly-born Sian also co-wrote 'Hot Right Now', the follow-up single for DJ Fresh, featuring Rita Ora, which gave the latter her first number 1 in February 2012.

3. Shirley Bassey. 'As I Love You' spent 4 weeks at number 1 in 1959, and in 2005, Kanye West sampled her 1972 James Bond theme 'Diamonds Are Forever' hit for his number 8 'Diamonds From Sierra Leone'.

4. Mary Hopkin. Her 1968 chart debut 'Those Were The Days' was produced by Paul McCartney, while her 1970 number 2 single 'Knock, Knock, Who's There?' was the UK entry at the Eurovision Song Contest in Amsterdam, where it finished second.

5. 'Buck Rogers', which peaked at number 5 for Feeder in January 2001. It was the sixth of twenty Top 40 hits for the band, who also reached number 5 in 2005 with 'Tumble and Fall'.

6. 'The Ballad of Tom Jones'. It was the seventh of nine Top 40 hits for Space, while Cardiff-born Cerys's only other solo hit was 'Baby, It's Cold Outside', her 1999 number 17 collaboration with … Tom Jones.

7. Goldie Lookin Chain. The Newport band counted Adam Hussain, Eggsy and Graham the Bear among their line-up, while former member Maggot appeared in Series 4 of *Celebrity Big Brother* in 2006.

8. Racing Cars. Formed in 1973, they enjoyed backing from the Chrysalis record label – home to Blondie and Jethro Tull – and supported Bad Company on tour, but never managed a second hit.

9. Charlotte Church. The former classical singer had six Top 40 hits between 1999 and 2006, though she was credited on the Jurgen Vries single as 'CMC', as her record label were concerned by her change of direction.

10. Scritti Politti. The group, who were fronted by Cardiff-born singer Green Gartside, had five Top 40 hits between 1984 and 1991, peaking with the 1985 number 6 'The Word Girl'.

NOW That's What I Call (Which) Country Answers

1. Australia. In May 2000, Melbourne duo Madison Avenue had their only Number 1 with 'Don't Call Me Baby', which knocked Britney Spears's 'Oops! … I Did It Again' off the top spot.

2. Canada. Sisters Natalie and Nicole Appleton were both born in Ontario, before moving to London, finding fame with All Saints and having three Top 40 hits as Appleton.

3. Denmark. Aqua's shaven-headed singer René Dif has a street named after him in his hometown of Bornholm.

4. Germany. Crazy Frog was originally known as 'the Annoying Thing' – 'his' number 1 single 'Axel F' was produced by Reinhard and Henning Reith, from German dance outfit Bass Bumpers.

5. Ireland. In 2018, Hozier released the single 'Nina Cried Power', featuring soul-music legend Mavis Staples, forty-six years after she made her chart debut with the Staple Singers on 'I'll Take You There'.

6. Scotland. Hue and Cry were a duo formed by brothers Greg and Pat Kane, from Coatbridge in North Lanarkshire. The band were named after the 1947 Ealing Studios film comedy starring Alastair Sim.

7. Sweden. Neneh Cherry is the step-daughter of American jazz trumpeter Don Cherry, while her own daughter Mabel had her first Top 10 single in August 2017 with the number 8 hit 'Finders Keepers'.

8. Trinidad and Tobago. In 2012 Nicki Minaj provided the voice for the woolly mammoth Steffie in the film *Ice Age: Continental Drift*. The cast also included Jennifer Lopez, Queen Latifah and Drake.

9. Wales. Cowbridge band The Automatic had their biggest hit in 2006 with 'Monster'. For legal reasons, in the US the band is known as The Automatic Automatic.

10. Belgium. Gotye is the stage name of Bruges-born Wouter de Backer. His 2012 single 'Somebody That I Used to Know' spent five weeks at number 1, though it remains his only hit single.

NOW That's What I Call a Theme Answers

NOW That's What I Call a Drink Answers

1. Hot Chocolate. They had their biggest hit and only number 1 with 'So You Win Again', which spent three weeks at number 1 in 1977. 'It Started with a Kiss' was first issued in 1982, when it reached number 5.

2. 'Milkshake'. It was the seventh Top 40 single for the artist born Kelis Rogers, and the first of three number 2 hits, to be followed by 'Trick Me' in 2004 and 'Bounce' by Calvin Harris featuring Kelis in 2011.

3. Brandy, who reached number 2 in June with Monica and 'The Boy Is Mine', and again in October with 'Top of the World' featuring Mase. On both occasions Irish quartet B*Witched held the number 1 spot.

4. 'Escape (The Piña Colada Song)' reached number 23 for Rupert Holmes but made number 1 in the US. The song has featured in a number of films, including *Shrek*, *Guardians of the Galaxy* and *Mars Attacks!*

5. All Saints, who entered the chart at number 1 in October 2000 with 'Black Coffee', making them only the second female group, after the Spice Girls, to achieve five number 1 singles in the UK.

6. Bucks Fizz. They first made number 1 in April 1981 with the Eurovision Song Contest winner 'Making Your Mind Up', and topped the chart twice in 1982 with 'Land of Make Believe' and 'My Camera Never Lies'.

7. 'Cold Water'. The song, which was co-written by Ed Sheeran, spent five weeks at number 1 beginning August 2016, but stalled at number 2 in the US.

8. R.E.M. Their biggest hit was the 2000 number 3 'The Great Beyond', though their 1993 number 7 hit 'Everybody Hurts' topped the chart in 2010 when it was recorded for the Helping Haiti charity project.

9. 'Tequila'. The number 23 single 'Tequila Sunrise' was the eighth of thirteen Top 40 hits for Cypress Hill, while 'Tequila' took Terrorvision to number 2 and gave them their biggest hit in January 1999.

10. 'I'd Like to Teach the World to Sing (In Perfect Harmony)'. The first of two chart-toppers for the New Seekers, it spent four weeks at number 1 in January 1972 and also reached number 7 in the US.

NOW That's What I Call Fashion Answers

1. Depeche Mode. Their name comes from a French magazine title, though the band hail from Basildon in Essex, where they played their first gig, at James Hornsby School, in 1980.

2. Roxette. Marie Fredriksson and Per Gessle had nineteen Top 40 hits between 1989 and 1999, including 'It Must Have Been Love', which reached number 3 in 1990 after it featured in the film *Pretty Woman*.

3. The Style Council. Formed by Paul Weller and former Dexys Midnight Runners keyboard player Mick Talbot, the band had their biggest hit when 'Long Hot Summer' reached number 3 in August 1983.

4. 'Style'. Orbital had their biggest hit with 'The Saint', a 1997 number 3 taken from the film of that name. Mis-Teeq reached number 2 twice, first with 'All I Want' in 2001, then with 'Scandalous' in 2003.

5. 'Dedicated Follower of Fashion' by The Kinks. The band's eighth Top 40 single begins 'They seek him here, they seek him there', a reference to the 1905 novel *The Scarlet Pimpernel* by Baroness Orczy.

6. 5 Seconds of Summer. The Sydney group's April 2014 number 1 was the thirtieth time an Australian artist has topped the UK singles chart, a chain that started in 1965 with the Seekers' 'I'll Never Find Another You'.

7. Bryan Adams. The song was co-written by producer Robert 'Mutt' Lange, who married singer Shania Twain in 1993. The couple had Bryan Adams's song '(Everything I Do) I Do It for You' played at their wedding.

8. 'The Model'. It was the biggest of nine Top 40 hits for the German quartet, who followed it up in March 1982 with the number 25 single 'Showroom Dummies'.

9. ZZ Top. 'Sharp Dressed Man' was the second of ten Top 40 hits for the Texan trio, who released their first single in 1969 and had their biggest hit with the 1983 number 10 'Gimme All Your Lovin''.

10. Sheena Easton. In 1981 she had her fifth Top 40 hit with the theme to *For Your Eyes Only*. In addition to 'U Got the Look', she also featured on Prince's 1989 number 27 single 'The Arms of Orion' from *Batman*.

NOW That's What I Call Food Answers

1. Meat Loaf. He had his biggest hit in 1993 with 'I'd Do Anything for Love (But I Won't Do That)', which spent seven weeks at number 1 and was the biggest-selling single of that year.

2. 'Life Is a Minestrone'. It was the sixth of the 10cc's thirteen Top 40 hits. After they left the band, duo Kevin Godley and Lol Creme released the singles 'Sandwiches of You' and 'Snack Attack'.

3. LadBaby. The version of Starship's 1985 number 12 by Mark Hoyle and his family was a charity fundraiser for The Trussell Trust foodbank organisation.

4. Norman Cook, who had a number 1 in 1986 with the Housemartins, 'Caravan of Love', and in 1990 with Beats International, 'Dub Be

Good to Me'. He had his biggest hit as Pizzaman with the 1996 number 18, 'Trippin' on Sunshine'.

5. DNCE. Fronted by Joe Jonas, the band's debut single reached number 4 in May 2016 and spent twenty-five weeks in the Top 40. The follow-up, 'Toothbrush', peaked at number 49 in September that year.

6. 'Peaches'. It was the Top 40 debut and the first of twenty-three Top 40 entries for the Stranglers, and the second and biggest Top 40 hit for Presidents of the USA.

7. 'The Day Before You Came'. Originally a number 32 single for ABBA in 1982, Blancmange's version spent three weeks at number 22 in August 1984. Their biggest hit was the 1982 number 7 'Living on the Ceiling'.

8. Fast Food Rockers, whose debut single 'Fast Food Song' spent two weeks at number 2 in 2003. Both singles were taken from the album *It's Never Easy Being Cheesy*.

9. DNA. It was the first and biggest of three Top 40 singles for duo Nick Batt and Neal Slateford, and the fourth and biggest of five Top 40 hits for Suzanne.

10. Bread. It was the third of five Top 40 singles for the band, who made their chart debut in 1970 with the number 5 hit 'Make It with You', which also provided Let Loose with a number 7 hit in 1995.

NOW That's What I Call A Girl Answers

1. Zig and Zag, who made their recording debut in 1990 with 'The Christmas No. 1', which duly topped the Irish singles chart that December. They had one more UK Top 40 hit in 1995 with 'Hands Up! Hands Up!'.

2. Girls Aloud. Their run of hits began with the Christmas 2002 number 1 'Sound of the Underground', which stayed at the top for four weeks before they were dislodged by another talent-show winner, David Sneddon.

3. The Tams. Originally released in 1964, 'Hey Girl Don't Bother Me' and their 1968 single 'Be Young Be Foolish, Be Happy' both charted in the seventies, when they were rediscovered by the northern soul scene.

4. 'Some Girls'. Racey's second Top 10 hit spent three weeks at number 2 in 1979, Ultimate KAOS reached number 9 in November 1994, while Rachel Stevens's 2004 number 2 was the second of five solo Top 10 hits.

5. The Chi-Lites, whose 'Homely Girl' reached number 14 in 1974, while 'Oh Girl' made number 14 in 1972. Their 1972 number 3 hit 'Have You Seen Her' also provided MC Hammer with a number 8 single in 1990.

6. Cheeky Girls, who made their debut with the number 2 hit 'Cheeky Song (Touch My Bum)', and followed it with '(Hooray, Hooray) It's a Cheeky Holiday', 'Have a Cheeky Christmas' and 'Cheeky Flamenco'.

7. Bombalurina, who spent three weeks at number 1 with 'Itsy Bitsy Teeny Weeny Yellow Polka Dot Bikini'. Fronted by DJ Timmy Mallett, the group also included Dawn Andrews, the future wife of Gary Barlow.

8. Haircut One Hundred with 'Favourite Shirts (Boy Meets Girl)', which spent two weeks at number 4 in November 1981. They had three more Top 40 hits, including 'Love Plus One', which peaked at number 3 in January 1982.

9. Pink (or P!nk, if you prefer). 'Most Girls' was her second Top 40 hit, reaching number 5 in September 2000, while 'Stupid Girls' became her thirteenth when it peaked at number 4 in April 2006.

10. Jim Dale. In addition to his eleven *Carry On* films, he also appeared in Walt Disney's 1977 film *Pete's Dragon*, and won a Tony Award in 1980 for his Broadway performance in *Barnum*.

NOW That's What I Call an Animal Answers

1. Katy Perry, who also mentions lions in her fourth number 1. In 1995 British boxer Frank Bruno marked his rise to world heavyweight champion by releasing a version of 'Eye of the Tiger', which peaked at number 28.

2. Ian Brown. 'Elephant Stone' was the fourth of his fifteen Top 40 singles with the Stone Roses, who had their biggest hit with the 1994 number 2 'Love Spreads'. His biggest solo hit is the 1998 number 5 'My Star'.

3. 'The Lion Sleeps Tonight', which was the third of four Top 40 hits for Tight Fit. The record featured singer Roy Ward, previously with City Boy, who had a number 8 hit in 1978 with '5.7.0.5.'

4. 'Gecko (Overdrive)'. DJ Oliver Heldens made his Top 40 debut in 2014 with the number 4 'Last All Night (Koala)' featuring KStewart. Becky Hill first rose to fame when she appeared on Series 1 of *The Voice*.

5. Manfred Mann. The 1966 single 'Pretty Flamingo' was one of three number 1 hits, along with 'Do Wah Diddy Diddy' in 1964 and 'The Mighty Quinn' in 1968. 'Fox on the Run' peaked at number 5 in 1968.

6. The Goodies. 'The Funky Gibbon' peaked at number 4 in April 1985. It was written by Bill Oddie, who performed onstage with The Who in 1972 and is a regular presenter of the BBC TV *Springwatch* programmes.

7. The Monkees. 'I'm a Believer' was the band's Top 40 debut, staying at number 1 for four weeks in 1967. It was written by Neil Diamond, as was their 1967 number 3 'A Little Bit Me, a Little Bit You'.

8. Seal, who featured on 'Killer', the 1990 number 1 by Adamski. His version of 'Fly Like an Eagle' peaked at number 13, while the original by Steve Miller Band failed to chart in the UK but reached number 2 in the US.

9. Crocodile. 'Crocodile Rock' was Elton's fourth Top 40 hit and spent

three weeks at number 5 in December 1972. The 1994 number 4 'Crocodile Shoes' was the third of seven Top 40 hits for Jimmy Nail.

10. Chipmunk. Born Jahmaal Fyffe, he made his chart debut in March 2009 with the number 21 'Chip Diddy Chip' and had five Top 40 hits that year, including 'Oopsy Daisy', which entered at number 1 in October.

NOW That's What I Call Music Answers

1. Madonna. 'Music' was her second chart-topper of 2000, following her cover of Don McLean's 'American Pie', recorded for the soundtrack of her film *The Next Best Thing*.

2. 'Let the Music Play'. Barry White peaked at number 9 in January 1976 with the seventh of his seventeen Top 40 hits, while the 1983 number 14 was the highest position achieved by the American born singer Brenda Shannon Greene.

3. The Beatmasters. Betty Boo, aka Alison Clarkson, had four more Top 40 hits, including the 1990 number 3 'Where Are You Baby?' In 2001 Alison co-wrote Hear'Say's number 1 debut single 'Pure and Simple'.

4. Village People. *Can't Stop the Music* has the dubious honour of winning the first ever Golden Raspberry Award for Worst Film in 1980, when it beat *Xanadu* starring Olivia Newton-John and Gene Kelly.

5. B*Witched. The quartet featured twins Edele and Keavy Lynch (sisters of Boyzone singer Shane), along with Lindsay Armaou and Sinéad O'Carroll, and the band's first four singles all reached number 1.

6. 'Play That Funky Music'. It was the only Top 40 hit for the band from Steubenville, Ohio, while Vanilla Ice would have another three, including 'Under Pressure (Ice Ice Baby)', a 2010 collaboration with Jedward.

7. 'Music Is My Radar'. It was Blur's twenty-second consecutive Top 40 hit, a run that began with 'There's No Other Way' in 1991, after their 1990 debut, 'She's So High', had peaked at number 48.

8. KDA. It is the only Top 40 hit for the DJ born Kris di Angelis, though it was Tinie Tempah's seventh number 1. Only his 2010 debut 'Pass Out' was a 'solo' project; the other six have all involved different collaborators.

9. Beach Boys. In total they have twenty-eight Top 40 hits, beginning with the 1963 number 34 'Surfin' USA', and including two numbers 1s with 'Good Vibrations' in 1966 and 'Do It Again' in 1968.

10. Bernard Edwards and Nile Rodgers of Chic. All three songs made the Top 20 in 1979, while 'Lost in Music' recharted in 1984 when it reached number 4, and again in 1993 when it peaked at number 14.

NOW That's What I Call Science Answers

1. Girls Aloud. The quintet's total of twenty-two Top 40 hits contained four number 1 singles, including their chart debut 'Sound of the Underground' and a cover of The Pretenders' 1994 number 10 'I'll Stand by You'.

2. 'Gravity'. The Embrace single peaked at number 7 in September 2004, and was one of eighteen Top 40 hits. 'Gravity' was the fourth Top 40 hit for Pixie, who made number 1 with her 2009 chart debut 'Mama Do'.

3. The Chemical Brothers. Noel featured on 'Setting Sun', which spent one week at number 1 in October 1996. The duo's other chart-topper, 'Block Rockin' Beats', relied on a sample from rapper Schooly D for vocals.

4. 'Ultraviolet'. It was McFly's eighth consecutive Top 10 hit, though the only one of their four double A-side releases that failed to reach number 1.

5. Orchestral Manoeuvres in the Dark. The single includes 'vocals' from a Speak & Spell device, an educational toy developed in the seventies to help children learning to spell.

6. Coldplay. 'The Scientist' peaked at number 10 in November 2002, and was covered by Corrine Bailey Rae for the soundtrack of the 2017 film *Fifty Shades Darker*.

7. 808 State. The partnership's other Top 40 hit was 'The Only Rhyme that Bites', which reached number 10 in July 1990 and sampled the theme music from the 1958 Western *The Big Country*.

8. The Undertones, who reached number 9 in May 1980 with 'My Perfect Cousin'. Their song also mentions The Human League, who wouldn't have their first Top 40 hit for another twelve months.

9. Pointer Sisters. 'Neutron Dance' reached number 3 in January 1985 for Anita, June and Ruth, who had their biggest hit with 'Automatic', which spent two weeks at number 2 in May 1984.

10. Westworld. Their only other Top 40 hit was 'Ba-Na-Na-Bam-Boo', which spent two weeks at number 37 in May 1987 and was featured on the soundtrack of the film *Planes, Trains and Automobiles*.

NOW That's What I Call a Boy Answers

1. 'Bad Boy'. The Marty Wilde song made number 7 and was his fifth consecutive Top 10 hit; the Gloria Estefan-fronted Miami Sound Machine reached number 16, while Skepta peaked at number 26.

2. Boy Meets Girl. The 1988 number 9 was the only Top 40 hit for George Merrill and Shannon Rubicam, though the duo also wrote Whitney Houston's number 1 'I Wanna Dance with Somebody (Who Loves Me)'.

3. Morrissey. Following his eighteen Top 40 hits with the Smiths, he made his solo debut with the 1988 number 5 'Suedehead', and had his biggest hit in May 2004 when 'Irish Blood, English Heart' reached number 3.

4. Phixx, whose version of 'Wild Boys' made number 13 in July 2004. The 2002 TV talent show resulted in the winning groups Girls Aloud and One True Voice, though the latter managed just two Top 40 hits.

5. Happy Mondays. 'The Boys Are Back in Town' and their biggest hit,

the 1990 number 5 'Step On', were cover versions of seventies hits. 'Step On' originally made number 4 for South African songwriter John Kongos in 1971.

6. Chesney Hawkes, who reached number 27 with 'I'm a Man Not a Boy'. It was the follow-up to 'The One and Only', which featured in the film *Buddy's Song*, starring Chesney alongside Roger Daltrey as his father.

7. Boy George, whose version of 'The Crying Game' was the theme to the 1992 Neil Jordan film of the same name. 'Don't Gimme No Lip Child', the B-side of Dave Berry's original 1964 single, was recorded by Sex Pistols for their album 'The Great Rock 'n' Roll Swindle'.

8. 'Oh Patti (Don't Feel Sorry for Loverboy)'. The fourth of five Top 40 singles for Scritti Politti, it peaked at number 13 in June 1988, and featured jazz legend Miles Davis.

9. 'Can't Take My Eyes off You'. Originally a US number 2 for Frankie Valli in 1967, the song was a hit for Andy Williams once again in 2002, when he recorded a duet version with Denise van Outen.

10. 'Bachelor Boy'. It was one of three number 1 singles featured in *Summer Holiday*, along with the title track and 'Foot Tapper', a fourth instrumental number 1 for the Shadows.

NOW That's What I Call News Answers

1. 'Read All About It', which spent two weeks at number 1 in November 2011. In February 2012, Emeli had her seventh Top 40 hit when 'Read All About It Part 3' peaked at number 3.

2. Traffic. The band had their biggest hit later that same year with 'Hole in My Shoe', which reached number 2, the same chart peak achieved by Neil from the BBC comedy *The Young Ones* with his 1984 cover version.

3. 'Express Yourself'. Madonna's single reached number 5 and was co-written with Stephen Bray, co-writer of her first number 1, 'Into the Groove'. Labrinth's single reached number 12, the sixth of his Top 40 hits.

4. The Jam. The only one of their Top 40 hits written by bass player Bruce Foxton, since 2005 it has been the theme music for the satirical TV panel show *Mock the Week*.

5. Dollar. In addition to 'Mirror Mirror (Mon Amour)', two of the duo's other hits peaked at number 4 – 'Love's Gotta Hold on Me' in 1979 and 'Give Me Back My Heart' in 1982.

6. Harry Styles. Of the five former One Direction members, Harry and Zayn both made number 1 with their solo debut singles, while Louis's stalled at number 2, Liam's reached number 3 and Niall's peaked at number 9.

7. 'Independent Women'. Their eighth Top 40 hit, it entered the chart at number 1 in December 2000 and was followed four months later by

their second chart-topper 'Survivor', which also spent one week at the top.

8. Feargal Sharkey. After seven Top 40 hits with the Undertones he had his biggest solo hit with 'A Good Heart', which spent two weeks at number 1 in November 1985.

9. 'Headlines (Friendship Never Ends)', which reached number 11 in December 2007 and was one of only two Spice Girls singles that didn't top the chart. The other was 'Stop', which peaked at number 2 in March 1998.

10. Phil Collins. It was the nineteenth of his twenty-seven solo Top 40 singles, in addition to another twenty-one with Genesis and contributions to many others, including Band Aid's 'Do They Know It's Christmas?'

NOW That's What I Call Red Answers

1. Simply Red. 'Fairground' spent four weeks at number 1 in October 1995, while 'Holding Back the Years' and 'If You Don't Know Me by Now' topped the US chart, though both peaked at number 2 in the UK.

2. The Rolling Stones. Their version of the song, first recorded by American blues musician Howlin' Wolf, was one of their three number 1 singles in 1965, and one of eight in total.

3. 'Red Dress'. Alvin's song was the second of his eleven Top 40 hits and the follow-up to his only number 1, 'Jealous Mind'. The Sugababes song reached number 4, one of their twenty-six Top 40 hits.

4. Red Dragon, a.k.a. Leroy May. 'Compliments On Your Kiss' was his and the Golds' only Top 40 hit. Gold is an adopted name and the pair born Brian Thompson and Patrick Morrison are not related.

5. Red Hot Chili Peppers, who twice stalled at number 2, with 'By the Way' in 2002 and 'Dani California' in 2006. Their 1991 song 'Under the Bridge' gave All Saints the second of their five number 1 hits.

6. Nena, who spent three weeks at number 1 with '99 Red Balloons'. Although the band had eight Top 40 singles in Germany, their only other UK chart entry, 'Just a Dream', peaked at number 70.

7. 'Snoopy vs. The Red Baron'. The Royal Guardsmen had one more Top 40 hit in 1967 with 'The Return of the Red Baron', while The Hotshots failed to live up to their name and were one-hit wonders.

8. The Drifters. Their run of hits began in 1960 with 'Dance with Me', and included the number 2 singles 'Save the Last Dance for Me' in 1960 and 'Kissin' in the Back Row of the Movies' in 1974.

9. Australian. Born in Melbourne, Daniel made his chart debut on Mark Ronson's number 2 single 'Stop Me', a reworking of the 1987 song by The Smiths 'Stop Me If You Think You've Heard This One Before'.

10. Redman. It was the third of four number 1 hits for Christina Aguilera, and one of five Top 40 singles for Redman that have also seen him collaborate with Beverley Knight, De La Soul, Adam F and Erick Sermon.

NOW That's What I Call the Planets Answers

1. Duran Duran, who made their chart debut with the 1981 number 12 'Planet Earth' and had the tenth of their thirty Top 40 hits with the 1984 number 9 'New Moon on Monday'.

2. Bruno Mars. He had his first 'solo' number 1 later in 2010 with 'Just the Way You Are (Amazing)', while B.o.B also had a second number 1 that year with 'Airplanes', featuring Hayley Williams of Paramore.

3. Venus. 'Venus in Blue Jeans' was the biggest of nine Top 40 hits for Mark Wynter between 1960 and 1964, while 'Venus' was the only Top 40 hit for Italian dance group Don Pablo's Animals.

4. 'To the Moon and Back', which reached number 3 for the Australian duo, the third of a run of ten Top 40 hits that began with the 1997 number 7 'I Want You'.

5. Inspiral Carpets. Their eleven Top 40 hits include their 1990 number 14 chart debut 'This Is How It Feels', and their biggest hit 'Dragging Me Down', which reached number 12 in March 1992.

6. The B-52's, who first got together at a Chinese restaurant in the southern US city. 'Planet Claire' failed to chart when first released in 1979 but peaked at number 12 after it was reissued in May 1986.

7. Kate Bush, whose version of 'Rocket Man' peaked at number 12 in December 1991. Elton's original stalled at number 2 in 1972, when it was kept off the top spot by T. Rex's fourth number 1, 'Metal Guru'.

8. Train. The number 10 single won a Grammy Award for 'Best Instrumental Arrangement' for British composer Paul Buckmaster, who also arranged the strings on David Bowie's 1969 chart debut 'Space Oddity'.

9. Beyoncé. 'Green Light' was the fifth single form her second solo album *B'Day*. The Neptunes, a.k.a. Pharrell Williams and Chad Hugo, have also produced hits for Nelly and Britney Spears.

10. Apollo 440. Their ten Top 40 hits between 1990 and 2000 include a second cinematic entry, with the theme to the 2000 remake of *Charlie's Angels*, which reached number 29 in December that year.

NOW That's What I Call Power Answers

1. 'Turtle Power'. The theme from the film *Teenage Mutant Ninja Turtles* spent four weeks at number 1 in 1990, though a second single, 'Undercover', only made number 92, and the band never had another hit.

2. The Power Station. They had two Top 40 hits in 1985, with the number 14 'Some Like It Hot' and a cover of the 1971 T. Rex number 1 'Get It On', which reached number 22.

3. 'The Power of Love'. Jennifer Rush spent five weeks at number 1 and

had the bestselling single of 1985. Huey Lewis reached number 11 that October then recharted in April 1986, when it peaked at number 9.

4. Electric Six. 'Danger! High Voltage' entered the chart at number 2 and was only denied the top spot by Girls Aloud's 'Sound of the Underground'. Their version of 'Radio Gaga' peaked at number 21 in December 2004.

5. 'Power to All Our Friends'. The UK came third at the eighteenth Eurovision Song Contest, which was held in Luxembourg and won by the host nation with 'Tu Te Reconnaîtras', performed by Anne-Marie David.

6. Roy Wood, who had previously fronted The Move before founding Electric Light Orchestra with Jeff Lynne. Roy left while the band were recording their second album and formed Wizzard.

7. Silk City. Mark Ronson had his first number 1 in 2014 with 'Uptown Funk', featuring Bruno Mars. Diplo founded Major Lazer, who made number 1 in 2016 with 'Cold Water', featuring Justin Bieber and MØ.

8. Atomic Kitten. Following 'Whole Again', their second number 1 single was 'Eternal Flame', a number 1 for The Bangles in 1989, while the third was 'The Tide Is High', a number 1 for Blondie in 1980.

9. 'Say What You Want', which gave Texas their biggest hit when it reached number 3 in January 1997. 'Powerless (Say What You Want)' was the fourth Top 40 single for Canadian singer Nelly Furtado.

10. 'Classical Gas'. It reached number 2 in the US, where it also won Grammy Awards for Best Instrumental Composition, Best Contemporary-Pop Performance (Instrumental) and Best Instrumental Arrangement.

NOW That's What I Call Radio Answers

1. Robbie Williams. 'Radio' topped the chart for one week in 2004, while 'Rock DJ' – which samples the strings from Barry White's 1977 single 'It's Ecstasy When You Lay Down Next to Me' – spent a week at number 1 in 2000.

2. Martine McCutcheon. In 1994 she scraped into the Top 100 with 'Lean on Me' by pop trio Milan, before finding fame in *EastEnders* and making her Top 40 debut with the 1999 number 1 'Perfect Moment'.

3. 'Last Night a DJ Saved My Life'. Both the original version by Indeep and the cover by Seamus Haji featuring KayJay peaked at number 13. In 2001, Mariah Carey recorded the song for her album *Glitter*.

4. 'Radioactive'. The Kings of Leon single reached number 7 and was their third to break into the Top 10; Imagine Dragons' 2012 number 12 was their chart debut; while the Rita Ora song peaked at number 18.

5. PJ and Duncan. The alter egos of Ant McPartlin and Declan Donnelly first made the Top 40 in 1994, and finally topped the chart in 2013

following a reissue of another 1994 single, 'Let's Get Ready to Rhumble'.

6. Taffy. She first achieved chart success in Italy, where 'I Love My Radio (Midnight Radio)' was a hit in 1985, before it was rerecorded for the UK market and renamed 'I Love My Radio (Dee Jay's Radio)'.

7. Edwin Starr. He made his chart debut in 1966 with 'Stop Her on Sight (S.O.S.)', which recharted two years later and peaked at number 11. He had his biggest hit in November 1970, when 'War' reached number 3.

8. 'Hello (Turn Your Radio On)', the fifth of six Top 40 singles for the duo, who had their biggest hit earlier in 1992, when 'Stay' spent eight weeks at number 1.

9. Canadian. Although the rock trio are yet to have a Top 10 single, three of their albums have peaked at number 3, including the 1980 release *Permanent Waves*, from which 'The Spirit of Radio' was taken.

10. Lolly. She had her biggest hit in September 1999, when her version of the Toni Basil song 'Mickey' reached number 4. She later became a presenter on children's TV and appeared in pantomime.

NOW That's What I Call the Blues Answers

1. Elvis Presley. Undoubtedly the Top 40 King of the Blues; in addition to 'Blue Moon', 'Blue River' and 'Indescribably Blue', add 'Blue Christmas', 'Moody Blue', 'A Mess of Blues' and 'Blue Suede Shoes'.

2. 'Fergus Sings the Blues' was the fifth of sixteen Top 40 hits for Deacon Blue. The Scottish band took their name from the Steely Dan song 'Deacon Blues', which appeared on their 1977 number 5 album *Aja*.

3. Pras. Born Prakazrel Samuel Michel, he had his biggest solo hit in July 1998 with the number 2 single 'Ghetto Superstar (That Is What You Are)', featuring ODB of Wu-Tang Clan and Mýa.

4. 'Blue Eyes'. The second of three Top 40 singles for Don Partridge, it reached number 3 in June 1968 and was his biggest hit. Elton's song peaked at number 8 and was his twenty-eighth Top 40 hit.

5. Moody Blues. Their 1964 chart debut 'Go Now' was a number 1 hit, but they were denied a second chart-topper when 'Back Home' by England World Cup Squad 70 kept 'Questions' at number 2.

6. Delta Goodrem. In her native Australia, Delta's debut album spent twenty-nine weeks at number 1 and produced four number 1 singles, beating the three from fellow *Neighbours* alumni Kylie Minogue's debut album.

7. The Equals. Their six Top 40 hits include the 1968 number 1 'Baby Come Back', which topped the chart again in 1994 when it was covered by Pato Banton featuring Ali and Robin Campbell of UB40.

8. The Blues Brothers. Their only hit single, it was sung by John Belushi and Dan Aykroyd as Jake and Elwood Blues, while the backing band included Steve Cropper and 'Duck' Dunn of Booker T & the MGs.

9. Paul Young, who first had chart success in 1978 with Streetband on their number 18 single 'Toast'. In 1983 his version of 'Wherever I Lay My Hat (That's My Home)' spent three weeks at number 1.

10. Bobby Vinton with 'Blue Velvet'. In the US it reached number 1 in September 1963, but it failed to chart in the UK until October 1990, when it peaked at number 2 behind Maria McKee's 'Show Me Heaven'.

NOW That's What I Call Royal Answers

1. Queen, whose six number 1 singles include collaborations with David Bowie and Five. They also reached number 31 with the Miami Project and 'Another One Bites the Dust', and number 32 with the Muppets and 'Bohemian Rhapsody'.

2. 'Dancing Queen' by ABBA. The fourth of their nine number 1 singles, it spent six weeks at the top in 1976 and recharted in 1992, when it reached number 16.

3. 'King for a Day'. The Thompson Twins' single reached number 22 in November 1985 and was their tenth Top 40 single, while Jamiroquai reached number 20 in December 1999 and had their sixteenth Top 40 hit.

4. Roger Miller. In 1976, comedian Billy Howard had a number 6 hit with his parody single 'King of the Cops', which included impressions of TV detectives of the day, including Columbo, Kojak and Ironside.

5. Lorde. Born Ella Yelich-O'Connor in New Zealand, her debut single 'Royals' spent seventeen weeks in the Top 40. Lorde had her third Top 40 single in 2017, when 'Green Light' reached number 20.

6. Princess. All four of her Top 40 hits were written and produced by Stock, Aitken and Waterman. In 1990, Princess sang on Vanilla Ice's album *To the Extreme*.

7. Wamdue Project, who appeared on the initial list for Best British Newcomer at the 2000 BRIT Awards, before organisers had to withdraw the nomination on account of the band being American.

8. KC and the Sunshine Band. They had their biggest hit in 1983 with 'Give It Up', which spent three weeks at number 1, while their 1979 number 3 'Please Don't Go' was covered by KWS for their own 1992 chart-topper.

9. Queens of the Stone Age. The band had their biggest hit with the 2002 number 15 'No One Knows', which included Foo Fighters' Dave Grohl on drums. It was nominated for Best Hard Rock Performance at the 2003 Grammys, but lost out to Foo Fighters 'All My Life'.

10. 'The Crown'. The full-length version ran for almost eleven minutes and featured rapped verses by Byrd, an American DJ, with additional vocals from Stevie Wonder and R&B singer Crystal Blake.

NOW That's What I Call School Answers

1. Busted. The first of eight consecutive Top 5 singles for Charlie Simp-

son, James Bourne and Matt Willis, the video included future Eurovision entrant and Sugababes member Jade Ewen playing a schoolgirl.

2. 'Another Brick in the Wall (Part II)'. It was Pink Floyd's first chart single since 'See Emily Play' made number 3 in 1967. Islington Green reportedly received a payment of £1,000 for their children's contribution.

3. The Korgis, whose original version, just called 'Everybody's Got to Learn Sometime', peaked at number 5. Baby D's biggest hit came in November 1994 when 'Let Me Be Your Fantasy' spent two weeks at number 1.

4. 'Mull of Kintyre' by Wings. With bagpipes and drums of the Campbeltown Pipe Band, it spent sixteen weeks in the Top 40, nine of those at number 1, and sold over two million copies.

5. 'This Used to Be My Playground', which reached number 3 in the UK but became Madonna's tenth number 1 in the US. Madonna also appeared in the film, playing 'All the Way' Mae Mordabito.

6. 'School's Out'. The only number 1 for Alice Cooper, it spent three weeks at the top in 1972. Karen 'Daphne' DiConcetto and Celeste Cruz had their biggest hit with 'Ooh Stick You', which reached number 8 in 2000.

7. Level 42. Their eighth Top 40 hit, 'Lessons in Love' spent three weeks at number 3 and reached number 12 in the US, where their biggest hit was the number 7 'Something About You', which peaked at number 6 in the UK.

8. 'Baggy Trousers' by Madness. It was the fifth of their Top 40 hits, spending eleven weeks in the Top 40, the longest stay for any of their singles. The promo video was filmed at Islip Street School in Kentish Town.

9. Jeannie C. Riley. In the US, it made Jeannie the first woman to top both the all-encompassing *Billboard* Hot 100 and the Country Singles Chart, a feat that wasn't repeated until Dolly Parton's '9 to 5' in 1981.

10. Girlschool. The three-song collection spent two weeks at number 5 in February 1981, and included a version of 'Please Don't Touch', originally a Top 40 hit for Johnny Kidd & the Pirates in 1959.